Live It, Learn It

The Academic Club
Methodology
for Students with
Learning Disabilities
and ADHD

by

Sally L. Smith
Founder/Executive Director
The Lab School of Washington
and Baltimore Lab
Director, Master's Degree Program in
Special Education: Learning Disabilities
School of Education
American University
Washington, D.C.

·P A U L·H·
BROOKES
PUBLISHING CO.®

Baltimore • London • Sydney

Paul H. Brookes Publishing Co.
Post Office Box 10624
Baltimore, Maryland 21285-0624

www.brookespublishing.com

Typeset by Integrated Publishing Solutions, Grand Rapids, Michigan.
Manufactured in the United States of America by
Victor Graphics, Baltimore, Maryland.

The case studies described in this book are based on the author's actual experiences.
Individuals' names and stories are used by permission or identifying details have been
altered to protect confidentiality.

Library of Congress Cataloging-in-Publication Data

Smith, Sally Liberman.
   Live it, learn it: the academic club methodology for students with learning disabilities
and ADHD/by Sally L. Smith.
     p.   cm.
   Includes bibliographical references and index.
   ISBN 1-55766-683-0 (pbk.)
   1. Learning disabled children—Education—United States.   2. Attention-deficit-disordered
children—Education—United States.   3. Student activities—United States.   4. Lab
School of Washington (Washington, D.C.)   I. Title.
   LC4705.S65 2005
   371.94—dc22
                                                     2004027589

British Library Cataloguing in Publication data are available from the British Library.

Contents

About the Author

 **Sally L. Smith** is the Founder/Executive Director of The Lab School of Washington®, which she designed in 1967 for children and adults with learning disabilities. She replicated The Lab School's program in Baltimore in September 2000. Baltimore Lab began with 18 students and has grown to 100 students in first through ninth grades for 2004–2005. Since 1976, Professor Smith has also been a Professor in the School of Education at American University in charge of the Master's Degree Program in Special Education: Learning Disabilities.

Professor Smith believes that everyone can learn, and she has designed teaching approaches involving all of the art forms and experiential education to teach academic skills to children and adults. Her Academic Club Methodology™ has been overwhelmingly successful with Lab School students since the school's inception. The Methodology builds storehouses of knowledge, vocabulary, fluency of language, and critical thinking—things that good readers develop from prolific reading—in poor readers and nonreaders.

Professor Smith is a national leader in the field of learning disabilities. In April 2001, American University gave her a medal for 25 years of outstanding service. She was recognized as a Principal of Excellence and presented with the Distinguished Educational Leadership Award by *The Washington Post* in November 1999. In May 1999, Professor Smith was recognized by Birmingham-Southern College as a "Woman of Distinction." She was also the first recipient of the Celebrating Abilities Award for Outstanding Contributions to the Field of Learning Disabilities presented by the Learning Disabilities Association of Georgia in October 1997. In May 1995, Professor Smith was honored with the American University Faculty Award for Outstanding Scholarship, Research, and Other Professional Contributions. She received the LDA Award from the Learning Disabilities Association of America (LDA)—the highest honor given in her field—in February 1993 for recognition and appreciation of outstanding leadership in the field.

Professor Smith is one of the elected specialists on the Professional Advisory Board of LDA and served for 6 years as an elected member of the Professional Advisory Board of the National Center for Learning Disabilities. From 1988 to 1999, she worked as a consultant on learning disabilities to the State Department Family Liaison Office, and from 1990 to 1994, she was a member of the Advisory Board of the "I Have A Dream"® Foundation in Washington, D.C. Professor Smith also served on the U.S. Task Force on the Definition of Developmental Disabilities in 1976–1977. She has testified as an expert witness before the Senate Committee on Labor and Human Resources. In addition, she was a member of the Advisory Council on the Arts in Education for the National Endowment for the Arts.

Professor Smith has run workshops throughout the United States and Canada as well as in Greece and Switzerland (for the European Council of International Schools). In July 2003, Professor Smith served as the graduation speaker for the Tasis Hellenic International School in Athens, Greece, and was invited by the U.S. Embassy in Athens to hold a 3-hour workshop for teachers and parents titled "Stop the Blaming: It's the Nature of the Condition of Learning Disabilities."

In January 2002, Public Broadcasting System (PBS) produced four films demonstrating the teacher training techniques Professor Smith originated and uses at American University and the Lab Schools. The series *Teach Me Different! with Sally Smith* won the Telly Award in the education category in 2002. In 2003, the series won the Silver International CINDY (Cinema in Industry) Award from the International Association of Audio Visual Communicators.

As the author of nine books and a number of articles in professional magazines, Professor Smith has mastered the art of translating difficult clinical issues into popular language. Her best-known books are *No Easy Answers: The Learning Disabled Child at Home and at School* (Bantam, 1995) and *Succeeding Against the Odds: Helping the Learning Disabled Realize Their Promise* (Tarcher/ Perigee, 1993). *Succeeding Against the Odds* was the recipient of the New York Orton Dyslexia Society's 1995 Margot Marek Book Award. Another of Professor Smith's well-known books, *Different Is Not Bad: Different Is the World* (Sopris West, 1994), explains disabilities for young children and is widely used in inclusive classrooms. In 1996, both *No Easy Answers* and *Different Is Not Bad* were selected to receive the 1996 Parents' Choice Award. The predecessor to *Live It, Learn It,* Smith's *The Power of the Arts: Creative Strategies for Teaching Exceptional Learners* (Paul H. Brookes Publishing Co., 2001), presents arts activities and their effectiveness with children with learning disabilities, attention-deficit/hyperactivity disorder, and language disorders as well as children who are at risk for failure. Professor Smith's article titled "What Do Parents of Children with Learning Disabilities, ADHD, and Related Disorders Deal With?" appears in the May/June 2000 issue of *Pediatric Nursing*.

Professor Smith hopes to establish another Lab School in the near future. She also plans to take advantage of her Academic Club Advisory Service to help other schools employ her Methodology.

Acknowledgments

Once again, I thank one of my dearest friends in the world, Elisabeth Benson Booz, who joined me in Bungalow 18 at Elounda Beach in beautiful Crete and initially edited this opus. I appreciate your enthusiasm, your understanding of the material, your great sense of humor, and the adroit way your red pen edited my purple scrawl. I am grateful for the time, energy, and clear thought you exerted on my manuscript. You made it better. *Thank You.*

To Diana Meltzer, my treasured Special Assistant and Workshop Co-Coordinator, who has typed all of these words, you have my profound appreciation. Not only did you have to decode the purple pen scratches, but you did it with such good humor and a smile. *Thank You* for helping in all kinds of wonderful ways to ensure that I finished the book and didn't lose pages or paragraphs along the way. I am also grateful to Moire Scherl for some typing, reproducing, generally readying the manuscript for the Publisher. It was a hoot and a howl to work with you.

To all of the Academic Club Leaders I have worked with, you have my admiration and affection. I know how hard it is to program for 182 days of teaching, and you do it beautifully every single day. My particular thanks go to The Lab School of Washington Club Leaders Amanda Wolfe, Gina Van Weddingen, Donald Vicks, Noel Bicknell, Sarah Lowenberg, and Amy Aden for sharing so many of your activities with me and allowing me to include some of your materials in this book. I love you all. I love your passion for this kind of teaching.

To Junior High teachers, Katie Clark and Nancy Rowland, who have spent many years at The Lab School teaching through the Academic Club Approach, I admire the degree of deep involvement you engender from your students through the enticing creative programming you provide. *Thank You* for your excellence. *Thank You* Marguerite Delaney for developing so beautifully the Junior Year Internship Program.

To Baltimore Lab Club Leaders: Ursula Marcum, Laura Parkhurst, and Susan Rome, I am extremely impressed with the Academic Clubs you teach and have taught for several years. *Thank You.*

To Lois Meyer, Head of College Counseling and Workshop Co-Coordinator, I offer very deep appreciation for going over the final manuscript with me. It took your precious time and energy to do this very painstaking review, and I *Thank You.* You witnessed my impatience and annoyance in checking every word. You not only demonstrated great patience and a depth of understanding, but you also used your critical thinking, for which I am profoundly grateful.

A special *Thank You* to the following staff members who have read the manuscript and commented on it: Dr. Luanne Adams, Head of Psychological Services; Dr. Lindy Rosen, Head of Speech-Language Pathology; Betsy Babbington, Head of Development and former Academic Club Leader; and Roya Rassai, Registrar and Quantitative Analyst.

A profound *Thank You* to The Lab School of Washington and Baltimore Lab staff members for using the Academic Club Methodology so well and thus allowing our students to learn with joy and excitement. I am particularly grateful to Peter Braun, Karen Duncan, Neela Seldin, Noel Kerns, Sally Seawright, Dick Meltzer, Robin Dulli, and Susan Rome for making sure that the Academic Club Methodology and hands-on teaching permeate both Lab Schools.

To Board Chairs, Susan Hager and John Clifford; to Corporate Committee Chairs Bill Mattox and Mimi Dawson; and to Finance Committee Members of the Board of Trustees, Pauline Schneider, Rick Nadeau, Bruce Drury, Antoine van Agtmael, Fred Brennan, and Charlie Jacobs; you have my grateful appreciation for helping to keep The Lab School of Washington and Baltimore Lab thriving. *Thank You* to all of the Board Members who so kindly volunteer their time and effort and stand solidly behind our unique approaches.

I am especially grateful to American University administrators and to my colleagues in the School of Education who have given me the full-time opportunity since 1976 to educate teachers in my style of teaching and learning. It has helped that you have expected me to keep on researching, developing new ideas, and publishing. Your support is important to me!

Finally, I am indebted to the great Master of Modern Art, Robert Rauschenberg, for being a constant source of inspiration, creativity, and kindness. Since 1994, your Rauschenberg Day at The Lab School have enriched the lives of our students, our faculty—all of us. It has been an Academic Club of its own. *Thank You*, Bob.

To all the little Clubbies over the years who have whispered their passwords in my ears, told me excitedly about their Academic Club lives, and brought me projects that were created in Clubs, you have nourished my fervent belief that this is a valid way to learn, and that it is learning for a lifetime of inquiry. *Thank You*.

To **Gary Smith,**
who forced me to think differently
Thank You My Friend

To **Nick Smith,**
who tutored me with his artistic eye
Thank You My Friend

To **Randy Smith,**
who contributed brilliant ideas for
birthday parties and Academic Clubs
Thank You My Friend

To **all of The Lab School of Washington
and Baltimore Lab Club Leaders,**
who bring magic, excitement, and
profound knowledge into schooling
Thank You

1

What Is the Academic Club Methodology?

Most people are familiar with learning through textbooks. Because this teaching style is so prevalent, many people don't realize that there are other successful ways to learn. In fact, students deemed "underachievers," "slow learners," or "nonlearners" in traditional classrooms can thrive if taught using an alternative approach. This book is intended to show you how a dramatic framework employing all of the arts can be used as the central component of formal education.

WELCOME TO THE CLUB!

To illustrate this concept, let me walk you through a lesson based on the Academic Club Methodology™. Let's pretend we are undergraduate students studying educational principles. We will begin by immersing ourselves in the pretend world of the Educational Philosophers Club.

You will play the role of John Dewey. I will be Jean Piaget. Laverne is going to be Maria Montessori. Look at Don! He is a great Jerome Bruner, and Pete wants to play Howard Gardner. Harry and Alonzo are already dressed in impressive academic robes and look distinguished in their roles as Johann Pestalozzi and Rudolf Steiner. They help three other Club Members into their robes so they can play the parts of Rabindranath Tagore, Lev Vygotsky, and Ted Sizer.

Standing at the door of the Academic Club is our teacher, who is dressed in a toga and is playing the role of Plato. We each whisper the secret password, *paradigm,* into Plato's ear as we enter. The dimly lit classroom is set up as a Symposium Room with high-backed chairs and a huge table. I find my chair with Jean Piaget's name on it and a symbol—four stair steps, representing Piaget's four stages of cognitive development. Your chair has John Dewey's symbol, a stylized picture of two children building a city with blocks because Dewey believed that children construct knowledge best from activity. Maria Montessori's symbol is a wooden rectangle with bright-colored pegs to place in the proper holes. The other Club Members have meaningful symbols on their chairs, as well.

Our meeting begins with an opening ritual. We stand in semidarkness and recite in unison a quotation from William Butler Yeats comparing education to the lighting of a fire. Then, we light our collective fire by turning up the classroom lights.

Our teacher holds up a picture of Plato, and there is a poster-size picture of Plato's mentor, Socrates, on the wall behind our teacher. A picture of Plato's famous pupil, Aristotle, is at our teacher's feet. Our teacher reads a passage from *The Republic.*

> *Calculation and geometry and all the other elements of instruction . . . should be presented to the mind in childhood; not, however, under any notion of forcing our system of education.*
>
> *Why not?*
>
> *Because a free man ought not to be a slave in the acquisition of knowledge of any kind. Bodily exercise, when compulsory, does no harm to the body; but knowledge which is acquired under compulsion obtains no hold on the mind.*
>
> *Very true.*
>
> *Then, my good friend, I said, do not use compulsion, but let early education be a sort of amusement; you will then be better able to find out the natural bent. (Plato, 360 B.C.)*

As we start our discussion of Plato's passage, my contribution as Swiss psychologist Piaget is to point out that children develop at different speeds. They need to be taught at their own levels. Those who think on a concrete level must be taught by concrete means—no matter what their age—before they can use higher-level thinking. Don, in the role of Harvard psychologist Bruner, believes in "discovery learning" and says that the best introduction to a subject is the subject itself. He promotes the view that students must be given a chance to make guesses and disagree with each other. They should be allowed to find their own way to solve problems. You, as American reformer Dewey, state vehemently that children must learn by doing.

When we all have had a chance to add to the discussion, Plato summarizes our contributions. We all agree that children must be actively involved in whatever they are learning. Plato then gives us a project to do in small groups or alone, as suits our learning style. We choose our materials as our educational philosophers would, selecting from cardboard and masking tape, a mound of clay, foam, and string. Our assignment is to design a classroom that will most enhance learning for third graders. Later, we will adapt or change our models to meet the needs of eighth graders.

Despite our clumsy fingers, we continue to build our models because artistry is not the main point. The conceptual use of space is what counts. We have begun the task today with the materials at hand; tomorrow or the next day, we will share our finished models with each other and give our rationale for designing them the way we did. We can present this rationale in writing or orally. My model uses curtains to make the room circular and places students close to the teacher. Pete, as Gardner, wants his model to be like a museum. Alonzo, as Tagore, wants his classroom to be outdoors under a tree.

The next activity is a choice between playing a teacher-made board game called Choose Your Path or a computer game that is a more complex version of Choose Your Path. Several of us overcome obstacles and ponder choices as we move our markers on a colorful board, which represents a historic progression from a one-room schoolhouse, to highly standardized classrooms, to open learning spaces, and on to new technological worlds that will change our conceptions of schools. Other Club Members cluster around a computer monitor to look at regions of the world and locate education theorists, such as Tagore in India, Pestalozzi in Switzerland, and Vygotsky in Russia.

We end this Academic Club session by celebrating Montessori's birthday. We each have Italian flags and relief maps of Europe that we made last week. Today, we will paint the models, frost a birthday cake that is shaped like the Italian boot, and listen to Italian music. We arrange our classroom to reflect Montessori's model, play with her recommended materials, and talk about her reasons for using these materials. Each of us toasts Laverne, as Montessori, citing a fact about her contribution to educational reform in the past and projecting her possible contributions to the future.

Just as we end the session, we show our deep respect for our Club Leader, Plato, who believed that the beginning of learning is wonder. We quote in unison from Plato's *Theaetetus 155d3*, "Wonder is the feeling of a philosopher, and philosophy only begins in wonder." Then, we take off our academic robes, return to our own identities, and move on to another activity.

AN ALL-INCLUSIVE TEACHING METHOD

You have just experienced a tiny glimpse of an Academic Club. As you can see, this methodology is highly intellectual and highly structured. Focused pretend play that incorporates all of the senses is used to build identification with a character, to learn about that character, and to explore the context in which the character lived and what he or she believed. Through a total environmental approach, the Academic Club allows a person to learn a number of topics and amass a storehouse of information. A Club Member engages in at least four kinds of activities within the 50-minute session and uses several different intelligences. The subject matter chosen for an Academic Club is appropriate to the interests and developmental level of the children.

The Academic Club Methodology employs:

- Active learning
- Project learning
- Contructivist learning
- Discovery learning
- Hands-on learning
- Responsive learning
- Multisensory learning
- Concrete learning
- Authentic assessment
- Interdisciplinary learning
- Cooperative learning
- Multicultural learning
- Reciprocal teaching

Figure 1 is a visual statement of the Academic Club Methodology.

I designed the Academic Club Methodology in 1966 to use with youngsters from inner-city Washington, D.C., who were failing in their current classrooms. The following year, I founded The Lab School of Washington® in order to educate my son with severe learning disabilities and other students like him. The Academic Club Methodology became the basis of a new way of teaching at The Lab School because it enabled each child to feel like an intimate part of history and a vital part of any topic being studied. It gave each child a voice and demanded intense participation, which was important because many of the students were passive in their previous classrooms.

I chose the word *club* to give a sense of membership, belonging, ownership, and privilege to these children who often felt left out and wanted desperately to be included. I called the clubs *academic clubs* because the program is highly academic. Challenging intellectual material is presented through visual, hands-on, and concrete means. I developed passwords, routines, rituals, and dramatic frameworks to help students focus and pay attention, as well as to organize the group into a tight unit.

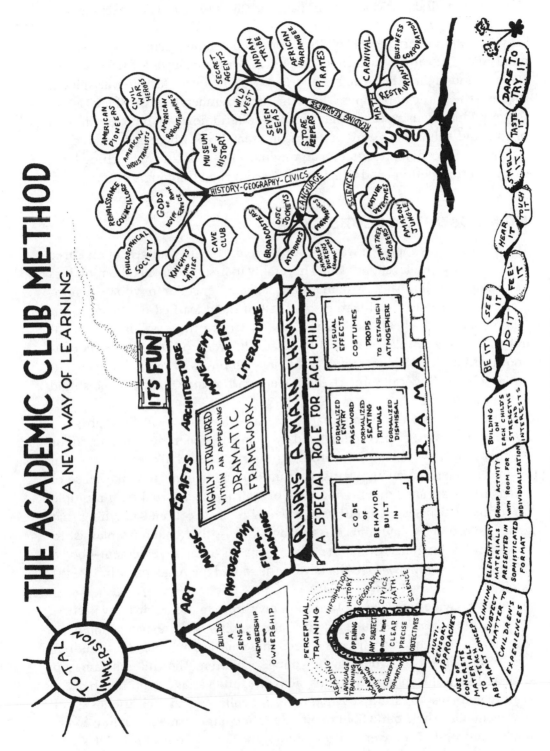

Figure 1. Visual statement of the Academic Club Methodology. Copyright © 1972 by Sally L. Smith.

Children find participating in Academic Clubs to be fun and exciting, and they get the opportunity to learn sophisticated material that is not usually taught to elementary school children. For example, the teacher of the Knights and Ladies Club at The Lab School, known as Lord Don, leads Sir Jeremy, Lady Rachel, and eight other Knights and Ladies with severe learning disabilities through the Battle of Hastings. Then, the Club Members recreate the 231-foot Bayeux Tapestry using paper and paint and collect information on the amount of land and animals to record in their Domesday Book. These children receive a classical education presented in an original way. This kind of teaching leads to long-term retention and a lifetime of learning and thinking.

HOW ACADEMIC CLUBS BEGAN

The power of this approach was first shown to me by the youngest of my three sons, who was intelligent but failed miserably in first grade. This situation was not unique. Traditional classroom lessons failed other children who were non-readers and untraditional learners; yet, all of them learned one way or another outside of school. I asked myself, "What are these children doing at home, on the sidewalk, or in their backyards in order to learn? How can children learn a great deal in camps, outdoor programs, and special projects but not at school? How can some children feel smart outside of school and stupid in the classroom?"

It became obvious to me that they learned a great deal through play: by building things; by pretending; and by acting out what they saw, heard, or touched. They were learning through the arts. These children were using drama, puppetry, drawing, crafts, rhythm, and movement to make sense of things that fascinated them. They were organizing their world with multiple art forms, which served as effective teaching tools. I realized something that great philosophers thousands of years ago knew—that children's play is, in fact, serious learning. Children's play demands total involvement—body, mind, and soul. *Involvement* is the key. At the root of the Academic Club Methodology is total involvement.

The basic idea of clubs evolved from my three children's birthday parties. Each party had a theme, such as secret agents, pirates, Greek gods, and Civil War heroes. My children's friends adored these parties, and the older children vied to be helpers at parties for the younger children. The children came up with all kinds of helpful suggestions, activities, and variations on the themes. For my youngest son's Jungle Party, the older children and their friends spent a week making the ground floor of our home and our outside porch into a veritable rainforest. They went to the library and found books on jungles and looked up rainforests in encyclopedias. They did their research to make it believable and thrust themselves into the roles of explorers led by David Livingstone. The children called each other on the telephone with ideas for the Jungle Party activities, such as Pin the Tusks on the Elephant, Following Animal Tracks, scavenger hunts, and Camouflage Hide-and-Seek, and they gave suggestions for stuffed animal prizes.

What struck me most was the depth of the children's involvement. I wondered how this passion for learning and deep involvement could be brought into schools, particularly for students who were failing under traditional instruction. Too many students had become passive learners who waited for things to be done *to* them and *for* them, for some kind of magic to enlighten them; it rarely did. The poor listeners, nonreaders, bad mathematicians, nonspellers, and failures at written language tended to feel that they were hopeless students, when they were not. Many unsuccessful students at school were excellent thinkers. They just thought differently. They did not rely on rote memory or verbal thinking, which tend to be bases of traditional instruction.

MANY INTELLIGENCES, MANY INTERESTS

My Academic Club experiences, which began in the 1960s, were confirmed by Dr. Howard Gardner's theories in the 1980s. Gardner, who is a professor of education at Harvard University, is one of the foremost experts of a new approach to assessing human intelligence called *multiple intelligences*. In his book, *Frames of Mind: The Theory of Multiple Intelligences* (1983/1999), Gardner describes eight different types of intelligence, of which no one takes priority over any other:

- Musical intelligence (which gives great composers and performers to the world)

- Spatial intelligence (which produces artists, sculptors, and architects)

- Bodily-kinesthetic intelligence (which brings forth dancers and athletes)

- Interpersonal intelligence (which is drawn on by the world's greatest leaders from Alexander the Great to Gandhi to Nelson Mandela)

- Intrapersonal intelligence, or empathy and insight (which produces psychologists, teachers, and healers)

- Nature and outdoor intelligence (which produces forest rangers, zoo keepers, agriculturists, and veterinarians)

- Linguistic intelligence (which gives rise to writers, journalists, and orators)

- Logical-mathematical intelligence (which is the intelligence of scientists and mathematicians)

Most nontraditional learners use one of Gardner's intelligences or other intelligences (e.g., "street smarts") that Gardner did not write about. *Street smarts* are demonstrated by children who enter a room and in minutes know where everything is, who get an instant feeling for interpersonal dynamics, and who intuitively know which adult to ask for which favor. The existence of Gardner's types of eight intelligences explains how a child who fails in school can achieve astonishing success as an adult; he or she does not have to follow the rules of a logical-linguistic system as exists in most schools in the 21st century.

Like Gardner, I saw how the magic of the children's play involved every part of the children's being. I watched how the children working on the Jungle Party became entranced with learning about jungles and rainforests. The party brought out their critical thinking, their creativity, and their thirst to know more. Our birthday parties drew on all of Gardner's intelligences plus more. I saw children who were considered to be slow learners rise to become top-of-the-heap leaders in preparing our birthday parties. They were excellent problem solvers. Some were visual thinkers and could see in their mind's eye how to transform rooms to fit specific themes. Others had a keen sense of drama and knew how to convey knowledge theatrically. I saw distractible youngsters with severe attention disorders concentrate well through this total immersion approach that dunked them into learning.

Learning through experience is a cornerstone of the Academic Club Methodology for both students and teachers. The great American educational theorist Dewey believed the teacher's job was to select the kinds of experiences that would encourage discovery, exploration, and a spirit of inquiry and to place children in these settings.

WHY THE METHODOLOGY WORKS

By experiencing the past through playing roles, making decisions, and debating consequences, children naturally begin to relate the past to the present. They consolidate and internalize their understanding of history through selective play in an Academic Club. Studying the past prepares these students to understand the present and plan for the future.

The Academic Club Methodology educates students in depth and across disciplines. It works well with learners with severe disabilities and also excites typically developing learners. Its success rests on the identification of teachers who can use the Academic Club Methodology to teach, the training of those teachers, and the support and supervision of those teachers.

Since 1967, I and the other teachers at The Lab School have seen that Academic Clubs work. We have watched students with extremely severe learning disabilities go on to college. In fact, 90% of The Lab School students attend college, and I am convinced that their large storehouses of information, their large vocabularies, their critical thinking, their ability to relate history to present times and to the future, and their memories of complex content derive from being taught through the Academic Club Methodology.

The wonderful thing about the Methodology is that it is adaptable to different school environments. It can be used with children from elementary school through high school and by teachers who teach a single subject area or multiple subjects. The two variations of the Methodology are called the Method and the Approach. The *Academic Club Method* is highly stylized with a clearly delineated structure and is typically used by teachers of elementary school students. It encompasses multiple subject areas and involves elaborate props. Behavior management is structured around the dramatic framework of the Academic Club and a series of props as learning tools. Academic content is acquired through total immersion, learning through all of the senses, project learning, and active and discovery learning.

The appealing dramatic framework of the Academic Club Method includes

- A decorated door that depicts the theme
- A password
- Total room decorations that convey the topic
- Costumes
- An opening ritual
- Special seating
- A dramatic cover that gives the teacher authority
- A specific role for each child
- A behavior code
- A closing ritual

The *Academic Club Approach*, like the Method, is experiential, hands-on, and personalized; however, it does not have the required, delineated structure of the Academic Club Method. The Approach still uses drama, most art forms, multisensory approaches, and concrete materials to teach abstract concepts and to deeply involve students, but it does not require the total immersion of the Method. This generalized use of the Academic Club Methodology is typically used for older students (middle and high school) in a single subject area. Students do use props as learning tools but may or may not wear costumes and don't give a password upon entering the room. The Approach does not warrant a particular room or a curtain that is designated to recreate a time period or special situation. Instead, students get deeply involved in the topic by using different intelligences. The Approach employs project learning, active and discovery learning, and experiential education.

The Approach, like the Method, demands precise teaching objectives for each activity and a means of evaluation to assess if the activity meets its objectives. Both the Method and the Approach require the teacher or Club Leader to develop original materials, such as diagnostic-prescriptive games or resources

hyperactivity disorder, and these students learn best in classes of 8–10 students. With our youngest students with the most severe disabilities, we have held Academic Clubs as small as 5–6 students. Inclusive classrooms of 25–30 students, however, can also use the Academic Club Methodology effectively.

Academic Clubs at The Lab School usually run 45–50 minutes per day. When Clubs were used in a public school only once a week, they lasted more than an hour and a half for each Club period. Because of the intensity of instruction, students are only involved in one Academic Club during the school day. Ordinarily, Clubs meet daily during the academic year and do not change by semester.

This book explores the elements of the Academic Club Methodology and helps prepare you to put them into action in your classroom, school, after-school program, and/or religious program. I hope that this book inspires you to employ this unique and successful approach with your students!

2

Why the Academic Club Methodology Works for Students with Learning Disabilities and ADHD

Charles hated school. He had been to four of them. Although he felt good about himself at home and in the neighborhood, he felt bad about himself at school. Charles didn't feel stupid when he was in the Cave Club learning about hominids. At dinner at home, he discovered he knew more about Paleolithic man than his older brother.

Marie wanted to hide in the back row in class and not be called on to speak. However, she felt important and needed as Assistant Manager of the Storekeepers Club.

Norman had what they called a motor mouth; he talked all of the time, and his body moved relentlessly. This perpetual chatterbox was the Barker in the Carnival Club who kept spinning the big bicycle wheel and luring visitors into the carnival with promises of prizes and wondrous sights within.

Alexandra said whatever popped into her mind without thinking. Then, she became Secret Agent 005 in the summer school Secret Agent Club. The teacher, Captain 007, reminded the agents to think before they spoke and not to give away secrets. Alexandra demonstrated more control of what came out of her mouth.

Kim was disorganized, could not read or write at age 9, and had a poor memory for facts. As Isis, the Goddess of Wisdom, in the Egyptian Gods Club, Kim loved seeing postcards of what her Goddess looked like. She made masks so she could recognize her Goddess, listened to the myths featuring her Goddess, and then made a pop-up book of her own about one of the stories featuring her Goddess.

Joey didn't know his left side from his right or forward from backward, and he frequently got lost in the large school building. But he always felt safe in an assigned seat in the Pirates Club on the main deck in the circle made of red tape. He reveled in the opening ritual holding out his skull and crossbones flag to points of the compass at the Pirate Chief's command, "All pirates north. All pirates south. All pirates east. All pirates west. All pirates stand tall."

Laura learned everything visually. She didn't think in words, but in pictures. In the Knights and Ladies Club, she knew that the feet of her Club Leader, Lord Don, measured exactly 1 foot. In order to visualize the length of the famous Bayeux Tapestry, she took a roll of toilet paper and asked Lord Don to step out exactly 231 feet (heel to toe).

Marco was disorganized. He was always losing something, forgetting his belongings, and looking disheveled. He responded with alacrity to lining up for his Club. He liked the feeling of entering a room in order, having an assigned seat, and having a defined place in his group. It helped him pay attention.

Kevin was unfocused much of the time. All of his report cards said that if he could focus, he would be able to show how smart he was. In the Cave Club, Kevin acted a dramatic role, wore his caveman costume, whispered a password into the teacher's ear, and participated in a ritual opening; he could leave all of the distractions behind him. The ritualistic beginning demanded that he, as part of the group, say, "We slowly rise up like *Homo erectus.* We use our hands like *Homo habilis* (gestures with hands). We speak and communicate like *Homo sapiens,* and count one, two, three! Greetings, Wise Elder." This ritual grabbed his attention and held it.

Abigail, who was a visual thinker, could draw ideas better than speak about them. She was talented in art and very original; she loved being a member of the Renaissance Councillors Club. Her role was to be Leonardo da Vinci, which she enjoyed because da Vinci made many ingenious inventions during his life and constantly drew his ideas. Abigail found that she could draw her own ideas, too, and she aimed to invent new contraptions to make life easier for human beings. She studied birds and how they flew and related these concepts to airplanes. Her next project was to look carefully at insects to see what could be invented from studying their movements.

BUILDING SELF-ESTEEM

The preceding examples show how the Academic Club Methodology was successful with children with moderate to severe learning disabilities and/or attention-deficit/hyperactivity disorder (ADHD) as well as children at risk for academic failure. The Methodology 1) demanded total involvement, 2) helped them to focus, 3) set clear boundaries for them, 4) taught them in ways that did not rely heavily on language abilities, 5) introduced complex material in an unintimidating manner, and 6) introduced complex material in ways that promoted long-term retention. It helped the children thrive in school and showed them that success was not only possible but also expected. Without such success, though, these children would have experienced devastating consequences.

Traditionally, the biggest battle we face with nonreaders or poor readers is rebuilding their sense of self-worth; these students tend to feel bad about themselves. They are very aware of their academic shortcomings. In fact, adults with reading difficulties often admit that they knew something was wrong with them as early as kindergarten. When children notice that they cannot do what other students do with ease, they taste the bitter herbs of defeat year after year in school. This disappointment leads them to create defense mechanisms to keep others from seeing their inadequacies. They put on "masks" to avoid pain felt from teasing or their own recognition of their failures. As a result, energy does not go toward learning but toward protecting self-worth through various defense mechanisms. Some children become class clowns who make everybody laugh in order to deflect attention from their difficulties. Others become "know it alls" who put everybody else down in an effort to conceal their own flaws. A child may become a Good Samaritan who runs errands so that he or she will not have to do any schoolwork. Nonreaders often pretend that they do not want to read.

Fortunately, many children with learning disabilities and ADHD shine in areas of school where the instruction is not verbal and/or logical-mathematical. Adults with reading difficulties often had childhood experiences of competence and mastery in the arts. For example, 30-year-old Ricardo said, "I hated school except for art and music. I was alive then. Then, people could see the person I was at home, in the summertime, everywhere but at school."

Drama can be especially comforting for children with learning disabilities and ADHD because it allows them to pretend that they are someone else. Children who are withdrawn in traditional classrooms often become extroverts when placed in the dramatic framework of an Academic Club. If they are afraid to say something wrong and risk failure, they feel protected by the Academic Club's dramatic cover, by their Club role, and by the dramatic theme of the Club. They dare to guess or say what they think because their character is the one speaking in the Academic Club. Through "childhood magic," a Club Member becomes a character and can then feel that the character is the one making mistakes. Therefore, a student who comes across as flat or emotionless in a traditional classroom may show animated reactions in the Academic Club.

The arts are also important for students with learning disabilities and ADHD because people who work in the arts often find unorthodox ways to teach youngsters. Ingenuity at problem solving, resourcefulness, and flexibility—all skills that are greatly needed to work with children with learning disabilities—are common traits among artists. Practicing artists usually engage in activities with a contagious enthusiasm. They often become excited by the challenge of trying to reach and teach children who puzzle other adults. Their richness of style, depth, originality, and ability to create things from whatever resources are available make them uniquely suited to teach children who resist usual school practices. Many artists/art teachers have become Academic Club Leaders. Teachers who are most comfortable in the use of arts and concrete approaches are particularly attracted to the Methodology.

The Methodology also builds on the strengths of teachers. The same Academic Club can be taught successfully in different ways by drawing on each teacher's special talents. For example, one Renaissance Club was taught for a number of years with students taking on roles of famous artists and the Club Leader acting as the great patron of the arts, Lorenzo De Medici. A different Renaissance Club Leader decided to explore poetry by reading Dante's *Inferno* to the Club Members and providing an exciting visual exploration of Dante's levels of the Inferno. Still another Renaissance Club Leader, who was a multi-talented artist and musician, decided to give one Club Member the role of a Renaissance musician, Josquin des Prez, a genius 15th-century composer who changed the medieval view of music as a craft into the High Renaissance idea of music as an art. Another Club Leader gave a Club Member interested in science the exciting role of Galileo. In this way, the Academic Club Methodology can help both students and teachers feel successful.

CHARACTERISTICS OF CHILDREN WITH LEARNING DISABILITIES

Although you probably know some students who have experienced failure in traditional classrooms, you may not understand the specifics of their learning difficulties. This section presents some of our findings about children with learning disabilities at The Lab School. For instance, we have found that children with learning disabilities are neurologically immature. They act their age in some ways and not in others. These children look typical but don't learn typically. Their responses and behavior are often more appropriate for much younger children, and they often lack basic skills that are usually acquired in the preschool years, such as sorting information into categories; differentiating by color, shape, and size; and integrating several things at once. These skills are the foundations necessary for academic learning, so these children are unsuccessful in traditional classrooms. Through a panoply of art forms, youngsters with learning disabilities can learn to sort information, differentiate, and integrate, and they can enjoy aesthetic experiences that can lead to future pleasures as audience members and/or artists. They can be successful in school and employment.

Children with delayed development live in a world of *disorder*. They have a hard time controlling their attention and actions. What they need from the outside world is *order*. Through the arts and Academic Clubs, children can put order into their world, make sense of what they know, relate past experiences to the present, turn muscular activity into thought, and put ideas into action.

Many children with learning disabilities and ADHD have trouble integrating several processes at once and need to do one thing at a time. Children with ADHD, for example, may look as though they are not paying attention to anything, but, in fact, they are attending to every stimulus around them. These children are bombarded by every sight, sound, and movement in the room. They cannot assign priorities or tell themselves which tasks are most important, less important, and unimportant. They give equal importance to all things and do not set priorities, so they are overwhelmed by too much information at once. Everything going on in the classroom distracts these children from paying attention to what they are there to do—learn! Children with ADHD are not yet equipped to automatically filter out irrelevant and unnecessary stimuli; however, the ritual activities of lining up for an Academic Club, whispering the password, putting on a costume, getting props, and sitting in an assigned seat help them focus. The very structure of the Academic Club is an ally to the weak control systems of children with learning disabilities and ADHD.

The Academic Club Methodology is designed to meet the needs of students with concentration and memory problems, learning disabilities, and ADHD, as well as students who are at risk for failure. It does so by producing immediate results, eliciting total student involvement, and drawing on students' strengths— all processes that can also be used for children without learning difficulties. Reading, writing, and research components can be added to the Methodology and emphasized when the Methodology is used with typically developing children.

The Methodology was designed for nonreaders, nonwriters, and unpredictable students. The basic goal is to build on students' strengths, but it takes detective work on the part of the teacher to filter out what students do well. It may be something in the academic realm, such as visualization, good conceptualization, or good listening or language skills. Often, students do not have obvious talents, and teachers have to dig deeper to discover the student who is the "best finder" of lost objects, "the quickest fixer" of things, the most thoughtful, the most original, the one with the best sense of humor, or the one who connects ideas well.

Experiential learning through hands-on projects in the Academic Clubs requires a frequent change of pace, alternating very active learning with listening and discussion. Club Leaders try to produce visible results in short time periods because Club Members may be impatient, unable to concentrate, or very impulsive. With miniprojects, students can physically point to their results and explain what they had to do first, next, and last. This ability is important for children who have trouble with sequences and order. In addition to miniprojects, several in-depth projects are planned for the entire year. Through these projects, students learn that producing great results takes time, intense thought, planning, and continued energy.

HELPING CHILDREN TO FOCUS

Instead of an expanding world that includes unlimited opportunities, free choices, and as many options as possible, children with learning disabilities need boundaries in order to learn effectively and to create fully. The Academic Club teacher and the structure of the Club must become the focusing agent for these children. The programming and material must also help children to concentrate, discriminate, and set priorities.

Academic Clubs give children with learning disabilities and ADHD the parameters and borders to organize what they wish to express. Because these children need a time, a space, and a place for all things, the Methodology provides clear, precise directions given one at a time. Use of drama helps to screen out distractions. For children who need help locating their own bodies in space, arranged seating is a blessing. A Secret Agent sits on the chair with his or her secret agent number (e.g., 007) marked on it, an Egyptian God sits in front of a special column with his or her logo, a Medieval Knight sits on a pillow with his heraldic symbol on it, and a Disc Jockey sits by his or her specific compact disc.

Children who often miss the main point need to know their goals. If they cannot visualize well, then a model or a demonstration can provide direction before they work on their own. If children have weak memories, then they need help learning to make pictures in their minds to remind them of information. If they cannot deal with sequences, they need to be shown explicitly what to do first, next, and last in order to understand the parts that contribute to the whole and the order of procedure. The Academic Club Methodology seeks to provide these children with the help they need.

SETTING CLEAR BOUNDARIES

In order to meet the needs of children who are overloaded with stimuli that is unscreened from their senses, the Academic Club Methodology places limits on the amount of materials, work, time, procedures, space, and words used. Abstract concepts are taught through concrete materials. For example, teaching young children about the North Atlantic Treaty Organization (NATO) can be done by using this basic concept: countries stick together to build resources and fight common enemies. Students can form designs using designated yellow, orange, and red pieces of paper that symbolize NATO countries. Children do not have the option to use other colors because these colors are not designated to symbolize NATO.

Basic skills, such as dealing with left–right and forward–backward directions, are presented in more mature forms that nevertheless have clear boundaries. In the Pirates Club, all pirates step forward, then turn north, south, east, and west as part of their opening ritual. The teacher always plays the role of an authority figure and is clearly in charge. The teacher, as Captain Hook or Mary Beth, a famous woman pirate, is the only one who has the authority to command the pirates. The structure of the roles of students and teachers create clear behavior expectations. Discipline is handled within the same framework, so a Secret Agents Club would have "agent rules," an American Indian Tribe would respect its "elders," and a Renaissance Councillors Club would use "council" discipline. The Academic Club also provides order and structure through the specific way the room is entered, the prescribed seating arrangement, the ritualistic opening ceremony, the limit of only three or four activities presented within the 50 minutes of Academic Club time, and the formal dismissal. Children with learning disabilities and ADHD thrive in this environment because they are given such clear limits and prescribed codes of behavior.

TEACHING THAT DOES NOT RELY HEAVILY ON LANGUAGE ABILITIES

Many children with learning disabilities also experience language problems (Catts & Kamhi, 1999; Dillon & Dodd, 1994; Vellutino, 1979). About 85% of the students at The Lab School have moderate to severe language learning disabilities. The Academic Club Methodology is designed to help children who are unable to read or express themselves well to actively participate in their education. Instruction draws on multiple intelligences, visual, and other senses to relay content. Primarily, the Methodology uses a visual, concrete approach through which children see, recreate, and visualize materials and develop artwork or projects. Being immersed in a historical period (e.g., American Pioneers Club, Livingstone's Explorers Club) or a dramatic theme (e.g., African Market Club, Computer Programmers Club) demands the use of every resource that Club Members have. A child's body, mind, and spirit are all active in an Academic Club setting.

Club Members develop their language skills while immersed in the topic. The Club Leader reads to them and shows them artwork and photographs relevant to the topic. Children also discuss the projects they work on, use passwords, and participate in a vocal dismissal procedure. Computer CD-ROMs and short films may be introduced occasionally to give an overview of a topic (e.g., castles in medieval times) or to reinforce a project the students have just finished (e.g., sculpting gargoyles). Learning by doing is the starting point, but activities are usually followed by discussion and questions.

MAKING EACH CHILD FEEL INCLUDED

When I designed the Academic Club Methodology, I chose the word *club* carefully. It implies membership, belonging, and ownership. Also, everything presented in a Club is academically based—thus, the name *Academic Clubs*. Academic Clubs are groups in which each person has a recognized place. By their very nature, Clubs are noncompartmentalized—the arts, the subject matter, the concepts, and the ideas all relate to one another, reinforce one another, and funnel toward the same objectives. Children with learning disabilities tend to be egocentric (i.e., unable to see through another person's perspective), so they have trouble working in groups in traditional classrooms. The magic of Academic Clubs, however, is that their dramatic framework and use of pretend play encourage children to naturally work as a group.

Club activities also allow room for individualization. Because the Methodology uses concrete materials and project learning, a teacher can place children in subgroups according to their strengths. Activities can be adapted for students with motor and/or visual–motor skill difficulties. One subgroup can create a large project out of heavy cardboard or wood while another makes a miniature or small project out of pipe cleaners.

The Methodology not only builds on children's strengths but also aims to give them a positive image of themselves. Each student is given a role—a dramatic cover—of a successful person, such as Curator of Housing in the Museum Club, John D. Rockefeller in the Industrialists Club, or Larry King in the Newscasters Club. In addition, students are given attention and praise for everything that they do well. Very specific praise is given; tokens, certificates, medals, and other visible signs of appreciation are part of the daily routine. The message is: We like who you are, what you are, and the way you are behaving and thinking. Thus, children get feedback through positive reinforcement rather than through disapproval of negative behavior.

INTRODUCING COMPLEX
MATERIAL IN AN UNINTIMIDATING WAY

The Academic Club Methodology is designed to entice children, to capture their imagination and enthusiasm, to build on their love of pretend play, and to offer them fun and success in learning by immersing them in the atmosphere of a given historical period (e.g., Cave Club; Gods of Ancient Egypt, Greece, and Rome; Knights and Ladies Club of the Middle Ages; the Renaissance Councillors; the Philosophical Society) or plunging them into a real-life experience (e.g., Smokey the Bear Nature Club, Magician's Club, Tarzan's Jungle Club, Western Gold Mining Club). The Methodology is based on the theory that children can be taught what they need to know through the very things that interest them most.

Any subject can be taught through an Academic Club; it is gently woven into a dramatic framework and approached through the arts, literature, science, logic, history, geography, and civics. Creative problem solving is demanded from both teachers and students. Although instruction may look very informal, when done properly, academic objectives for a Club are carefully programmed and rigorously reviewed. The step-by-step teaching is reflected in ongoing written reports that are part of the Club's record-keeping procedure. Objectives, activities, and comments on individual and group behavior are documented by the teacher in daily reports that are used regularly for reference.

The Academic Club Methodology is designed to stretch bright minds and tap students' imagination in the classroom while subtly teaching the mechanical skills of reading, spelling, handwriting, and arithmetic. Students do not feel overwhelmed because of their deep involvement in their learning and because of the Methodology's ability to help children use multiple resources to learn. Academic Clubs draw on the full range of children's experiences and relate subject matter to their lives. Clubs relate the past to children's present lives and show children cause-and-effect relationships as well as the steps from planning to action. In addition, abstract concepts are presented in a concrete, understandable way.

The Methodology challenges children's intellect as far and as fast as possible so that students are guaranteed success. Club Members can learn specific readiness skills that they did not master at a younger age because the Club Leader tailors instruction to suit Members' abilities. Students are not overwhelmed but, instead, are offered an interesting and manageable topic to explore. Concepts that would be too complex for students to tackle in traditional classrooms are easily investigated using the Academic Club Methodology and presented in ways to promote retention over a lifetime.

The following example illustrates how one Renaissance Club Leader introduced Dante's *Inferno* to her group of 10-year-olds. She had each student produce a Pocket Inferno made from a watercolor paint set with 10 paint wells and a lid. The paint set served multiple purposes during the project. The watercolor paint was removed from the wells, and nine of the wells became graphic organizers, representing the nine circles of the Inferno. As sections of Dante's poem were read aloud, the Pocket Inferno provided an anchor to which Club Members could tether new vocabulary or abstract concepts. Each well symbolized a different level of the Inferno and a particular behavior deserving of punishment. In this way, the concepts of cause and effect and the law of retribution were reinforced.

The Pocket Inferno provided the location for each student to create symbols for concepts. In the wells, the students built small mixed-media sculptures from clay, found objects, hot glue, and paint. Students were allowed to create original symbols for each action and circle of the Inferno. They had to choose carefully because the well was small and because some ideas would not make good symbols. Club Members were encouraged to look for examples in their own lives and then convert them into sculpture. Some concepts were simple to create images for, such as violence and gluttony; others, such as sullen, traitor, and fraud, challenged the students to search for examples— and, in the process, better internalize their vocabularies. One student found it easy to make a figure that was feeding itself with two hands to represent *gluttony,* but he struggled with how to depict *traitor.* However, when another Club Member said, "It's like turning a back on a friend," he made a statue of a person turning his back on the American flag.

These Pocket Infernos also provided students with a visual prompt for a presentation to their peers. This prop helped the students become more confident presenters. In addition, the project helped students sequence information, which is a skill that students with learning disabilities need to practice. Those who have experienced Pocket Infernos can recall the information on Dante many years later; it is painted in their minds.

EXPECTED RESULTS

The Academic Club Methodology is designed to pave the way for a lifetime of critical thinking and to build language and huge storehouses of information for children. Since 1967, students at The Lab School have become so well educated that the knowledge they acquire becomes a part of their being. When they go on to college, the knowledge they have learned through Academic Clubs is refreshed by textbooks and history courses.

Former Lab School students tell us how much the Academic Clubs helped them throughout their education. They explain that they relived their roles and pictured their Academic Clubs when they were in classes discussing relevant information and when they were in Europe seeing the cathedrals, monuments, buildings, archways, and art they had studied at The Lab School. They tell us that allusions to Greece and Rome in literature make sense to them. Art history classes bring "old friends" back to them, as do architectural design, archeology, anthropology, and cultural anthropology.

Too often, children with learning disabilities are not taught classic literature or serious content because they cannot read. I believe that the Academic Club Methodology's focus on this content explains why so many students of The Lab School have succeeded in colleges in the social science area. With the Academic Club Methodology, it does not matter that a child cannot yet read or that his or her writing is far behind. Students are taught history, geography, civics, science, and literature in ways that they will learn it and integrate the knowledge in their constantly increasing storehouse of information. Children who previously only knew academic failure are certain to find success with this approach.

3

How to Keep Students
Engaged in Learning

*Why Students Have Few
Behavior Problems in Academic Clubs*

Behavior management is a common problem in schools. Instruction that relies on lecture tends to alienate learners with language disorders, learning disabilities, and attention-deficit/hyperactivity disorder (ADHD). Fortunately, Club Leaders, for the most part, do not have to deal with behavior problems. This chapter explores the reasons why students have few behavior problems in Academic Clubs. It clarifies the responsibilities and tasks of Club Leaders and explains how to plan a 6-week Academic Club. The chapter ends with an example of one Academic Club in action.

TYPICAL CAUSES OF NEGATIVE STUDENT BEHAVIOR

Many students need to do an activity first before they can listen to a short lecture. The needs of students who are nonreaders or poor readers are often overlooked in schools. Common behavioral techniques, such as making contracts with students, taking away students' free time, removing students from favorite activities, sending students to detention, and calling students' parents, often do little to prevent future misbehavior.

Negative behavior occurs when children with learning disabilities, ADHD, and language problems do not feel as if they belong. In classrooms in which they have failed over and over to read, write, spell, do math, follow instructions, or take timed tests, these children allow their frustration, anger, guilt, and profound fear of failure to manifest itself in behavior problems. Hyperactivity, impulsiveness, distractibility, and a weak attention span, which tend to be neurological problems, also add to these students' difficulties, leading them to regularly disrupt groups and pick on other students. Boredom resulting from failure to understand the material frequently turns into unfriendly behavior.

There are many reasons why children in Academic Clubs exhibit few challenging behaviors. First, Club Leaders invite children into a beautifully decorated room and a dramatic setting. Children get to play roles of successful characters, not themselves (e.g., Joey or Amy failing in the classroom). The Club has a secret password, and the word *secret* excites children. Students have to say the password, put on a costume, and recite an opening ritual in order to belong to this exciting group, but once they belong, they are "in"! Being somebody else allows children to risk failure—for, after all, their characters will fail, not them. This phenomenon is similar to how children feel with puppets because children magically assign any failure to the puppets, not to themselves. With less fear of failure, children tend to lower their defenses and become more available for learning. When they feel more content with themselves, they do not need to act out and cause trouble in a group. Hence, children who are known to have behavior problems in their general education classrooms become active learners in Academic Clubs and rarely act out or exhibit negative behaviors.

STUDENTS FEEL SAFE

Children usually become intensely involved in an Academic Club if they feel secure enough to throw themselves into an activity and learn; their Academic Club relies on their participation. The Academic Club setting has a tight structure. The Club Leader has an authoritative role, such as Captain Dan, Lord Don, and Ranger Gina. The rules are clear within the dramatic framework. In a Cave Club, Wise Elder (Club Leader) sets the rules and assigns seats for each student on fur mats. The Hominids (Club Members) learn procedures for acquiring material, for storing material, and for playing games. In the Museum Club, the Club Leader is Director of the Museum, and Club Members are employees. Sometimes, the Museum Club Leader is the head of the Museum Association of America, and Club Members are each directors of a different museum. In some Academic Clubs, Council Discipline provides the structure, such as in the Renaissance Councillors Club, where Lorenzo de Medici leads the Council to adopt certain rules and regulations.

With hands-on learning, experiential education, project learning, and activity learning, all of a Club Member's different intelligences are brought into play. Visual thinkers, children who learn best through body motion, and children who learn through rhythm and music can learn in an Academic Club setting. Many children with severe learning disabilities have not experienced much success in learning, but with the Academic Club Methodology, they find that they can sure get used to it! Success takes care of a lot of behavior problems. Club Members don't feel stupid in their Academic Clubs. They don't feel like "Mr. Big Failure," as one child labeled himself. They play roles of successful people in their clubs, experience success in their Academic Clubs, and carry that sense of success with them to other activities.

STUDENTS RECEIVE SPECIFIC PRAISE

The Academic Club Methodology advocates giving specific praise for behavior that Club Leaders want to see. When teachers reward positive behavior, students learn when they are exhibiting appropriate behavior—behavior that fits the situation—and are encouraged to behave the same way in the future. The Club Leader might say things like: "Leonardo da Vinci is not saying a word as he gets ready to enter the room; good!" "I like the way Michelangelo is sitting still." "I can see Della Robbia has his eyes on me!" "Ghiberti is standing tall."

Club Members are also given tangible rewards. Brunelleschi may receive a florin for risking failure to give an answer aloud. Lord Don may give out medallions, precious stones, and the Ring of Nobility for effort, correct answers, and kindness to others. These rewards reinforce children's sense of self-worth and attempt to help them build more self-confidence and higher self-esteem.

Built into the Academic Club Methodology is the Club Leader's respect for the students and the students' respect for one another. The Museum Director will point out how helpful Curator Michael has been to a colleague and make sure that all Club Members realize that this behavior is valuable and important in the Museum. This praise may encourage Curator Juan to offer help to Curator Jake as he puts together an exhibit. The Museum Director will quickly give Curator Juan a small certificate or card picturing an ancient monument, wall carvings, or a famous mural. As you can see, the Museum Director does not take for granted cooperative, focused behavior.

The Lab School and Baltimore Lab, a division of The Lab School of Washington, each have a huge bulletin board with the label "random acts of kindness." Any time a faculty member hears a child saying something kind or sees a student doing a helpful act for a classmate, this behavior is written about and put on the bulletin board for all to see. Thoughtfulness and kindness are valued.

STUDENTS HAVE SPECIAL MEMBERSHIP

Because each Academic Club has a secret password and is only experienced by the Club Members and their Club Leader, students can, as a group, reject disruptive behavior and promote cooperative, peaceful behavior. Youngsters who are known to tease, bully, or distract others behave appropriately in their Academic Clubs. Although students with ADHD still exhibit restless behavior and excessive movement, Academic Club activities apply excess movement toward activity learning. In the Park Rangers Club, for example, Rom, who usu-

ally is very hyper, was assigned the role of Trainee Rom, instructed to frequently get up and check the hall for unwanted animals. The Storekeepers
Club's Clerks used up excess energy by making products, placing them on
shelves, and walking through the aisles to check or order products. The Pirates
Club also channeled children's restless energy by demanding that all the Pirates follow the Pirate King and walk the plank. The Pirates had to salute their
Pirate flag to the north, south, east and west and do frequent aerobics or cal-
isthenics to keep strong.

To counter distractibility and help members keep focus, the Academic
Club Methodology insists on using tactile objects. The Cruiseship Members
and their Captain used compasses. Employing cards with pictures and symbols
to guide them, the Aristocrats Travel Club Members went on a pretend safari
to a famous animal park, Ngoro-Ngoro, in Tanzania one week. Another week,
they went to the Taj Mahal in India. They also went on trips to the Leaning
Tower of Pisa in Italy, Machu Picchu in Peru, the Pyramids of Giza in Egypt, and
Mount Rushmore in South Dakota. They stamped their homemade passports
with these pictures and symbols. The Circus Club and Carnival Club had all
kinds of appropriate props placed around the room that demanded to be
touched, jumped on, guided by a wheel, or could not be entered without
climbing into or out of an apparatus.

STUDENTS' FASCINATION MODIFIES THEIR BEHAVIOR

In Academic Clubs, students are usually fascinated by what is going on and do
not want to miss any of the activities. Their attention is on the Academic Club
activities because they are intensely involved; as a result, they do not feel as if
they need to act out to gain adult or peer attention. The ethics of the Academic Club are that Club Members must be cooperative, help one another, and
enjoy each other's successes. Youngsters rarely feel compelled to violate this
code. There are also so many enticing activities in the Academic Club, such as
those that involve unusual movements, gestures, tastes, and colorful and exciting projects, that children rarely have time to get out of order. Students with
the toughest reputations are usually no trouble in an Academic Club.

CLUB LEADERS ADAPT
ACTIVITIES TO MEET STUDENTS' NEEDS

The Academic Club Methodology can be used on a daily basis with students
with oppositionally defiant behavior, obsessive compulsive disorder, Tourette
syndrome, ADHD, learning disabilities, and severe language problems. The
Methodology engenders cooperation from these students because Club Leaders make appropriate adaptations for students to be included in all activities.
By paying careful attention to the learning difficulties of students that may pro-

duce behavior problems, Academic Club Leaders often can prevent problems. For example, if the rest of the class is cutting out an emblem, sewing on leather, or gluing mosaics, a Club Leader may simplify the assignment or give a different, but equally important, assignment to a youngster with poor eye–hand coordination and visual-motor problems. A Club Leader may teach students with poor articulation or trouble speaking to clap or stomp out the syllables of a word. Pointing to various parts of the body or to common objects may also help students remember a word or phrase. For example, touching their necks helped Magicians Club Members remember their password, *necromancy*.

A student with Tourette syndrome may make barking sounds and exhibit various tics that frighten peers. Other students may worry that they will develop the same uncontrollable behaviors. However, if the Club Leader chooses one area in which this child performs well (e.g., art, photography, music), the student with Tourette syndrome can shine. Gradually, other children will lose their fear of the student.

When a student with obsessive compulsive disorder has trouble stopping an activity when asked to because he or she wants to make sure the project is absolutely perfect before considering it finished, the Club Leader can give the child tasks that have clear points of completion (e.g., puzzles that are completed when they are assembled into a whole). Another option is that when it is time for the next activity, the Club Leader can use a dramatic approach to transport the child forward and to take the child's mind off of the present activity. The Club Leader can say something such as, "We will be going on a hunt for rocks with hieroglyphics on them! All eyes ready! Go!"

CLUBS IMPROVE STUDENTS' SELF-WORTH

Students with language-based learning difficulties need activity learning, and when they receive what they need, few behavior problems arise. Six-year-old Maria, known as Blue Wind in Cave Club, used to cry every time she got frustrated. Then, Wise Elder (Club Leader) asked her to hold tightly onto her fur jacket the next time she felt like crying. Wise Elder also asked the other Cavemen to help Maria by noticing when she was clutching her jacket and helping her to feel better about herself. After a while, Maria stopped crying, and her fellow Cavemen were as proud of her as she was of herself. A similar technique worked with Rodney (known as Grey Cloud) who tended to yell and stomp his feet every time he felt frustrated.

Alexis talked incessantly in the Travel Agents Club. He wanted to punch the tickets that each Travel Agent gave him, but he could only do so if he could control his talking. Alexis decided to limit his talking so that he could keep up with his job of collecting tickets.

Joachin was afraid that he could not make a good enough mask in the African Market Club. His Club Leader decided to pair him with Alicia, who was an artist and enjoyed working on group art projects. Together the two Merchants were able to make a mask that they both were happy with.

The preceding stories show how simple techniques to improve self-worth were used to correct behavior problems. Many behavior problems relate to a child's feeling of worthlessness, but negative feelings diminish if a child learns that he or she is not "stupid" or "bad at everything." For children who have been abused, have experienced emotional loss, or have endured a traumatic experience, however, self-worth is not as easy to repair. Nevertheless, these children respond well to the Academic Club Methodology. Our experience at The Lab School is that when we tailor instruction to the children's developmental levels and ensure that these children can succeed, the children exhibit less negative behavior and are able to work cooperatively as part of a group.

SPECIFIC TASKS OF A CLUB LEADER

Club Leaders have many tasks. These include using dramatic roles, employing hands-on learning techniques, demonstrating through concrete objects, approaching topics from any angle, assessing Club Members' skills, creating hooks for memorization, personalizing information, solving problems, and rewarding positive behavior. To test their knowledge, students play diagnostic-prescriptive games created by their teachers; formal written testing does not convey what students who cannot read or write know.

Using Dramatic Roles

Club Leaders need to make the Academic Club setting so real via their enthusiasm and imagination and sense of drama that each Club Member believes that he or she is transported into the chosen setting. As mentioned previously, the root of the Academic Club Methodology is total involvement, so the main challenge for Club Leaders is fully engaging each child's body, mind, and spirit. The Academic Club Leader always takes on a dramatic role that has great authority. Visitors to the Academic Club should be included in the dramatic cover. A visitor to the Secret Agent Club might be designated a Captain from another agency. In the Storekeepers Club, a visitor could be Marketing Manager or Vice President in Charge of Sales.

Using Hands-On Learning Techniques

Club Leaders structure their curricula to rely on hands-on learning, simulation, experiential projects, and group activities. Some of these activities may include using playdough to create relief maps and playing teacher-made board games. Active learning precedes discussion. For example, children would create relief maps, then discuss the different geographic features shown on the maps. The order of activities is: Look, Do, Analyze, Talk. Everything is kept visual and concrete; tactile, movement-oriented activities are used whenever possible.

Demonstrating Through Concrete Objects

In every case, abstract principles should be taught through concrete objects, such as using scales to demonstrate the principle of "balance of power." Elastic pulled in three different directions by three different students can be used to represent America's "checks and balances" system. One student can represent the legislative branch of government, another the judicial branch, and the third the executive branch. When the students each pull on their piece of elastic, they affect the other pieces of elastic, just as the different branches of government affect each other.

Approaching Topics from Any Angle

Club Leaders should have a broad, cross-disciplinary grasp of the academic materials they are teaching. For instance, the Industrialists Club's Leader should not only know American history from the 1700s to 1900 but also should know about the stock market, banking, world history, the role of women, the use of child labor, early legislation, and the past and current U.S. political climate. Every project and every concept can be approached from many different angles. The whole pool of knowledge that Club Leaders have accumulated through their research can be brought into play.

Assessing Club Members' Skills

Because of the wide variety of Academic Club activities, events, projects and so forth, a Club Leader has a broad opportunity to observe and assess Club Members' strengths and weaknesses. This kind of systematic analysis can lead to more effective matching of a child to appropriate activities. The Academic Club can also provide the Club Leader with a great deal of diagnostic information. For example, consider the password used to enter the Club. If a child remembers it right away, he or she probably has a good short-term memory. If the child knew the password but can't remember it after a period of a few weeks, he or she may have a long-term memory problem. If the child produces the syllables of the password in reversed order or in a confused order, he or she may have a sequencing problem. If a child has difficulty coloring, pasting, and cutting during an Academic Club activity, then he or she may have visual-motor problems. To improve a child's skills by programming imaginative activities for him or her in his or her specific areas of difficulty is a great challenge, but doing so will guarantee the child's success. What a child can do or likes to do indicates his or her strengths. What a child hates to do or has trouble with shows his or her problem areas. All of the arts provide opportunities for teachers to gain this diagnostic information about their students.

At The Lab School and Baltimore Lab, the knowledge that children have gleaned is assessed through dramatic reenactment, discussion related to a project, and diagnostic-prescriptive games. Teachers also listen carefully to what students say while creating artwork.

Creating Hooks for Memorization

Because Academic Clubs are usually designed for nonreaders and nonwriters, Club Leaders need to find ways to trigger memory that do not rely on the written word. Other senses (e.g., touch, taste, smell, hearing) can be summoned for this task. Teachers have to choose a visual hook on which children can hang information. For example, when teaching about how the United States advanced from an agrarian economy to an industrial economy, a Club Leader can have Club Members make a machine out of objects such as pipe cleaners, ping-pong balls, paper towel holders, baskets, straws, and paper clips. As a group, the students can problem-solve and try out ideas until they create a machine that repeats an action five times, which will prove that the machine works. This activity creates a picture of a machine in the Club Members' minds when they hear the words *Industrial Revolution*. This image becomes the *hook* that helps children recall information about that topic.

Personalizing Information

Whenever possible, the information behind the facts taught in an Academic Club should be linked to the daily lives of the children. The Club Leader should seek out and add the human element to their lessons. For example, what is home life like for an East African fisherman? Have any biographies been written about Nana of the Market? Teachers should search for nuggets of information that fascinate children and provide insight into the straight facts. Children love juicy details, such as descriptions of despicable characters. They like to know about family dynamics, conflicts, and collaboration. They love to learn when an important person did something wrong or "bad." Club Leaders need to go to original sources, such as biographies, autobiographies, and documentaries so that they can present children with the detailed knowledge they crave. Searching for details, one Club Leader found that one industrialist sent his own wife to jail when she disobeyed him and that another man was called "The Mephistopheles of Wall Street."

Solving Problems

Problem-solving abilities are important because Club Leaders are always figuring out different ways to teach the same thing, analyzing tasks, and tailoring the approach to fit different children. Curiosity and interest on the teacher's part fosters curiosity and interest in students. One of the magical aspects of teaching in an Academic Club is setting up situations in which children can discover their own pathways and solutions. One Renaissance Club Leader had children observe birds, as Leonardo da Vinci did, and devise flying machines that they could later compare with da Vinci's invention.

Rewarding Positive Behavior

Club Leaders should pay attention to good behavior, cooperation, and small acts of kindness by students and give recognition through specific praise or tokens appropriate to the Academic Club's theme. Some tokens include "seeds" for Cavemen (to be eaten or planted), "valuables" (painted glass pieces) for Knights and Ladies, "florins" (ancient Italian coins) for the Renaissance Club, "Employee Award Certificates" for the Museum Curators, and "stocks" or play money for the Industrialists. Ways to promote desirable behavior within the dramatic framework of the Academic Club include the Code of Chivalry in the Knights and Ladies Club, Tribal "Code of Honor" in the American Indian Club, and the "Honesty and Service" motto in the Storekeepers Club. Club Leaders can demonstrate inappropriate behavior within the dramatic framework of the Academic Club so that the students have the opportunity to correct their teacher's behavior. This activity guarantees great laughter all around!

HOW CLUB LEADERS BECOME BETTER TEACHERS

Many teachers do not realize that cognitive development is connected to behavioral interaction. Children who exhibit inappropriate behavior need their teachers to check their cognitive development and devise methods of teaching that suit their individual needs. Without such help, children feel so bad about themselves and so confused that they opt to disrupt classes and keep others from learning rather than expose how little they actually know. Because teachers usually receive little training in this area, the Academic Club Methodology helps them become better teachers. Success for children requires task analysis of what is being taught along with an analysis of each child's strengths and weak areas. Club Leaders commit to differentiated instruction to teach through each Club Member's strengths and intelligences.

Club Leaders also benefit from the demand for original research in order to set up an Academic Club. They gain a fund of knowledge and an enthusiasm for the subject that transmits itself to the children. Teachers' sensibilities are heightened, and their intellectual curiosity is stimulated. Usually, the research freshens their interest in finding new vehicles for presenting material. Club Leaders have to try out new pathways, even if an occasional activity fails to meet their expectations. They are carried along by their fascination with the topic, their growing fund of knowledge, and the enthusiasm of their Club Members. They become accustomed to using different intelligences when teaching a Club and tend to think more visually and less linguistically as time goes on. They frequently discover unsuspected talents in themselves and in their students as they use their own resourcefulness in new ways.

An Academic Club Leader cannot rely on last year's curriculum. Of course, some of the material can be recycled and refashioned, but new children necessitate that the Club Leader add different material and make new adaptations. The Club Leader's curiosity tends to lead to unexplored areas that can be used both in research and in teaching. A dynamic Club Leader who has a commitment to inquiry and uses all of his or her senses and intelligences cannot help but become an even more extraordinary classroom teacher. I have seen this transformation happen since The Lab School's founding in 1967. Consider the comments of Sally Montanari, The Lab School's first Club Leader. Montanari was a scene and costume designer as well as an actress.

> *My first Club was the Renaissance Councillors Club, set in one of the most exciting periods of history. My fields are art and drama; I am not a historian by training, but I became so excited about the Italian Renaissance when we talked about it as the context for a Club that I began reading everything about the period that I could lay my hands on. I took armfuls of books out of the public library. I visited museums and art galleries—Washington is an absolute treasure trove—and I borrowed records of Renaissance music. I got completely immersed in it, just as children in a Club do, and I could hardly wait to share it. I was learning so much and making so many new connections—which is what learning is all about.*

When she was asked how she could teach something as abstract as history to children with learning disabilities, Montanari answered:

> *It's very difficult because history is all out of sight, hidden away in the past, and it's hard for children to grasp, especially when they have a very poor sense of time, as these children do. This is where the Club Methodology is so fantastic— it sets the children right down in the middle of history, it allows them to 'be' real characters from another age and live the experiences of those times. They make the decisions that faced those historical figures, and then they check their own decisions and judgment against what really happened. History is no longer a distant abstraction; it is related to real people and the lives of these children.*

The props and decorations and costumes make the period come alive and help the children to visualize and remember. For instance, I got the idea from portraits in the National Gallery that many scholarly people in the Renaissance wore red velvet hats. So it occurred to me that the children could wear red hats as a visible sign of their own interest in learning. We took colored photographs, like portraits, of the children in their red hats and set them in a display beside prints of Renaissance portraits, and they all looked so much alike you wouldn't believe it! Clubs help children link a new experience to what they already know. When we studied the great painters of the Renaissance and saw how they began to put backgrounds into their pictures, that led us naturally to the concept of perspective, which is a hard one. So we all went out on the street, red hats and all, and looked at the telephone poles; we measured them as they appeared to get smaller and closer together way down the road, and the children really understood how perspective works in this concrete way, measuring it themselves. They don't forget it, either.

Montanari used original sources as much as possible. She found material describing how the Council in Florence made decisions about ownership of property or declarations of war. She had her students ponder a problem before the Council and then compare their own judgments with the verdict of history. For example, a metal called *alum* was discovered near the village of Voltera in Italy. Alum could be used to keep dyes from washing out of wool cloth. Lorenzo de Medici wanted to run the mines himself and collect the profits directly. The villagers wanted to send the revenues to Lorenzo de Medici after they mined, processed, and sold the alum. The Renaissance Council debated the problem and voted unanimously to let the villagers run the mines. When Montanari read what the real Florence Council had done, the Club Members were excited because they had voted the same way. To the children's disgust, de Medici had taken over the mines anyway. The children understood completely the anger of the villagers. After delving further into the history, they felt a little better because they found out that de Medici had learned from his early mistakes. Later in his life, he listened carefully to the Council of Florence and worked with them cooperatively.

The Club Members were most impressed by de Medici's sponsorship of great artists. One parent of a 10½-year-old Renaissance Club Member told us that when he and his wife went to a museum to see an exhibition of Henri Matisse's work, their son asked, "Would Lorenzo de Medici have sponsored Matisse? If so, then he has to be a great artist!" His Academic Club knowledge served as a way for him to evaluate the quality of an artist. The transfer of knowledge to everyday life was an educational objective that was accomplished through the Renaissance Club. Through the Academic Club Methodology, an excellent Club Leader inspires students to transfer knowledge and carry it with them for the rest of their lives.

PLANNING A SIX-WEEK ACADEMIC CLUB

The Academic Club Methodology calls on all of the resources teachers can muster. It demands robust mental activity, passionate interest, a well of imagination, willingness to work hard, and use of all of the intelligences defined by Gardner (see Chapter 1). The preparation for a successful Academic Club is rigorous and begins by teachers listing the concepts and basic information that they want children to absorb. A topic must be identified and researched in depth; however, the research is not limited to books and written materials. Visiting museums, watching films, reviewing reliable web sites, and meeting with people familiar with the topic are essential. Other forms of research include handling artifacts, tasting food, and listening to music or topic-related sounds. Teachers must immerse themselves totally in the topic and use all of their senses. This extensive inquiry helps them become so comfortable with the subject matter that information flows out of them and enables them to create an authentic make-believe world that will mesmerize their students.

Planning an Academic Club must be meticulous. Academic Club activities involve concrete objects or experiences. Concepts are introduced through visual, tactile, or physical activities that are within the realm of children's experiences. Instruction uses concrete activities to scaffold the development of abstract and other higher-order thinking skills. For example, to convey the notion of mummification in the Egyptian Gods Club, one Club Leader gathered apples, paring knives, and plastic wrap. The students cut apples in half, wrapped one half in plastic wrap, and left the other half open to the air. Club Members checked the apples the next day to find out what happened. They discovered that the uncovered half of the apple was discolored and wrinkled, whereas the one inside the plastic wrap was well preserved. From the concept of preservation, the Club Leader easily proceeded to a discussion of mummification.

Six-week Academic Clubs are planned in "chunks" of concepts. Three weeks may be spent on one aspect of the topic, while one week may be spent on another aspect. A few days may be all it takes to review some material. In addition, ongoing projects or a special subject may be explored each week. No matter how teachers plan to teach the concepts, the program must be flexible enough to accommodate the unexpected interests of the students. Children's fascination with a certain aspect of a topic may make a teacher decide to lengthen the exploration of a subject, or the teacher may find new information that he or she decides to add as the Academic Club evolves. The Methodology has no imposed set of lessons for specific topics or specific days because ideas of the past day relate to the present day's lesson, and often a subject is broadened to include many art forms and literature. Teachers bring their unique interests and strengths to an Academic Club, so one teacher may pursue a particular topic more in depth than another teacher might. Although the basic content remains stable, teachers are free to shape the curriculum as they wish.

Teachers create their own materials from various sources to teach children who have trouble reading and gaining information from books. Club Leaders become storytellers who share information they have learned from original written sources (e.g., biographies, histories). They illustrate this information with photographs, pictures, and art projects.

The Academic Club Methodology's curriculum grounds students by giving them individual roles through which they can experience the time period being studied. The children become highly motivated to find out about themselves (i.e., their characters). They thus acquire a meaningful, concrete schema to develop as they learn content that relates to their characters.

ONE ACADEMIC CLUB IN ACTION: AFRICAN MARKET CLUB

The following story shows how one third-grade teacher planned an Academic Club and put it into action. The teacher's students were interested in their African heritage, so she decided to create a Summer Academic Club on the subject. She began by going to the library and looking on-line for materials about Africa. She found too many ideas to explore, so she limited herself to two novels, some poems, and a photography book on Africa. Later, she read some appropriate children's books. She visited a nearby museum of African Art, studied African artifacts, and wrote to the embassies of Kenya, Tanzania, Cameroon, and Senegal for information. (Some Club Leaders find it helpful to focus on one country but still continue researching surrounding countries, tribes, and regions.) She also found that travel guidebooks were a wonderful source for pictures, facts, and regional maps.

The teacher's cousin knew a young Ghanaian doctor living in her city, and the doctor showed the teacher some of the textiles and carvings that his family had sent him from Ghana. He also lent her two beautiful photography books on the natural wonders of Africa and on African markets. These books helped her discover that she could create an African Market Club and serve as Nana, the Chief Organizer of the Market.

As the teacher continued her research, she focused on African cultures and markets. She looked at African products in stores and museums, ate at an Ethiopian Restaurant, and listened to recordings of African drumming. She also attended a performance by a Cameroon dance troop, where she reacted enthusiastically to the stirring movement, bright costumes and colors of the dancers, and the energy and the spirit of the dance troop.

Creating the Setting

Transforming the classroom into a believable African Market took some ingenuity. The teacher used one large curtain painted in bright colors with African scenery: market stalls, acacia trees, animals prowling, and Africa's highest mountain (the snow-capped Mount Kilimanjaro). Because the teacher was not an artist, she discussed her wishes with an art teacher, who helped her paint the curtain. They drew vivid images from various parts of East Africa on the curtain to set the tone. The teacher contemplated how she could decorate the door to the classroom to make it an African Entrance: a jungle, a mask, tribal dancing, or products from an African Market. She decided to use Kenya's coat of arms, with the word *harambee* on the bottom. *Harambee* is a Swahili word for "pull together." Around the door, she placed images of Kenya. Tables in the classroom were covered with African cloth so that they could serve as booths for students selling handmade papier-mâché vegetables, fruits, bread, sweets, meat, fish, instruments, and sculptures.

Costumes

Costumes are an important part of an Academic Club. For the girls, the teacher chose dazzling, highly patterned African cloth that they could wrap around their waists. The girls also made headpieces as a group project. For the boys, the teacher chose hats made of African materials with African cloth wound around them and a sash. Because wearing jewelry is very important in many African tribes, the boys made tribal jewelry to represent their Club role and to give themselves a sense of ownership and identity.

Defining Roles

The teacher, as Nana, was powerful, savvy, shrewd, kind, and helpful to others. She studied Swahili names so that she could give each Club Member a Swahili name. Then, Nana defined the roles that the Club Members would be assigned, which corresponded to a defined booth in the Market. Her research uncovered the following typical East African people who owned booths at the market.

- Drummer
- Musician (finger harp or xylophone)
- Sculptor, Wood Carver
- Weaver of Baskets and Hats
- Weaver of Clothing and Textiles
- Painter
- Storyteller
- Poet
- Dollmaker
- Jewelry Maker

- Fruit Seller

- Vegetable Seller

- Sweets Seller

- Bread Maker

- Hair Specialist

- Dancer

- River Trader (Boatman)

- Fish Seller (Fisherman)

- Safari Guide (works with maps)

- Money Man (in charge of money exchanges)

Nana then decided which role would be appropriate for each Club Member.

Code of Behavior in the Market

Nana reinforced the make-believe atmosphere of the African Market Club at all times. She stayed in character and maintained the students' characters, too. Children's real names were never used in the Club.

Because the African Market Club would not succeed if she dropped out of character, Nana devised a code of behavior that she explained to the Club Members as follows: "Nana is in charge of the Market. She expects cooperation. Everyone will help everyone else. Nobody fights, hurts, or steals from another person. Nana knows they are all good people. Nana cares about each one."

If a Club Member had to be sent out of the classroom for a time-out or cool down, it happened within the dramatic framework of the Club. Nana sent offenders out of the Market to sit in a quiet place under a baobab tree or guard against lions outside the door. Sometimes, she gave them a market-related task for a few minutes, such as sorting colored counting sticks or shells, which were used as money. Serious misbehaviors were dealt with by the Tribal Chief, the school principal.

Rewards were also given in character. At the beginning of the Academic Club experience, Nana explained to Club Members the behavior that was expected and that they could earn rewards. The African Traders would receive local money (counting sticks or shells) to invest in new merchandise or barter for rare goods. Nana also assured them that she wanted to give them praise and rewards. In addition, Nana Shillings, coins made from tin foil or bottle tops, were used as a form of behavior modification. The Club Members needed shillings to participate in activities, and they tried to earn as many Nana Shillings as possible. Losing Nana Shillings via fines was punishment for misbehavior. Club Members enjoyed trading Nana Shillings for arts and crafts as well as sharing them with friends to ensure their participation in certain projects.

Establishing a Password

Nana chose *harambee* as the password for each Club Member to whisper in her ear upon entering the Market. Upon leaving, Club Members said *uhuru*, Swahili for "freedom and liberty." Words such as *baobab tree, Tanzania, Olduvai*, and *Kilimanjaro* were alternate choices for passwords. Another entry ritual that Nana considered was shaking hands and saying *jambo* ("hello") to three people, including Nana. On exiting, Club Members would shake hands and say *kwaheri* ("goodbye") to three people, including Nana.

Activities on the First Day

On the first day, the Club Members created identification badges by placing their photographs on index cards with an African-design border. The Club Members' Swahili names were listed on the badges. This activity gave Nana time to talk with each youngster and discover his and her interests and strengths in order to determine what booth would be perfect for each child. Each booth had the symbol of a fisherman, musician, storyteller, or other African trader so that the students could find their booths easily. As the days progressed, each child worked at his or her booth in the Market. They wore their costumes and identification badges and sat behind their stalls.

POSSIBLE CONCEPTS LEARNED IN AN AFRICAN MARKET CLUB

The preceding example of the African Market Club shows the preparation involved in planning an Academic Club. You may be wondering what concepts can be taught in an Academic Club. Let's consider some of the concepts that can be taught in an African Market Club. First, Club Members can learn what the African continent looks like, such as the fact that East Africa is bordered on the right side by the Indian Ocean. They can also learn geographic features of East Africa including Mount Kilimanjaro, grasslands (where the animals roam), Lake Victoria (second-largest freshwater lake in the world), Mombasa (a big port), and Nairobi (city located a mile high on the equator). Another topic of interest is the Sahara Desert (the world's largest desert) in Northern Africa.

Club Members can learn about African plant and animal life. Baobab trees are the best known trees in Africa. Sometimes, they are called the "upside-down tree." They also may be the oldest life forms on the African continent. Acacia trees are some of the hardiest trees in Africa. Unique African animals include giraffes, lions, hyenas, African elephants, zebras, gnus, rhinoceroses, hippopotamuses, and wild dogs.

The country of Kenya can be studied. A fun fact is that Kenya is not unbearably hot, even though the equator runs through it, because much of its elevation is a mile high. Mombasa, which is at sea level, has cool sea breezes to keep away the heat. Tribes of Kenya include the Kikuyu tribe (the main tribe of Kenya of which Club Members can be "honorary members") and the Maasai tribe (whose members are great runners).

Trading is an important part of African culture. Students can explore the ways that East Africans trade and what they trade. They can also explore the difference between trade, barter, and the use of money.

The arts are also very important in East Africa. Africans love to dance, and they communicate through music. Wonderful carvings, statues, masks, and dazzling patterns of cloth are all products of Africa that will appeal to Club Members. Storytelling and myths are also important in Africa.

Finally, children can explore the history of African countries. Although the countries in East Africa are now self-governed, they were once colonies of England and Germany. Students can learn what a colony is and how East Africa became free.

POSSIBLE PROJECTS FOR AN AFRICAN MARKET CLUB

The Academic Club Methodology relies heavily on project learning and hands-on activities. This section uses the example of the African Market Club to explore some special projects that Club Members can work on during their 6-week summer program.

In Week 1, the following activities might be used:

- Walking on a map of Africa drawn on the floor
- Weaving baskets with brightly colored raffia
- Making African masks
- Telling African stories with pictures and colors

Week 2 might include the following activities:

- Making a 5-foot baobab tree out of papier-mâché
- Telling African stories without pictures and colors
- Making a relief map of Africa
- Making a geography Bingo game with special features of East Africa and playing it
- Learning how East Africa was colonized by Great Britain and Germany

During Week 3, students can enjoy the following projects:

- Making African symbols and designs in clay
- Printing symbols on cloth
- Acting out how East Africa was colonized and became free
- Telling African stories with music/percussion instruments or singing
- Describing messages sent across great distances by drumming

Week 4 might be designated as Safari Week with the following activities planned:

- Studying East African animals

- Collecting a menagerie of African animal photographs from magazines such as National Geographic and creating a wildlife mural

- Creating animals that may be found in the jungle out of papier-mâché

Week 5 might be filled with the following activities:

- Listening to African animal myths and stories

- Making up stories of animal life

- Telling stories through dance

- Learning an East African dance with heavy drumming

Finally, Week 6 would provide a review of the special features of Africa. Students could plan an East African festival in the Market with singing, dancing, storytelling, and products from all of their booths.

Academic Clubs, such as the African Market Club, allow Club Leaders to teach students in a way that leads to the students' success. Through careful preparation and planning, Club Leaders create a dramatic framework that minimizes negative behavior and maximizes content explored in class. The Academic Club Methodology is equally beneficial to teachers, as it encourages them to explore original sources, think creatively about instruction, and share with students their enthusiasm for the subject matter.

4

The Sequence
of Academic Clubs
at The Lab School
and Baltimore Lab

As a teacher, you are probably most comfortable lecturing to students or asking them to read about a topic and repeat the information back to you. You may not have needed to search for other ways to help your students learn. But how do you teach history, geography, and civics to students who are nonreaders or poor readers and, in many cases, poor listeners? Sequences and order cause great difficulties for students with learning disabilities. Different teaching strategies are needed to help these students be successful in the classroom.

As discussed previously, tangible objects can serve as keys to learning. Touching, feeling, seeing, smelling, and tasting objects can facilitate the flow of knowledge. Mental hooks—pictures in the mind—prompt the recall of material and help students see the whole picture, whether it is cause and effect or the essence of a certain time. Thus, when students create a working machine out of toilet-paper holders, pipe cleaners, Ping-Pong balls, rods, and tape, the machine becomes an image that represents the change from an agrarian society to the Industrial Revolution. Sequenced photographs or children's drawings on cards can help students with learning disabilities explore the order of events. Because these youngsters need constant practice sequencing events, the Academic Club Methodology provides many opportunities to investigate order and sequencing. The more ordering and sequencing, the better they learn!

HOW CLUBS FORM A LOGICAL PROGRESSION

The progression of the Academic Clubs taught at The Lab School and Balti-more Lab also follows a logical sequence. The historically based Academic Clubs are taught in a 5-year sequence that caters to children's interests. The content of the Clubs progresses from the Old Stone Age; to the Gods of An-cient Egypt, Greece, and Rome; to the Knights of the Middle Ages; to the Re-naissance; and to the Museum Club, which leads up to the discovery of Amer-ica. The final Academic Club is now the American Industrialists Club, but in the past, it has been the American Immigrants Club or the American Revolu-tionaries Club. Thus, Lab School students in kindergarten or first grade—who are "primitive" (beginning) learners on the threshold of literacy—study early man in the Cave Club. As students progress through elementary school—and mature as learners—their Academic Clubs progress through civilization to the founding of America, the Civil War, and the Industrial Revolution.

After the Cave Club, 7- and 8-year-olds (second or third graders) are taught classic literature. These children are fascinated by superheroes, so they love to hear myths of the ancient world as well as *the Odyssey* and *the Iliad*. Because most children this age love pretending to be Superman, Wonder Woman, or one of the Powerpuff Girls, we assign them the omnipotent, all-powerful role of an ancient Egyptian, Greek, or Roman God.

Nine- and ten-year-olds at The Lab School explore the adventure, chiv-alry, and valor of the Middle Ages. They begin by learning about *Beowulf,* then about the Battle of Hastings, the Bayeux Tapestry, The Domesday Book, and the *Canterbury Tales.* Through project learning, reenactments, and the creation of architectural models, the children form a mental hook that helps them or-ganize information they learn from hearing medieval literature and seeing medieval artwork.

Around 10–11 years of age, Lab School students move on to the light of the Renaissance, which was centered in Florence, Italy. Students meet the great artists of the time and learn about trade and exploration. Children of this age are stimulated by the wonder of art and exploration, so this Academic Club is appropriate for them.

Students age 11 or 12 then join the Museum Club, in which they are Curators or Directors of different museums reporting to the Director of the Museum Association of America (Club Leader). They learn about the Meso-potamians, the Babylonians, the Phoenicians, the Minoans, the Hebrews, the Muslims, the Christians, the Hindus, the Buddhists, the Chinese, and the Por-tuguese. They also learn about the Spanish explorers, who discovered the new world, and about the birth of the United States. Students create museum arti-facts, organize each exhibit, learn about different cultures, hear the literature of each culture, and examine relevant artifacts and photographs. Thus, the students get a full overview of the beginnings of civilization and what events led to the creation of the United States.

In the early years of The Lab School, we offered the Philosophers Club, in which students played such characters as Voltaire or Locke, as an Academic Club for 11- and 12-year-olds. The curriculum was designed to help students understand the principles each philosopher stood for and witness the continuity of ideas that inspired America's Founding Fathers. As years passed, however, more and more Lab School students had moderate to severe language-based learning disorders. These students had great difficulty debating ideas, so we had to create the Museum Club as a less abstract and less verbal alternative. Because the Museum Club was more concrete and visual, students were more successful in this Club than in the Philosophers Club.

The final Academic Club at The Lab School and Baltimore Lab takes place when students are in sixth grade. The Club studies the early history of the United States, including the War of Independence, the Civil War, and the change from an agrarian to an industrial economy. For many years, this final Club was the American Revolutionaries Club or the American Immigrants Club. In recent years, however, it has become the American Industrialists Club because the youngsters are so interested in money. They hear so much about the U.S. economy that they are eager to explore this topic. In the American Industrialists Club, each student becomes a famous Industrialist and traces the background of his or her character, following the character from the beginning of the United States, through the Civil War, and into the Industrial Revolution. Students learn about the character's bad practices as well as the honorable ones. They study the great legacy each industrialist has provided.

This Academic Club is a work in progress. For example, Madame Walker, the first woman Industrialist, has recently been included, and Club Leaders would like to add more women Industrialists. Despite its evolving nature, the American Industrialists Club has been a success because the sixth graders love identifying with their characters, who are multimillionaires. We have found that they do not forget the material they learn in this Academic Club. They carry it with them to middle and high school, where they can apply it to textbook learning.

Throughout the progression of Academic Clubs, Club Leaders place an emphasis on critical thinking. Club Members are placed in many problem-solving situations and are faced with questions such as:

- How did cavemen discover fire?

- What happens when someone like King Edward the Confessor promises his crown to two different princes?

- Why did Dante need nine levels in the Inferno to punish the Seven Deadly Sins?

- What did the use of concrete allow the Romans to do with their architecture that the Greeks could not do?

- How did Henry Ford's moving assembly line transform American industry?

Celebration, laughter, and rejoicing fill the venue of every Academic Club because of the wonders of humankind and the ingenious adaptations to hardship that abound. Through their thoughtful answers, Club Members demonstrate that they are learning a great deal through play; making things; pretending; and reenacting what they have seen, heard, and touched. As Club Members probe the history, geography, and civics of each historical period, their understanding of the world and of themselves grows.

NO TEMPLATE FOR ACADEMIC CLUBS

No single way exists to organize and run an Academic Club. There is no exact template to follow. Every Club Leader brings ideas, talents, and interests to the Club. Every Club Leader chooses ways to achieve the academic goals of the Club. Since 1967, The Lab School has seen a whole array of approaches to the core Academic Clubs. For example, the Renaissance Club can be made up of only visual artists or it can include musicians and, also Dante and Galileo. Perhaps in the future, an inspired Club Leader will tackle the Renaissance in northern Europe, which was centered around Erasmus. The sky is the limit for what can be done in an Academic Club.

The descriptions of Academic Clubs that follow show one teacher's interpretation. They are not blueprints. Please use these suggestions to spark your own imagination.

Cave Club

- **Age group:** 6–8 years old; first graders

- **Purpose:** In the Cave Club, students study the evolution of man throughout the Old and New Stone Ages. The students explore prehistory, prehistoric humans, and prehistoric animals through a structured, multisensory approach to learning. The students examine both the physical and the social adaptations of early humans as they coped with changes in the environment from the African Savannah to the end of the Ice Age in Europe. They also are immersed in the environment of prehistoric times by wearing customary skins, performing daily opening and closing rituals, making prehistoric tools and weapons, and examining early human survival skills. The study of the development of humans, from Australopithecus to *Homo sapiens,* establishes the starting point for the development of many academic skills, such as knowledge of history, archaeology, geology, geography, science, the enhancement of vocabulary (through a daily password), the ability to see cause and effect relationships (the adaptations of humans and animals), the ability to compare and contrast (lifestyles of the past and present), and an increased social awareness (cooperation as a means of survival).

The Cave Club year is divided into five segments, each with a clear focus. One Club Leader divided the year into these five segments:

1. Establishing the time (Earth up to the appearance of humans) and setting (Africa)

2. Beginnings of human development

3. Old Stone Age (Paleolithic)

4. New Stone Age (Neolithic)

5. Paleontology and archeology

Another Club Leader had the following segments:

1. Establish the time and setting

    *   Decorate the room as a cave

    *   Discuss a time period of prehistory highlighting the major events in the evolutionary process (i.e., Earth begins, plants, simple animals, dinosaurs, mammals, humans)

    *   Discuss paleontology and archeology

        Establish the differences between the two sciences

        Examine fossil types

        Study scientific reconstruction samples

2. Introduce the beginnings of human development

    *   Establish Africa as a point of departure

    *   Distinguish between past and present

    *   Introduce Australopithecus

3. Continue human development

    *   Introduce *Homo erectus* (e.g., lived 2 million years ago)

    *   Introduce *Homo habilis* (e.g., explore tool making)

    *   Introduce *Homo sapiens* (e.g., first modern human)

    *   Develop group sense of survival skills

    *   Explore hunter/gatherer lifestyle and social structure

4. Discuss the Old Stone Age—Paleolithic

    *   Introduce different types of Paleolithic villages

    *   Discuss humans traveling beyond Africa

        Homo erectus and *Homo sapiens*

Java and Peking man (e.g., identify on map, discovery of fire, more advanced tools and clothing, Neanderthals)

Cro-Magnon Man (e.g., *Homo sapiens sapiens*, instinct versus reason, artistic boom)

5. Discuss the New Stone Age—Neolithic
    *   Discuss agriculture
    *   Learn about domestication of plants and animals

Specific Items Studied

Club Members learn about the evolution of planet Earth from a hot, molten ball circling the sun, to the creation of oceans, to the beginning of life. Life first existed in the water and then on the land. Primitive vegetation led to the age of dinosaurs and to the coming of mammals and humans. Club Members create a timeline.

They learn about adaptations life forms made to the changing climate at the end of the last Ice Age. Humans were able to begin planting crops and learned to domesticate animals. They also began living a settled life. Animals had a wider range of lifestyles because some did not like the warmer climate and others learned to live with humans. Many more plants could grow in the warmer climate.

Finally, students learn about the evolution of humans from Lucy (Australopithecus) over millions of years to *Homo sapiens*. They study hunting and gathering. The woolly mammoth was hunted by Neanderthals. *Homo sapiens* used settled farming and tamed wild animals.

Characters, Costumes, Passwords, and Rituals

On the first day of the Cave Club, the main task is to have students invent caveman names for themselves. The Club Leader, Wise Elder, helps Club Members who have difficulty. It is helpful to encourage Club Members to use the first sound of their own name when creating caveman names because they will have a much easier time remembering their new names. Wise Elder can also use a drum to help isolate the syllables of each Club Member's name. Children usually come up with really creative caveman names. For example, a child named Greg invented the name Ga Ti. A child named Sam invented the name Soom I No. Another child liked to rhyme, so his name was Ingo Jingo. Sometimes, Club Members match their first names to pictures, such as Joe Good Earth, Sarah Winding River, Matthew Majestic Mountain, or Tom Tall Sky. In one Cave Club, the members picked their favorite color and matched it to a naturally occurring phenomenon (e.g., Blue River, Green Vine, Yellow Sun Light).

Another system for choosing names is to give each child a prehistoric animal name:

- Climbing Paramys
- Dire Wolf
- Ferocious Smilodon
- Fierce Daphoenus
- Galloping Eohippus
- Giant Megatherium
- Woolly Mammoth

After Club Members have chosen their names, Wise Elder makes nametags out of heavy paper cut in the shape of a bone. Nametags can also be made by using wood-burning tools to brand cutout leather circles. Poster board miniature caves with caveman names on them can also be made. Each child should get comfortable with seeing his or her new name in print. Each child may also receive a mat, which will be stored on a shelf in the classroom. If the child's caveman name is an animal, his or her mat can match the coat of the animal (e.g., Galloping Eohippus had zebra-like striped cloth).

On the first day, Club Members also learn the secret password used to enter the Academic Club. The password is whispered in Wise Elder's ear and captures the spirit of the Academic Club. Sample passwords include:

- Cro-Magnon Man
- Hominid
- Neanderthal
- Opposable thumb
- Fossils
- Savannah
- Paleolithic
- Prehistoric
- Archeology
- Ancestor
- Agriculture
- Descendant

Because children with learning disabilities tend to have difficulty remembering information, the passwords usually have accompanying movements to aid with memorization. For example, students learn *Hominid* by tapping their feet on the floor—hom * in * id—because it means a creature walking on two feet (bipedal). The point of passwords is to achieve immediate focus on the material and to learn new vocabulary.

The opening and closing rituals are very helpful for keeping Club Members focused and in control of themselves. The opening ritual begins with the whole group crouching in a circle around the fire with the lights out. Club Members recite the following lines as they perform the actions shown in brackets:

"We slowly rise up like Australopithecus." [Children rise to a standing position.]

"We use our hands like *Homo habilis*." [Children raise their hands and wiggle their fingers. Then, they tap their chests twice and wiggle their fingers again.]

"We travel like *Homo erectus*." [Children pretend to carry a pack over one shoulder. Then, they tap their chests twice and tap their backs three times.]

"We speak and communicate like *Homo sapiens*." [Children point to their foreheads and mouths. They tap their chests twice and their temples three times.]

After this speech, the Wise Elder says, "Greetings, Hominids!" The Club Members return the greeting by saying, "Greetings, Wise Elder!"

The Club Leader then takes the fire stick toward the fire and says, "Now, I light the fire with my fire stick." As the Leader turns on the light switch, he or she says, "and we have light!" Counting "1, 2, 3, 4," the Wise Elder lowers the fire stick four counts.

Although the closing ritual is brief, it helps students collect themselves before returning to their other classes. It is designed to keep the students focused and in control because they tend to be so distractible and impulsive. The Fire Keeper brings out the make-believe fire. The Club Members stand around the fire while Wise Elder passes out their fire sticks, which have been made as a small individual project from sticks covered with red, yellow, and orange tissue paper. Club Members maintain eye contact with Wise Elder, who then nods to each of them to place the stick in the fire. Then, as a group, Club Members say, "Now, we have fed the fire to keep it alive. Now, we may go hunt."

Skills Emphasized

One of the wonderful things Club Members learn is relationship skills. During other classes, Club Members remember their membership in the clan and try to protect and root for each other. The responsibilities of being a Club Member are emphasized. Class discipline is set by Wise Elder but reinforced by clan responsibility and the fact that survival depends on the clan sticking together.

Other skills that Club Members learn include:

- Reading readiness (e.g., decoding messages, cave paintings)
- Language development

- Rhyming

- Memory (visual and auditory)

- Eye–hand coordination (e.g., coloring, ceramics, weaving, doing papier-mâché)

- Sequences (e.g., sequence from Australopithecus to *Homo habilis* to *Homo sapiens*)

- Thinking skills (e.g., cause and effect, reasoning, classifying)

- Symbolism (e.g., Lascaux Caves)

- Understanding the parts that make up the whole (e.g., making a fishing or agricultural village)

- Cooperation, kindness, helpfulness, and sensitivity to each other's needs

Sample Activity: Prehistoric Tarpit

Objective: Students will create a prehistoric environment.

Materials:

- Elmer's glue

- Hot glue gun

- Small plastic cups

- 8.5" x 11" sheet of cardboard

- Grass (fake moss)

- Trees (fake garland)

- Small plastic animals (e.g., tiger for a saber tooth cat, elephant for a woolly mammoth, horse for a galloping eohippus)

- Black powdered tempera paint

- Brown tempera paint

- Popsicle sticks

- Spoon

Procedure:

1. In the middle of the cardboard sheet, trace the bottom of the small plastic cup.

2. Paint the cardboard brown, making sure to leave the circle unpainted. One coat of paint usually dries in 10 minutes.

3. Glue the plastic cup's bottom to the unpainted circle with the hot glue gun.

4. Use moss to symbolize grass. Elmer's glue can be used if children have the motor skills to hold and squeeze the bottle. If not, hot glue may be used by the Club Leader.

5. Construct trees out of the garland, which should be made with gardening wire so that it bends easily.

6. Use the hot glue gun to attach the trees to the cardboard.

7. Pour Elmer's glue into the cup.

8. Mix a tablespoon of the powdered paint into the glue in the cup.

9. Let students mix the paint with a Popsicle stick.

10. Place the animal in the cup. It can hang halfway out of the cup for a more dramatic effect.

Background Information for Teachers

American Museum of Natural History. (1993). *The humans: Human origins and history to 10,000 B.C.* New York: Weldon Own Pty Limited.

Andrews, P., & Stringer, C. (1989). *Human evolution.* London: Cambridge University Press.

Johanson, D.C., & O'Farrell, K. (1990). *Journey from the dawn: Life with the world's first family.* New York: Early Man Publishing Co.

Lewin, R. (1988). *In the age of mankind.* Washington, DC: Smithsonian Institution.

Nida, W.L. (1929). *Fleetfoot the cave boy.* Chicago: Albert Whiteman. [out of print]

Picq, P. (1996). *Lucy and her times.* New York: Henry Holt and Co.

Scarre, C. (1993). *Timelines of the ancient world.* New York: Dorling Kindersley.

Steck V. (1989). *History of the world: Prehistoric and ancient Europe.* Austin, TX: Raintree Publishers Limited Partnership.

Stidworthy, J. (1986). *When humans began.* Morristown, NJ: Silver Burdett.

Illustrated Books to Show Students

Bell, R.A. (1991). *The big golden book of cavemen.* New York: Western Publishing.

Berger, M. (1986). *Prehistoric mammals: A new world.* New York: GP Putnam's Sons.

Berger, M. (1988). *Early humans: A prehistoric world.* New York: GP Putnam's Sons.

Brandenberg, A. (1996). *Wild and woolly mammoths.* New York: HarperCollins Publishers.

Colville, B. (1990). *Prehistoric people.* New York: Doubleday.

Haines, T. (2001). *Walking with prehistoric beasts.* New York: Dorling Kindersley.

Lauber, P. (1998). *Painters of the cave.* Washington, DC: National Geographic Society.

Merriman, N. (1989). *Eyewitness books: Early humans*. London: Dorling Kindersley Limited.

Books to Read to Students

Angeletti, R. (1999). *The cave painters of Lascaux*. New York: Oxford University Press.

Brett, J. (1988). *The first dog*. New York: Harcourt Brace Jovanovich.

Bush, T. (1995). *Grunt the primitive cave boy*. New York: Crown Publishing.

Gerrard, R. (1990). *Mik's mammoth*. Hong Kong: Sunburst Books.

Nida, W.L. (1929). *Fleetfoot the caveboy*. Chicago: Albert Whiteman. [out of print]

Nolan, D. (1989). *Wolf child*. New York: Macmillan Publishing.

Films, Videos, and CD-ROMs

A Neanderthal's World Video (Discovery Channel)

Apeman: The Story of Human Evolution [Four tapes] (A&E Home Video)

Before We Ruled the Earth (Discovery Channel)

The Ultimate Guide: Iceman (Discovery Channel, 1998)

Land of the Mammoth (Discovery Channel)

Prehistoric Animals (Dorling Kindersley, 1997)

Prehistoric Life (Dorling Kindersley & BBC Worldwide, 1996)

Raising the Mammoth (Discovery Channel)

Smilodon (Discovery Channel)

Walking with Prehistoric Beasts (Discovery Channel)

Music

Dawn Until Dusk: Tribal Song and Didgeridoo (Australian Music International)

Liph'iginiso (Ladysmith Black Mambazo)

Gods Club

- **Age group:** 7–9 years old; second graders
- **Purpose:** The children in Gods Club are introduced to the history, geography, architecture, culture, government, art, and science of the ancient Egyptians, Greeks, and Romans. The main events include mythology, the development of written language, inventions, and the influence of these civilizations on our present one. The dramatic framework, in which each child assumes the role of a God, encourages children to experiment freely and participate in activities that teach content and

strengthen readiness skills. The Gods all have distinct characteristics and areas of influence that empower the children to expand their activities. Because the Gods are related to one another, as in a family, the roles tend to foster cooperation between them.

The Gods Club uses the arts and dramatization to study the Egyptian civilization and mythology. Greek and Roman mythologies and cultures follow. The year begins in Egypt, where students learn about the growth of societies around rivers and specifically how the Nile River was vital to the growth of Egyptian civilization. The Nile River is painted on the floor in the middle of the Club room, just as the Nile flows through the middle of Egypt. Egyptian life, including the centrality of their gods to beliefs about life and afterlife, is explored through observing how their myths encouraged stability and continuity in their culture. Daily Egyptian life is depicted through books, art projects, and role-playing activities. Club Members note which inventions and practices continue to be used today. The literature and myths of the Egyptian Gods are studied.

During the second trimester, students learn about the evolution of religion from Egyptian to Greek culture. Geographic, social, political, and religious differences are explored. Students learn about the various Greek Gods; read and discuss myths; and learn about the Trojan War, *The Iliad,* and *The Odyssey.* They study the difference between democracy (e.g., government in Athens) and autocracy (e.g., government in Sparta). They discover the contributions of Alexander the Great, who laid the cultural and linguistic foundation for the Roman Empire.

During the third trimester, students explore the interplay and transition of Greek to Roman culture. Club Members explore the Roman Empire's political, social, and religious concerns. Roman myths and the *Aeneid* are presented with puppets. Arches and aqueducts are made. In addition, the development of law is studied and a comparison is made to the current U.S. government.

Specific Items Studied

In Egypt, students learn about the Egyptian Gods and their myths. They also learn how the Pyramids and the Sphinx were built. Other concepts include:

- Importance of trade
- Importance of irrigation
- Invention of the *shaduf*
- Making of and the use of papyrus
- Rosetta Stone
- Hieroglyphics
- Mummification

- Valley of the Kings

- Famous Pharaohs

When students begin the section about Greece, subject matter includes Mount Olympus, the various Greek Gods and their myths, and Heracles's Trials. Sometimes these trials are studied during the Roman section because Hercules is the Roman name for the Greek man, Heracles. Other topics are the following:

- *The Iliad* and *The Odyssey*

- Trojan War

- Difference between Athens and Sparta

- Architecture (e.g., columns) and pottery

- The Agora, the Polis, democracy

- The Olympics

- Alexander the Great

In the final section, Rome, students learn about the Roman Gods and their myths. They also learn about Julius Caesar and Cleopatra. They learn about the Roman leaders (Caesar) and Roman numerals. Other subjects explored are:

- Roman Forum, Coliseum, Circus Maximus

- Use of concrete and how it changed architecture

- Arches and domes

- Roman law and its relation to democracy

- Aqueducts

- Mosaics

Characters, Costumes, Passwords, and Rituals

During the Egypt trimester, the Academic Club Leader might be the Pharaoh's Vizier, Queen Cleopatra, or the all-powerful Sun God, Re. Students may become very confused if the Club Leader changes his or her name for each trimester, so one Club Leader opted to remain Cleopatra throughout the three Academic Clubs.

Possible student names, based on Egyptian Gods, include the following:

- Anubis—God of Embalmers

- Bastet—Goddess of Joy

- Horus—God of Light

- Isis—Goddess of Magic or Goddess of Wisdom

- Nut—Goddess of the Sky
- Osiris—God of the Dead
- Ptah—God of Crafts
- Sebek—God of Waters
- Thoth—God of Scribes

The costumes of the Gods can be white togas. The Club Leader's costume may be more elaborate. For example, Queen Cleopatra's costume may be jeweled, and she may wear an elaborate headband with a gold scarf attached to it. This headpiece is called a *names* and is worn with a *collar* around the neck. The all-powerful Re may be a radiant sun in yellow cloth with an appliquéd sun sewn on to a toga.

Sample passwords to be used for Egypt include

- Nile River
- Delta
- Shaduf
- Pyramid
- Sphinx
- Scarab

The opening ritual begins with the Club Leader standing at the delta of the Nile, holding the crook and flail. He or she gestures to the first student to the left, who identifies him- or herself (e.g., "I am Hathor, Goddess of Music"). Each child presents him- or herself, ending with the Club Leader saying, "I am the Pharoah's Vizier [or Cleopatra or Re]. May the Nile bless us." For the closing ritual, students line up and say, "As we float down the Nile, toward the Great Sea, may the Nile bless us!"

During the Greek trimester, which typically begins in early January because Egypt begins when school starts, some Club Leaders choose the role of Socrates, a wise Greek sage who was always posing questions. "The Gods" never forget the name of Socrates or what he stood for because they use the name for many months. Socrates wears a shawl over a simple toga. Greek Gods wear headbands with a symbol. For example, Apollo has a sun on his headband. Athena has an owl on hers. Club Members may sit on mats in front of a column with their symbol on it or may sit on mats around a traditional hearth in the center of the room. Club Members hold "attributes of power," which are their symbols. Zeus holds thunderbolts. Poseidon holds a trident. Athena holds an owl and a spear.

The names of the Greek Gods are:

- Aphrodite—Goddess of Love and Beauty
- Apollo—God of Light

- Ares—God of War

- Artemis—Goddess of the Moon, Wild Animals

- Athena—Goddess of Wisdom, Art, and Science

- Demeter—Goddess of Grain

- Hades—God of the Underworld

- Hephaestos—God of Fire

- Hera—Queen of the Gods, Zeus's wife, Goddess of Marriage

- Heracles—God of Victory, God of all Commercial Enterprises

- Hermes—Messenger of the Gods

- Poseidon—God of the Sea

- Zeus—Ruler of the Gods, God of the Sky

Some sample passwords for the Greek Gods Club are:

- Acropolis

- Atrium

- Corinthian

- Delphi

- Doric

- Marathon

- Olympiad

- Oracle

During the opening ritual, Club Members might say the following lines: "From Mount Olympus, from the wine-dark sea, the Gods of Greece assemble. I am Zeus, King of the Gods. I am Hera, Queen of the Gods (list all Club Members' characters). May we rule with wisdom and courage." The closing ritual involves Club Members holding a large torch and saying, "May the light of ancient Hellas bring us back safely tomorrow." The torch provides a visual link to the rebirth of Greek and Roman ideas, which is the opening ceremony of the Roman Club, along with the switching on of the lights in the room.

The third trimester, Rome, is typically presented after Spring vacation. As mentioned previously, Club Leaders may choose to play one character (e.g., Queen Cleopatra) for all three Academic Clubs or to be a different character (e.g., Julius Caesar, Augustus Caesar). Togas and laurel wreath crowns are appropriate costumes for Club Members and Club Leaders.

The names of the Roman Gods are:

- Apollo—God of Light

- Ceres—Goddess of Grain

- Diana—Goddess of the Moon, Wild Animals
- Hercules—God of Victory, God of all Commercial Enterprises
- Juno—Queen of the Gods, Jupiter's wife, Goddess of Marriage
- Jupiter—Ruler of the Gods, God of the Sky
- Mars—God of War
- Mercury—Messenger of the Gods
- Minerva—Goddess of Wisdom and Art and Science
- Neptune—God of the Sea
- Pluto—God of the Underworld
- Venus—Goddess of Love and Beauty
- Vulcan—God of Fire

Sample passwords include:

- Arena
- Aqueduct
- Circus Maximus
- Coliseum
- Gladiator
- Romulus and Remus
- Triumphal arch

During the opening ritual for the Roman Gods Club, students recite the following: "From the banks of the Tiber, from the Seven Hills, the Gods of Rome assemble. I am Janus, God of Beginnings and Endings (list all of the Club Members' characters). May we rule with strength and honor." The closing ritual involves students saying, "May we rule with strength (make fist) and honor (place fist across chest)."

Skills Emphasized

The skills emphasized during the Gods Club include the following:

- Understanding symbolism (hieroglyphics)
- Studying inventions (e.g., building of the pyramids, simple machines)
- Vocabulary development
- Memory
- Eye–hand coordination (e.g., making a shaduf to irrigate the river)
- Learning the geography of the Mediterranean
- Relating preservation to mummification

- Pattern recognition and formation (drawing meanders, emphasis on symmetry and balance)

- Thinking skills (e.g., comparing the government of Athens to Sparta)

- Math skills (learning Roman numerals)

Sample Activity: The Gifts of the Nile

When the Greek historian Herodotus visited Egypt, he wrote detailed descriptions of amazing sights, and he described Egypt as "The Gift of the Nile." By involving the students in the drama of a boat ride down the Nile, discovering gifts as they go, the teacher seeks to make Herodotus's abstract comment a more concrete reality for the students.

Objective: Students will discover the importance of the Nile River to the growth of Ancient Egypt by becoming familiar with the resources or "gifts" that the Nile offered to the Egyptians.

Materials:

- Blue contact paper cut to the approximate shape of the Nile River and stuck to the floor of the classroom to serve as the Nile River

- A boat made from cardboard boxes and big enough to hold three or four students

- Eight boxes wrapped as presents with varying wrapping papers and ribbons. In each box, place a representation for one of the following gifts of the Nile and a card with the name of the gift printed on it: 1) water (glass jar of blue-dyed water); 2) soil (container of dirt); 3) papyrus (small piece of papyrus); 4) mud brick shelters (small mud brick made of clay); 5) transportation (small typical Egyptian boats); 6) clothing (small linen tunic); 7) animals (miniature ducks and fish); and 8) food (real pita bread and grapes)—should be the biggest box.

- Chart made of poster board with a picture of each gift and a space next to the picture left blank for the name of the gift to be added during the activity.

- Cards numbered 1–8

Procedure:

1. Randomly distribute the gifts over the length of the Nile River.

2. Shuffle the numbered cards, and have each child select a number.

3. Tell the students that they will be going on a boat ride down the Nile River. Discuss how important the Nile River was to the ancient Egyptians. Introduce the phrase "Egypt is the Gift of the Nile."

4. Invite the students to come into the boat and float with you down the Nile. The size of the boat determines the number of students who can ride at one time. Lead the sailors to "stroke" together to help the boat "move." Stop and exclaim over the gifts, urging the students in numerical order to choose a "gift." Each child

may choose any gift *except* the largest gift, which is reserved for the last child.

5. After the student has chosen a gift, he or she opens it and shares its contents with the rest of the class. The student adds the card with the name on it to the chart posted on the wall. Each child keeps his or her gift for the remainder of the class period.

6. The last student chooses the food gift, opens it, and shares the gift with the rest of the class. At the teacher's discretion, the children may eat the snack at that time or keep it for later.

Sample Activity: Greek Column

Objective: Students will learn the three basic parts of a Greek column (base, shaft, and capital) and the three basic capitals (doric, ionic, and corinthian).

Materials:

*   Pictures of doric, ionic, and corinthian columns used in ancient architecture

*   Pictures of doric, ionic, and corinthian columns used in present-day architecture (preferably local buildings)

*   Optional—hat made from a shallow square gift box with a head-sized hole cut in the bottom; the sides are covered with paper, with a doric, ionic, or corinthian capital drawn on each of three sides

Procedure:

1. Show pictures of ancient temples with fluted columns topped by capitals. Tell the students that columns have three parts—the base, the shaft, and the capital. Point to the parts of the column as you name them. Explain that the doric column does not have a base but rests directly on the floor.

2. Show the students how columns are like their own bodies. The base is like their *feet* (ask them to stand with heels together and toes spread apart), the shaft is like their *body* up to the neck (ask them to stand tall and straight), and the capital is like their *head* with a fancy hat on it (say, "like the one I'm wearing," and put on the box hat).

3. Teach students a song to remember the parts of the column (To the tune of Head, Shoulders, Knees, and Toes).

    Base, Shaft, Capital . . . Capital
    Base, Shaft, Capital . . . Capital
    Doric (make straight line across forehead)
    Ionic (make "scrolls" on each side of head)
    Corinthian (make wild "vegetation" with hands)
    Base, Shaft, Capital . . . Capital

Sample Activity: Roman Arch

Objective: Students will learn how a Roman arch is constructed and maintained.

Materials:

- Sculpted, free-standing balsa wood arch pieces
- Additional balsa wood blocks
- Flexible plastic ruler

Procedure:

1. Show how an arch can support more weight than flat material. Hold a flexible ruler in both hands. Ask a student to press down on it with one finger. Next, bend the ruler upward (forming an arch), and ask the student to push downward again. Allow each student to try both. They will see the greater strength of the arch. Mention the force exerted by hands pushing against the ruler. Downward force is met by equal upward force from their hands. The ruler stays arch shaped because the hands exert an equal force against each side.

2. Using the teacher-made arch puzzle, show the students how the pieces are built upward from two square columns. Square block pieces are carefully shaped and balanced to gradually slope inward, creating the arch shape. Show the use of the wooden frame to support the arch. Finally, insert the keystone, and remove the frame. Explain that the keystone "locks" the arch in place and directs forces down and out. The arch will be part of a building or aquaduct that will supply the necessary counter force.

3. Next, have the student attempt to assemble a freestanding arch. These sculpted balsa wood pieces will duplicate in three dimensions what the puzzle demonstrated on a flat surface. As they assemble the pieces, they will assume that the insertion of the keystone will lock the arch in place, but it will fall down (because the arch needs to be incorporated into a wall to create a force pushing on either side). Additional balsa wood blocks should be available in sight but not next to the arch pieces. If necessary, guide the class in looking at where the forces may be acting on the blocks. Usually, someone in the class will think of walling in the arch on each side.

4. Admire the beautiful arch with the class!

Background Information for Teachers: Egypt

Bower, T. (2000). *The shipwrecked sailor: An Egyptian tale with hieroglyphics.* New York: Simon & Schuster.

Giblin, J.C. (1990). *The riddle of the Rosetta Stone.* New York: Harper & Row.

Hart, G. (1990). *Eyewitness books: Ancient Egypt.* New York: Alfred A. Knopf.

Hart, A., & Mantell, P. (1997). *Pyramids!* Charlotte, VT: Williamson Publishing.

Perl, L. (1987). *Mummies, tombs and treasure: Secrets of ancient Egypt.* New York: Clarion.

Illustrated Books to Show Students: Egypt

Cohen, D. (1990). *Ancient Egypt.* New York: Doubleday.

Crouch, W. (1990). *Life in ancient Egypt.* London: Derrydale Books.

Hart, G. (1990). *Eyewitness books: Ancient Egypt.* New York: Alfred A. Knopf.

Macaulay, D. (1975). *Pyramid.* Boston: Houghton Mifflin.

Books to Read to Students: Egypt

Aliki. (1979). *Mummies made in Egypt.* New York: Harper & Row.

Bower, T. (2000). *The shipwrecked sailor: An Egyptian tale with hierogylphics.* New York: Simon & Schuster.

Climo, S. (1989). *The Egyptian Cinderella.* New York: Harper & Row.

de Paola, T. (1987). *Bill and Pete go down the Nile.* New York: G.P. Putnam's Sons.

Harper, J. (1997). *Pyramid.* New York: Barnes & Noble Books.

Lattimore, D.N. (1992). *The winged cat.* New York: HarperCollins.

Lumpkin, B. (1991). *Senefer: A young genius in old Egypt.* Trenton, NJ: Africa World Press.

Murdoch, D. (1998). *Tutankhamun: The life and death of a pharaoh.* New York: DK Publishing.

Putnam, J. (1993). *Eyewitness books: Mummy.* New York: Dorling Kindersley.

Putnman, J. (1994). *Pyramid.* New York: Dorling Kindersley.

Stolz, M. (1988). *Zekmet the stone carver.* San Diego: Harcourt Brace Jovanovich.

Films, Videos, and CD-ROMs: Egypt

Ancient Graves: Voices of the Dead (National Geographic, 1998)

Egypt: Secrets of the Pharaohs (National Geographic, 1997)

Journey Through the Valley of the Kings (The Learning Channel, 2002)

Pyramid (Macaulay, D., Public Broadcasting Service, 1992)

Mysteries of Egypt (National Geographic, 1999)

Mummies Made in Egypt (Reading Rainbow, 1992)

Background Information for Teachers: Greece

Denton, G. (Ed.). (1992). *Eyewitness books: Ancient Greece.* New York: Alfred A. Knopf.

Gibson, M. (1977). *Gods, men & monsters from the Greek myths.* New York: Peter Bedrick Books.

Graves, R. (1993). *The Greek myths* (Vols. I & II). New York: Penguin Press.

Hart, A., & Mantell, P. (1999). *Ancient Greece!* Charlotte, VT: Williamson Publishing.

Schofield, L. (Ed.). (1997). *Discoveries library: Ancient Greece.* New York: Viking.

Illustrated Books to Show Students: Greece

Cohen, D. (1990). *Ancient Greece.* New York: Doubleday.

Evans, C., & Millard, A. (1985). *Greek myths and legends.* London: Usborne.

Grant, N. (1990). *The world of Odysseus.* London: BBC Educational Press.

Loverance, R. & Wood, T. (1995). *Ancient Greece.* New York: Penguin Group.

Books to Read to Students: Greece

Fisher, L.E. (1988). *Theseus and the minotaur.* New York: Holiday House.

Fisher, L.E. (1990). *Jason and the golden fleece.* New York: Holiday House.

Hoges, M. (1989). *The arrow and the lamp.* Boston: Little, Brown, & Co.

Films, Videos, and CD-ROMs: Greece

Ancient Civilizations for Children: Ancient Greece (Schlessinger Media, 1988)

Jason and the Golden Fleece (Troll Video)

Perseus and Medusa (Troll Video)

Theseus and the Minotaur (Troll Video)

Background Information for Teachers: Rome

Corbishley, M. (1989). *Cultural atlas for young people: Ancient Rome.* New York: Troll Associates.

James, S. (1990). *Eyewitness books: Ancient Rome.* New York: Alfred A. Knopf.

Roberts, P.C. (Ed.). (1997). *Discoveries library: Ancient Rome.* New York: Viking.

Sims, L. (1999). *A visitor's guide to ancient Rome.* London: Usborne Publishers.

Illustrated Books to Show Students: Rome

Crouch, W. (1990). *Life in ancient Rome.* London: Derrydale Books.

James, S. (1990). *Eyewitness books: Ancient Rome.* New York: Dorling Kindersley.

Macaulay, D. (1974). *City: A story of roman planning and construction.* Boston: Houghton Mifflin.

Miquel, P. (1985). *Life in ancient Rome.* Morristown, NJ: Silver Burdette.

Books to Be Read to Students: Rome

Corbishley, M. (1994). *Growing up in ancient Rome.* New York: Troll Associates.

Forman, J. (1976). *The Romans.* Morristown, NJ: Silver Burdette.

Waters, G. (1988). *Time train to ancient Rome.* London: Usborne.

Films, Videos, and CD-ROMs: Rome

Ancient Civilizations for Children: Ancient Rome (Schlessinger Media, 1998)

Ben-Hur (MGM/United Artists, 1959)—This movie contains an interlude selection during Part II that can be used during a Roman Feast.

Claudius: Boy of Ancient Rome (Encyclopedia Britannica Films)

Roman City (Macaulay, D., Public Broadcasting Service, 1994)

Knights and Ladies Club

- **Age group:** 8–10 years old; third graders

- **Purpose:** The academic objective of the Knights and Ladies Club is to teach the history and culture of Europe during the Middle Ages. Emphasis is placed on basic European and world geography, as well as the main events and cultural aspects of Medieval times. Sophisticated material such as *Beowulf* and the Magna Carta are introduced to the students.

By assuming historical roles, such as Serf, Peasant, Merchant, Page Squire, and Knight, students get to experience the social system of feudalism. Club Members learn about each group by changing characters throughout the year (e.g., they become Merchants to learn about Merchants; then, they become Page Squires to learn about Page Squires). Eventually, they all become Knights and Ladies, and they remain in these roles for the rest of the year. Their Club Leader remains the same character throughout the year (e.g., Lord Don, Overlord of the Knights and Ladies, Lady Eleanor of Aquitaine).

Although students get a chance to play characters at each social level, they are taught that the feudal system was like the caste system in India. A person born at a certain social level could not change his or her station in life. Students build a systematic structure with colored blocks that cannot vary as a model for this system.

Through drama, stories, and art, students learn about the history and culture of Europe during the Middle Ages. Feudalism, the rigid social system, and everyday life in a medieval village are dramatically recreated. The growth of central government in England is investigated as students learn about the role of the king, the Magna Carta, and the parliamentary system. Students also build towns. They explore the reasons for the growth and decline of towns by learning about invasions, period-appropriate technology, the form and function of guilds, religion, and the Black Death. Students explore life in medieval castles and learn why castles were built. In addition, they study the Battle of Hastings, which led to the creation of the Bayeux Tapestry. Finally, students study the Crusades, the *Canterbury Tales*, and early English history.

Specific Items Studied

Some topics that are explored in this Academic Club are:

- Calligraphy and illuminations
- Vikings
- Saxons
- Norman Conquest
- Black Death
- Gargoyles
- Ordeal by fire
- King Henry II—trial system
- Monasteries
- *Canterbury Tales*
- History of early English queens and kings
- Geography

Characters, Costumes, Passwords, and Rituals

The Club Leader (e.g., Overlord of Knights and Ladies) can dress in a long tunic. Peasants wear brown tunics, and Merchants wear jeweled tunics. Page Squires wear simple tunics. After the Knighting Ceremony, Knights and Ladies wear more elaborate tunics.

Some sample passwords used for entrance into the classroom include:

- Conquest
- Feudalism
- Illuminations
- Medieval
- Monks
- Plague
- Tapestry
- Tonsure

For the opening ritual, Club Members stand and say, "We, the [page squires, knights, etc.] of the [Court of the Round Table, Court of Fire, Court of

Ten, etc.] are all equal (cross arms or hold hands) under the monarchy that rules (lift arms) by divine right pledge (open arms) loyalty (fist over heart), bravery (make muscle), and truth (open hand)" The closing ritual involves Club Members saying, "Heart, Strength, Peace." They accompany these words with hand gestures. For *heart*, children place a hand over their heart. For *strength*, children make a fist, and for *peace*, children hold one hand up with an open palm.

Skills Emphasized

This Academic Club emphasizes vocabulary development, memory, sequential memory, and formulating questions. Club members also practice writing (e.g., calligraphy, illumination). Examples of questions that use Club Members' inductive and deductive thinking skills are:

- What did the Norsemen bring to the Saxons?

- Why was there conflict between the Saxons and the Normans?

- If you didn't live in a castle, where did you live?

- What was the justice system in the Middle Ages?

Activity: Making of the Bayeux Tapestry

Objective: Students will retell the story of the Battle of Hastings in the correct sequence. They will draw and sew their own replica of the Bayeux Tapestry.

Materials:

- Pencils, markers

- Sewing needles and assorted thread (e.g., red, brown, green, gold)

- Cotton/linen fabric cut into 6" x 3" strips

Procedures:

1. Present background information of the Battle of Hastings.

2. Brainstorm what a tapestry is, then explain how people used the Bayeux Tapestry to tell the story of the Battle of Hastings.

3. Assign students a major scene. Each scene can be assigned to an individual or group of students.

4. With pencils, sketch the major scenes on the fabric.

5. Use thread to sew over the pencil sketch outlines.

6. Use markers to fill in outlines and add details (e.g., chain mail on knights).

7. Have students put their scenes in the proper sequence.

8. When done, sew the strips together.

Background Information for Teachers

Brookfield, K. (1993). *Eyewitness books: Middle ages.* New York: Alfred A. Knopf.

Guy, J. (1999). *Medieval life.* London: Ticktock Publishing.

Price, M. (1988). *Medieval amusements.* Essex, England: Longman Group Limited.

Sauvain, P. (1986). *Do you know about castles and crusaders?* New York: Warwick Press.

Triggs, T. (1980). *The Saxons.* Morristown, NJ: Silver Burdett.

Illustrated Books to Show to Students

Howarth, S. (1993). *See through history the Middle Ages.* New York: Viking.

Howe, J. (1995). *Knights: A 3-dimensional exploration.* New York: Orchard Books.

Osband, G., & Andrew, R. (1993). *Castles: A 3-dimensional exploration.* New York: Tango Books.

Books to Read to Students

Aliki. (1993). *A Medieval feast.* New York: Harper & Row.

Caselli, G. (1986). *A Medieval monk.* New York: MacDonald & Co.

MacDonald, F. (1984). *Everyday life in the Middle Ages.* New York: MacDonald Education.

Films, Videos, and CD-ROMs

Castle (Macaulay, D.)

Cathedral (Macaulay, D.)

Music

"Ave Maria" sung by the Benedictine Nuns of St. Cecilia's Abbey

Gregorian Chant

Renaissance Club

- **Age group:** 9–11 years old; fourth graders
- **Purpose:** Renaissance Club introduces students to the rebirth of Roman and Greek ideas that flourished in Italy after the Middle Ages. The Club is staged in an environment that simulates Florence, Italy, the birthplace of the Renaissance. The Club Leader can be Lorenzo de Medici, and the Club Members can be Artist Members of Lorenzo de Medici's Council. Another option is for Club Members to be Florence Artist Guilds working for Lorenzo de Medici. Artist Guild membership is the result of their years of training in the workshops of master artists. Red velvet hats are symbols of shared guild membership. Guild membership was required to become a citizen of Florence. With citizenship comes voting rights and entry into political life.

Emphasis is placed on geography, main events, and cultural aspects of the period. By assuming the role of a famous Renaissance artist, such as Michelangelo or Leonardo da Vinci, students are encouraged to participate in activities that teach history, strengthen thinking skills, and explore an important cultural legacy. The students are usually so impressed with their characters that they thirst for as much knowledge as possible. Leonardo wants to know why he painted the Mona Lisa. Brunelleschi wants to know whom he competed against to design the Duomo, and Ghiberti is curious as to what else he sculpted besides "The Gates of Paradise." Even youngsters with poor memory skills do not forget any of the information about their characters. It is all personalized and becomes a part of their being. Being an important, productive character with an incredible legacy helps students feel good about themselves.

In this Academic Club, students learn about humanism and the buoyant optimism of the Renaissance while sculpting Michelangelo's "David" from student-made "marble." They study the emotions in Giotto's "Lamentation of Christ," learning about the fresco painting process and the departure from the somber art of the Middle Ages. They grind pigment and paint their own frescoes. The students experience the competitive spirit among artists to gain commissions from wealthy patrons when they sculpt bas-relief panels like the gilded bronze panels Ghiberti made for the baptistery doors (i.e., The Gates of Paradise). They learn how Renaissance science affected the future when they produce a life-size flying machine and Leonardo's ornithopter. They also study the engineering masterpiece the Duomo in Florence, designed by Brunelleschi. Students also study the Great Greek Revival and the development of important cultural centers such as Milan and Florence and famous ports for trade such as Venice and Genoa. The roles of the Church, guilds, women, scholars, and poets are explored as well as the works and lives of classical artists.

Another fun topic students explore is Michelangelo's frescoes in the Sistine Chapel. Painting the frescoes was a struggle. The Club Leader explains the techniques of painting with water-based pigment on wet plaster and tells of Michelangelo's reluctance to abandon sculpting because he saw himself as a sculptor. The Pope, however, commanded him to paint the Sistine Chapel. Frustration caused Michelangelo to chip off an entire finished section of the frescoes and to start over again! Although the student artists are not asked to reproduce the Sistine Chapel, they each are given watercolors and a box half filled with fresh plaster. They get to apply their imagination and skills to a totally new medium that is nonetheless well within their capability, and their fresh, colorful designs are taken home proudly. The organizational skills of planning, focusing, proceeding systematically and step by step, discriminating, and integrating all lead to success in making frescoes and are applicable to academic success in the classroom.

Specific Items Studied

The Renaissance Club year has eight sections of 3 or 4 weeks each determined by different artists, characters, and legacies, not by subject area. The following subjects are covered:

1. Florence—birthplace of the Renaissance

2. International trade and geography

3. Renaissance humanism

4. Renaissance architecture

5. Scientific innovations and inventions

6. Literature, language, and values

7. The Sistine Chapel

8. Artistic innovations

9. Daily life in the Renaissance

10. Parallel cultural developments in other regions of the world (e.g., fresco painting in Tibet during the 15th century is a superb example of cross-cultural comparisons)

Students also learn about the geography of Italy (e.g., the boot shape) in Europe. They learn how to sew by making membership hats. They study the revolution in banking (e.g., life of Lorenzo de Medici, Medici Bank), international trade (e.g., finding pigments for Giotto's fresco), and Renaissance architecture (e.g., Brunelleschi's Dome, Della Robbia's architectural ceramics). Renaissance music and dance (e.g., Josquin's music composition, instrument making) and literature and language (e.g., Dante's *Inferno*) are also explored. Artistic innovations examined include how Renaissance painting used perspective to create backgrounds of cities, landscapes, and topiary gardens.

Some other important topics are Renaissance scientific innovations/inventions (e.g., study of flight, machines, water, the body from Leonardo's *Codex*), Renaissance humanism (e.g., Michelangelo's David, da Vinci's Mona Lisa, Ghiberti's Gates of Paradise), and historical biography (e.g., lives of the artists and their peers). Students contrast past to present by figuring out what specifically was included in the Great Greek Revival that took place in the Renaissance. Finally, Club Members learn about the daily life in Renaissance times.

Characters, Costumes, Passwords, and Rituals

The Club Leader is typically the great patron of the arts, Lorenzo de Medici, and wears a royal purple velvet shawl bordered in gold. Club Members can wear red velvet hats like the artist Lippi, who was known for having discovered the concept of perspective in Renaissance times. They wear tunics that can be made of cloth or velvet. Every student is a well-known artist such as:

- Botticelli
- Brunelleschi
- Dante (poet)
- Ghiberti
- Giotto
- Leonardo da Vinci
- Luca Della Robbia
- Michelangelo
- Raphael

Other roles include Tintoretto, Caravaggio, Fra Angelico, and Josquin des Prez (musician).

Sample passwords for the Renaissance Club include:

- Ballatatoio
- Commission
- Contrapposto
- Galileo
- Humanism
- Linear perspective
- Ornithopter
- Patronage
- Restoration
- Sfumato

The opening ritual of the Renaissance Club begins outside the Renaissance door. Club Members say, "Bon Giorno, il Magnifico!" Then, they come inside and gather around the table. They say in unison, "From the darkness of the Middle Ages comes the light of the Renaissance to bring in the Modern World!" They may also enter a darkened room and say the word *light* as the lights turn on. The closing ritual involves Club Members saying, "The Renaissance; the rebirth of Greek and Roman ideas" as they leave the room.

Sample Activity: Commissioning Apprentices to Sculpt Michelangelo's "David"

Objective: Students can use the activity of making shoebox-size "Davids" to learn concepts of Renaissance humanism, art history, and geography while developing math skills (measuring, one-to-one correspondence), motor skills (sculpting with tools), and spatial organization skills (three-dimensional positive and negative space).

Materials:

- Three 8-quart bags of Vermiculite (garden supply)
- Two 25-pound bags of plaster of Paris (inexpensive at large home centers)
- 4 pounds of Portland Cement Mix
- Three 10" x 6" x 2" plastic food storage containers
- Large plastic bucket
- Pair of rubber gloves
- Large plastic bag

Procedure:

1. Prepare molds by lining the inside of the plastic food storage containers with sheets of plastic. Pieces of plastic must be large enough to cover containers with 6 inches extra on all sides.

2. Put dry ingredients in bucket: 3 quarts plaster, 3 quarts Vermiculite, and 1 cup Portland cement.

3. Wearing the rubber gloves, carefully and completely mix the dry ingredients by hand. Then, add 3½ quarts water. Quickly mix the materials with the gloved hands. Make sure to break apart all lumps and scrape the bottom of the bucket. A smooth, pancake batter-like consistency is the goal.

4. Material will set, so quickly pour equal parts into the waiting molds. Gently pull at the plastic sheet edges to create a smooth surface. Rinse the bucket promptly with water.

5. Wait one half-hour before removing the bricks from the molds, then carefully remove the plastic sheets from the bricks. Stack the bricks, and cover them with plastic. Wait one day before carving.

6. Using a knife tip, Club Members will outline the shape of David, making sure that his navel is in the middle of the block and that his head and feet extend to the top and bottom edges of the block of simulated marble. Have pictures of the actual David sculpture to use as a reference.

7. Using the tools, Club Members begin to remove the marble that is not part of the body (negative space). There are no rules in regard to how to sculpt or with what tools. This process is strictly trial and error, and each child will develop his or her own preference.

8. Through studying a picture of the real David, Club Members refine the details of the sculpture, such as the shape of the muscles and the hair.

9. Day by day, the bricks will steadily harden as they dry. When students are not working on the sculptures, cover the bricks in plastic to retard the drying rate. The sculpting material turns white when completely dry.

Note: Each day that the sculpting ensues, incorporate new information by reading the story of "David and Goliath," finding the town Carrara in the Alps in Italy where Michelangelo procured his marble, teaching the term *contrapposto,* and wearing newspaper hats like those worn by marble sculptors in Carrara today to keep the marble dust out of their hair.

Background Information for Teachers

Bergin, T.B., & Speake, J. (1987). *The encyclopedia of the Renaissance.* London: Market House Books.

Cohen, E.S., & Thomas, V. (2001). *Daily life in Renaissance Italy.* Wesport, CT: Greenwood Press.

Field, C. (1990). *Celebrating Italy.* New York: HarperCollins.

Lindqist, T. (1995). *Seeing the world through social studies.* Portsmouth, NH: Heinemann.

Roth, S.F. (1998). *Past into present: Effective techniques for first person historical interpretation.* Chapel Hill: University of North Carolina Press.

Setton, K.M. (Ed.). (1970). *The Renaissance maker of modern man.* Washington, DC: National Geographic Society.

Shlain, L. (1991). *Art and physics.* New York: Quill, William Morrow.

Steves, R. (2000). *Europe 101* (6th ed.). New York: Avalon Travel

Steves, R., & Openshaw, G. (2001). *Mona winks* (5th ed.). New York: Avalon Travel.

Stone, I. (1996). *The agony and the ecstasy.* (Renaissance ed.). New York: New American Library.

Strauss, S. (1996). *The passionate fact: Storytelling in natural history and cultural interpretation.* Golden, CO: Fulcrum Publishing.

Illustrated Books to Show to Students

di Medici, L. (1992). *Tuscany: The beautiful cookbook.* New York: HarperCollins.

Mancinelli, F. (1996). *The Sistine Chapel.* Florence: Vatican Museums.

Romei, F. (1994). *Masters of art: Leonardo da Vinci.* New York: Simon & Schuster Young Books.

Romei, F. (1995). *Masters of art: The story of sculpture.* New York: Macdonald Young Books.

Time-Life Editors. (1986). *Library of nations: Italy.* New York: Time-Life Books.

Venezia, M. (1991). *Michelangelo.* Connecticut: Children's Press.

Wings Books. (1992). *Michelangelo: The Sistine Chapel.* Avenel, NJ: Outlet Book Company.

Wood, T. (1993). *The Renaissance.* New York: Viking Press.

Books to Read to Students

Clare, J.D. (1994). *Italian Renaissance: "Living history" series.* San Diego: Harcourt Brace & Co.

Fritz, J., & Talbott, H. (2001). *Leonardo's horse.* New York: G.P. Putnam's Sons.

Galli, L. (1982). *Mona Lisa: The secret of the smile.* New York: Delacorte Press.

Guarnieri, P. (1998). *A boy named Giotto.* New York: Farrar Straus Giroux.

King, R. (2000). *Brunelleschi's dome: How a Renaissance genius reinvented architecture.* London: Random House.

Krull, K., & Hewitt, K. (1995). *Lives of the artists: Masterpieces, messes (and what the neighbors thought).* San Diego: Harcourt Brace & Co.

Langley, A. (1999). *Eyewitness books: Renaissance.* New York: Alfred A. Knopf.

Parillo, T. (1998). *Michelangelo's surprise.* New York: Farrar Straus Giroux.

Provensen, A. (1984). *Leonardo da Vinci.* New York: Viking Press.

Richtus, J.P. (1976). *The notebooks of Leonardo Da Vinci* (Vols. 1–2). New York: Dover Publishing.

Stanley, D. (2000). *Michelangelo.* New York: HarperCollins.

Films, Videos, and CD-ROMs

Agony and Ecstasy (Twentieth Century Fox, 1992)

Florence: Cradle of the Renaissance (Museum City Videos, V.I.E.W. Video, 1992)

Florence: Birthplace of the Renaissance (Educational Video Network, 1994.)

Hudson Hawk (Columbia Pictures, 1991)

Masterpieces of Italian Art Series: Birth of the Renaissance (Educational Video Network, 1990)

Masters of Illusion (Smithsonian Institution and National Gallery of Art, 1988)

Michelangelo: Artist and Man (A&E Home Video, 1994)

Music

Gentil Madonna: A Vision of the Italian Renaissance—London Pro Musica/Bernard Thomas (The United Recording Company, 1994)

Museum Club

- **Age group:** 11–12 years old; fifth graders

- **Purpose:** Students study ancient civilizations that have not appeared in the Academic Club sequence. The students end with learning about explorers such as Vasco da Gama, who led the way for Christopher Columbus and other explorers of the New World.

The purpose of the Museum Club is to review major periods of history beginning with the ancient civilizations and expanding into the earliest exploration for trade routes to the New World 4,000 years later. The Club Leader is Director of the Museum Association of America. The students are all Directors of different museums. Emphasis is placed on visual pictures of the civilization studied and seeking out progress in government, architecture, agriculture, technology, and communications. The lifestyle of each period is examined by looking at arts and crafts, tools, inventions, religion, science, language, clothing, and housing. Replicas of artifacts from each period of history are made and displayed in the Museum. At the end of each unit of study, an Exhibit Opening is held with each Curator speaking to visitors on one aspect of the exhibit.

The multisensory approach and hands-on activities encourage an understanding of the development of civilization. Children acquire classical knowledge, learn about cause and effect relationships, and develop problem-solving skills and expressive language.

The Museum Club devotes its first trimester (September, October, November, early December) to the ancient civilizations of 1) Mesopotamia (Sumerians, Babylonians, Assyrians); 2) Phoenicia (great traders of the Mediterranean); and 3) Crete (the home of Minoan civilization). The second trimester (January, February, March) examines the history of the Hebrews, Christians, Muslims, and Hindus. In the third trimester, most of the focus is on Buddhism, China, and China's 4,000 years of civilization. The Great Explorations of Portugal and Spain finish the term leading to exploration in America and the discovery of Native Americans and their new foods (e.g., potatoes, yams, turkey, corn), use of fertilizers, and use of smoking tobacco.

Specific Items Studied

Students learn that Mesopotamians

- Established cities and agriculture

- Installed an extraordinary irrigation system from the Tigris and the Euphrates Rivers

- Used the great legal system devised by Hammurabi from Babylon
- Were known for their temples called *ziggurats*
- Invented cuneiform on clay tablets
- Had a stock exchange

The Assyrians were known for savagery in warfare but were phenomenal artists and artisans, with splendid statues of winged bulls that became their emblem. Surrounded by cedar forests, the Assyrians made fleets of beautifully crafted boats. They were known for spreading the use of many Mesopotamian inventions to other countries.

Phoenicians were great navigators and traders who carried on commerce throughout the Mediterranean. They knew how to make a rare purple dye out of snails, and the fine purple cloth they produced was in great demand. The Phoenicians invented the alphabet.

The Minoans developed an advanced civilization on the island of Crete, as demonstrated by the Palace of Knossos discovered by archeologist Arthur Evan in 1903. Bulls played a big part in their art, religion, and sports. Children learn about the myth of the Minotaur (Minos's Bull) and design their own labyrinths and Minotaurs.

Students learn that the Hebrews believed in one God and that the first Hebrew, Abraham, left Mesopotamia with his wife, Sarah, and traveled westward. Club Members also learn about Abraham's two sons, Isaac and Ishmael. Other topics explored are the Exodus, the Ten Commandments, and the Diaspora.

The Hindus are studied as a culture with many gods, chiefly Brahma the Creator, Vishnu the Preserver, and Siva the Destroyer. Great Indian myths and stories, notably those in the Ramayana epic, are told and reenacted, and richly expressive Indian art and sculpture are an important element in the Museum Club.

When studying China, Club Members

- Learn symbols from the Chinese alphabet through calligraphy painting
- Learn how silk is made
- Construct a Chinese dragon
- Celebrate the Chinese New Year with Chinese dishes, green tea drunk from homemade bowls glazed with Chinese characters, and chopsticks

Finally, Club Members learn that the first great European explorers took to the sea from Spain and Portugal, searching for spices and trade opportunities. The Pope drew a Line of Demarcation to divide the world in half. Europeans came in contact with Native Americans, who had developed their own products and ways of life.

Characters, Costumes, Passwords, and Rituals

As the students enter the Museum Club, they assume the roles of staff from museums throughout Washington, D.C. The students assume the following jobs: Curator, Preparatory, Art Conservator, Archivist, Exhibit Designer, Development Coordinator, Exhibit Artist, and Education Coordinator. The Club Leader is the Director of the Museum staff.

The staff members wear work aprons that they silk-screen with the Museum Club logo. They also design and create their own name badges, which have their title, museum name, and photograph.

Sample passwords for the Museum Club include:

- Archaeologist

- Babylon

- Civilization

- Cuneiform

- Dynasty

- Exodus

- Gilgamesh

- Irrigation

- Ishtar Gate

- Mesopotamia

- Ziggurat

The opening ritual of the Museum Club involves Club Members saying, "Museums—windows onto the past and doorways into the future." The closing ritual involves students saying, "An unending dialogue between the past and the present."

Skills Emphasized

The Museum Club emphasizes the following skills:

- Increasing storehouses of knowledge

- Developing long-term memory through association

- Developing receptive and expressive language

- Sequencing of historical events

- Eye–hand coordination

- Thinking skills (problem solving)

- Research skills

- Making connections between artifacts created and their historical significance

- Step-by-step planning and organization

- Socialization skills

- Learning about how museums operate

Sample Activity: The Secret of Silk

Objective: Students will make silk paper.

Materials:

- Silkworm cocoons (can be ordered from a science catalog)

- Small heat-resistant plastic bowls

- Electric burner

- Small metal cooking pot

- Electric coffee urn to heat water

- 6″ x 6″ wooden frames

- Sizing or stiffening medium

- Brushes

- Slotted spoon

- Old towels

- Extra disposable bowls

Procedure

1. Fill the pot with water, and place it on the electric burner. Heat the water until it simmers. Warm additional water in the coffee urn.

2. Add the cocoons to the pot, and simmer them for about 10 minutes. This action loosens the sericin, or gummy substance that coats and binds the silk threads.

3. Give each student a wooden frame and a small bowl half full of warm water from the coffee urn.

4. Spread towels around the work space.

5. Using the slotted spoon, give each student a cocoon in his or her bowl.

6. Place the extra disposable bowls around the work space.

7. Have students pick up their cocoons and make a small hole with their fingers to remove the pupa. Place the pupae in the disposable bowls in the table.

8. Show children how to gently spread the fibers of the cocoon with the fingers of both of their hands until it is large enough to stretch over the wooden frame.

9. Repeat this process with five or six cocoons, and have children layer each co-coon on top of the others on the wooden frame. They should adjust the silk fibers to create even layers of silk.

10. Optional—to enhance the sheets of silk paper, small pieces of decorative fiber (dyed strands of silk, gold threads, gold leaf) may be added in between the lay-ers of silk.

11. Dry the silk paper overnight on the frames.

12. The next day, children can remove the silk from the frames. The silk may be ironed to flatten it out.

13. Children then should brush the silk paper with a coating of a stiffening medium (sizing, starch, thinned school glue)

14. Finally, students lay the silk flat to dry on a nonporous surface or over window screening.

Background Information for Teachers

Encyclopedia of world religions. (2001). London: Usborne Publishing.

Herbert, J. (2001). *Marco Polo for kids: His marvelous journey to China.* Chicago: Chicago Review Press.

Islam, a global civilization. (n.d.). Washington, DC: Embassy of Saudi Arabia.

Pauling, C. (1997). *Introducing Buddhism.* New York: Barnes & Noble.

Stockstad, M. (1995). *Art history* (Vol. 1). New York: Prentice Hall.

Illustrated Books to Show Students

Barnes, T. (1999). *The Kingfisher book of religions.* New York: Kingfisher Publi-cations.

Chatterjee, M., & Roy, A. (2002). *Eyewitness books: India.* New York: Dorling Kindersely.

Cotterell, A. (1994). *Eyewitness books: Ancient China.* New York: Dorling Kinders-ley.

Fairservis, W.A. (1964). *Mesopotamia: The civilization that rose out of clay.* New York: Macmillan.

Langley, M. (1996). *Eyewitness books: Religions.* New York: Dorling Kindersley.

O'Connor, J. (2002). *The emperor's silent army.* New York: Viking Publishing.

Pearson, A. (1992). *Eyewitness books: Ancient Greece.* New York: Dorling Kin-dersley.

Perring, S., & Perring, D. (1999). *Then and now.* Edison, NJ: Chartwell Books.

Shuter, J. (2002). *The Sumerians*. Chicago: Reed Educational and Professional Publications.

Stierlin, H. (2002). *Islamic art and architecture*. New York: Thames and Hudson.

Time-Life Editors. (1998). *Ancient civilizations*. New York: Time-Life Books.

Wilkinson, P. (2001). *Eyewitness books: Islam*. New York: Dorling Kindersley.

Yu, L.T.-T. (1988). *Chinese watercolor painting: The four seasons*. Cincinnati: North Light Books.

Books to Read to Students

Angeletti, R. (1999). *The Minotaur of Knossos*. New York: Oxford University Press.

Bahree, P. (1995). *The Hindu world*. Morristown, NJ: MacDonald and Co.

The children's illustrated Bible. (1994). New York: Dorling Kindersley.

Encyclopedia of world religions. (2001). London: Usborne Publishing.

Fisher, L. (1986). *The great wall of China*. New York: Macmillan.

Into the unknown: The story of exploration. (1987). Washington, DC: National Geographic Society.

Odijk, P. (1989). *The Sumerians*. Morristown: Silver Burdette Press.

Senker, C. (2002). *Judaism*. Columbus: McGraw-Hill Children's Publishing.

Shuter, J. (1998). *The Ancient Chinese*. Chicago: Reed Educational and Professional Publishing.

Time Life Books. (1998). *Ancient civilizations*. New York: Author.

Wilkinson, P. (2001). *Eyewitness books: Islam*. New York: Dorling Kindersley.

Music

Authentic Middle Eastern music, both instrumental and vocal

Calls to worship from mosques

Music from synagogues and Israeli folk music

Gregorian Chants (to represent Christianity)

Sacred Buddhist and Hindu music

Chinese folk music

Films, Videos, and CD-ROMs

Ancient Mesopotamia (Schesslinger Media Library Video)

Faith and Belief: Five Major World Religions (Knowledge Unlimited)

Islamic Art (Films for the Humanities, Princeton)

American Industrialists Club

- **Age group:** 11–13 years old; sixth graders

- **Purpose:** Club Members learn about American history from the 1700s to the mid-1900s. They learn about the 13 colonies, the reasons for the Revolutionary War, and the first industrialist (Eleuthere Dupont, who made the gunpowder used in the War of 1812). Another industrialist studied is Andrew Carnegie. The curriculum also includes topics such as the westward movement (e.g., Louisiana Purchase, Gold Rush, transcontinental railroad), the Industrial Revolution (e.g., man versus machine), the Civil War (e.g., Fort Sumter, underground railroad, Emancipation Proclamation, abolitionist), the stock market crashes (e.g., Black Friday), World War I (e.g., Central Powers versus the Allies), World War II (e.g., Pearl Harbor), and the United Nations.

Specific Issues Studied

Students learn about American history from 1776 to 1900, including American Independence, the Constitution, the agrarian economy, slavery, immigration, the transcontinental railroad, the westward movement, urban life, the Industrial Revolution and its impact on urban life, child labor laws, the beginning of labor unions, and anti-trust legislation. Questions explored include 1) Upon whom did the Industrialists trample to make their multimillions? 2) What legacy have they left for all of us? 3) Why did Carnegie establish public libraries? and 4) Why was Guggenheim a patron of the arts?

    Other issues studied include:

- U.S. geography

- U.S. government

- The Stock Market

- Plight of the poor

Characters, Costumes, Passwords, and Rituals

Club Members choose from one of the following industrialists from different time periods:

- Andrew Carnegie

- Eleuthere Dupont

- Henry Ford

- Jay Gould

- Meyer Guggenheim
- J.P. Morgan
- John D. Rockefeller
- Cornelius Vanderbilt
- Madame C.J. Walker (entrepreneur)

The Club Leader can be Madame History, Chairman of the Board, or the U.S. Secretary of the Treasury. During the 50-minute Club sessions, students hold board meetings, manage trust funds (recorded in ledgers), keep records concerning business and personal transactions, and study the Stock Market. They learn the difference between the Bull Market and the Bear Market. The value of each student's trust fund—which fluctuates according to each student's behavior and is subject to fines and rewards—is an excellent behavior management tool.

The American Industrialists can wear bowler hats. Girls may prefer to wear wide-brimmed hats covered with flowers and tiny veils. All Industrialists wear vests and carry briefcases that hold their important documents and money. Each Industrialist has a name plate carved on a wooden plaque that marks his or her place at the corporate table.

Sample passwords for the American Industrialists Club include:

- Abolitionist
- Assembly line
- Automation
- Commercial
- Corporation
- Enterprise
- Monopoly
- Philanthropy
- Secede
- Standardization

For the opening ritual, the Club Members say, "The meeting of the Industrialists Club is now called to order. All those present please signify by saying *Aye.*" The Club Leader then takes roll by saying each character's name (e.g., Carnegie, Ford). After taking roll, the Club Leader says, "The meeting of the Industrialists Club is now called to order."

For the closing ritual, the Club Leader says, "Is there a motion for this meeting to be adjourned?" The Club Leader calls on a Club Member (e.g., "I recognize Vanderbilt"). The Club Member answers, "I so move." The Club

Leader then asks, "Is there a second to the motion?" and calls on another Club Member. This Club Member replies, "I second the motion." The Club Member concludes the meeting by saying, "No further business will be considered."

Sample Activity: Building a Model Boat for Vanderbilt

Objective: Students will sand, paint, and assemble models of a Periauger, which was Vanderbilt's first boat.

Materials:

- Styrofoam for hull
- Sticks for masts
- Metal and plastic for rudder and spar
- Sandpaper
- Water-based paint and paintbrushes
- Paint markers
- Number decals
- Two 10' rain gutters
- Two sawhorses

Procedure:

1. Have the students line up outside the door in single file.
2. Ask each student to whisper the password *Periauger* to you as they enter the classroom.
3. Tell the students to take their places at the board table, and then open the meeting.
4. Hand out the boxes containing the materials for the boats to each student.
5. Tell students to label their materials.
6. Students should then mark the design of the ship on the Styrofoam hull and label where the mast, spar, and rudder will be placed.
7. Student should sand and imprint their hulls.
8. Explain that students should put several coats of water-based paint to the hull.
9. Help students apply a high-gloss acrylic enamel paint to the completely dried hull.
10. Prepare two 10' gutters on sawhorses for the students to have a regatta.

Background Information for Teachers

Buckley, S.W. (1996). *American history time lines.* New York: Scholastic Professional Books.

Bundles, A. (2001). *On her own ground: The life and times of Madam C.J. Walker.* New York: Washington Square Press.

Chernow, R. (1998). *Titan: The life of John D. Rockefeller Sr.* New York: Random House.

Cort, D. (1986). *Edwin Gould: The man and his legacy.* New York: Edwin Gould Foundation for Children.

English, J.A., & Jones, T.D. (1998). *Scholastic encyclopedia of the United States at war.* New York: Scholastic Trade.

Groner, A. (1972). *The American heritage history of American business and industry.* New York: Heritage.

Janis, H. (1999). *The Civil War for kids: A history with 21 activities.* Chicago: Chicago Review Press.

Josephson, M. (1962). *The robber barons: The great American capitalists 1861–1901.* Fort Washington, PA: Harvest Books.

Lacey, R. (1986). *Ford: The man and the machine.* Boston: Little, Brown & Co. [out of print]

Mosley, L. (1980). *Blood relations: The rise and fall of the Du Ponts of Delaware.* New York: Atheneum.

Strouse, J. (1999). *Morgan, American financier.* New York: Random House.

Vanderbilt, A.T, II. (1991). *Fortune's children: The fall of the house of Vanderbilt.* New York: Quill.

Wall, J.F. (1989). *Andrew Carnegie.* Pittsburgh: University of Pittsburgh Press.

Weisberger, B.A. (1966). *Captains of industry.* New York: American Heritage Publishing Co.

Illustrated Books to Show Students

Asher & Adams. (1976). *Asher & Adams' pictorial album of American industry.* New York: Routledge Books.

Cahill, M., & Piade, L. (Eds.). (1989). *The history of the Union Pacific, America's great transcontinental railroad.* New York: Smithmark Publishers.

Porter, G. (1992). *The worker's world at Hagley.* Wilmington, DE: Hagley Museum and Library.

Quimby, M.O. (1973). *Eleutherian Mills.* Wilmington, DE: Eleutherian Mills-Hagley Foundation.

Snell, C.W. (1960). *Vanderbilt mansion.* Washington, DC: Government Printing Office.

Thorndike, J. (Ed.). (1953). *Ford at fifty: An American story.* New York: Simon & Schuster.

Books to Read to Students

Aird, H.B., & Ruddiman, C. (1960). *Henry Ford: Young man with ideas.* New York: Macmillan.

Athearn, R.G. (1963). *The American heritage new illustrated history of the United States: Vol. 10. Age of steel.* New York: Dell Publishing Co.

Bowman, J.S. (1989). *Andrew Carnegie.* Englewood, NJ: Silver Burdett.

Bundles, A. (1991). *Madam C.J. Walker entrepreneur.* Philadelphia: Chelsea House Publishers.

Carratello, J., & Carratello, P. (1991). *Thematic unit Civil War.* Westminster, CA: Teacher Created Materials.

Clark, P. (1988). *Wars that changed the world: The American Revolution.* Tarrytown, NY: Marshall Cavendish.

Clark, P. (1988). *Wars that changed the world: The Civil War.* Tarrytown, NY: Marshall Cavendish.

Curtin, A. (1965). *Gallery of great Americans.* New York: Franklin Watts.

Fisher, D.A. (1949). *Steel making in America.* New York: United States Steel Corporation.

Gilbert, M. (1962). *Henry Ford: Maker of the Model T.* Boston: Houghton Mifflin.

Kent, Z. (1960). *The story of the New York Stock Exchange.* Chicago: Children's Press.

Kownslar, A.O., & Frizzle, D.B. (1967). *Discovering American history.* New York: Holt, Rinehart & Winston.

Large, L. (1935). *Little people who became great.* New York: Platt and Munk.

Mitchell, B. (1986). *We'll race you, Henry: A story about Henry Ford.* Minneapolis: Carolrhoda Books.

Redden, R. (1976). *Money.* London: Macdonald Educational.

Rutland, J. (1987). *The age of steam.* London: Kingfisher Books.

Films, Videos, and CD-ROMs

America's Castles II (A&E Television Networks and Centel Productions, 1995)

Andrew Carnegie Prince of Steel (Biography/A&E Home Video)

Citizen Kane (Warner Home Video, 1944)

J. Pierpont Morgan Emperor of Wall Street (Biography/A&E Home Video)

This is America, Charlie Brown series: The Building of the Transcontinental Railroad (Paramount Pictures, 1994)

The Rockefellers (Biography/A&E Home Video)

The Vanderbilts: An American Dynasty (Biography/A&E Home Video)

Music

Music and the Underground Railroad (Ascension Productions, 1988)

RESULTS OF ACADEMIC CLUBS

Nonreaders, poor readers, and students with language and attention problems become fascinated with history, geography, civics, and many related subjects through the Academic Club Methodology. They live through their characters, they feel important and intimately involved, and they learn complex material. Once they have learned the material, they tend to remember it for a lifetime!

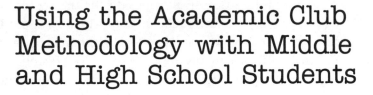

5

Using the Academic Club Methodology with Middle and High School Students

So far, you have explored how the Academic Club Methodology is used for elementary school students. Older students may not welcome the costumes, rituals, and passwords of Academic Clubs, but they do respond well to the in-depth, hands-on learning experiences of the Academic Club Approach. Teaching strategies that are part of the Approach include living history, hands-on geography, reenactments of literature, scientific investigations, and problem solving. Writing also plays an important part in the education of older students. This chapter explores some of the middle and high school subjects taught at The Lab School of Washington and at the Baltimore Lab: humanities, democracy, science, and Spanish. It also explains some excellent programs we have for older students, such as the School Store, Apprenticeship Program, Deadline Management Course, Rauschenberg Day, and whole-school learning projects.

HUMANITIES COURSE

Seventh graders at The Lab School have moderate to severe learning disabilities with major challenges in reading, writing, listening, memorizing, and focusing. Our Humanities Course is designed to let them explore three countries during the school year. For example, students have studied Morocco from September to the end of December, Brazil from January to the end of March, and Japan from April to June. Students use history, geography, archeology, civics, and various art forms to study these countries. They look at photographs, drawings, and artifacts; listen to the music of the country; hear the country's language spoken; meet at least one person from the country; view films and CD-ROMs about the country; and look on-line for information on the country—all to get a feel of the country's culture.

Consider the Humanities Course activities during the Morocco unit. Students explore geography by making a relief map of Africa and pointing out the northern part, where Morocco exists. They also make maps of Morocco and recreate the flag and various symbols of the country. The history and government of Morocco are also presented. Morocco's decades under French colonial rule are examined to see how much of the French influence remains in Moroccan life. Today's monarchy is acted out and contrasted with American democracy. Special features such as "The Casbah," the fortified marketplace in Fez; "Marrakesh" with its water carriers, snake charmers, and covered souk; "Casablanca" (made famous by the Humphrey Bogart movie); and the Moroccan capital of Rabat are studied. One year, a group sewed leather wallets, key ring holders, and sewing kits to look like Moroccan goods; another year, students constructed a 7-foot camel made out of papier-mâché.

One Humanities teacher, Katie Clark, introduced her students to the extraordinary work of the Berbers by showing traditional Berber symbols and designs. Students were given a piece of construction paper and instructed to create Berber carpet designs using paint, magic markers, gel pens, stencils, yarn, and their own creativity. They punched holes in the edges and fringed them with different colors of yarn, similar to real carpets. Then, using their carpet designs as their guides, they went to their computers and composed a brief story, description, or history of the symbols or patterns they used.

Humanities Course students also study the configuration of neighboring countries to Morocco, the Moroccan economy, and current issues (e.g., independence for Western Sahara). They listen to well-known Moroccan poetry or short stories along with Moroccan music. The culmination of all of these activities is a recreated Moroccan Restaurant. For 3 days, parents, friends, school faculty, and volunteers are invited to sit at highly decorated tables; eat couscous, vegetables, Moroccan salad, bread, and baklava; and drink mint tea. Some students prepare Moroccan music or perform a Moroccan folk dance; others are responsible for making the all-purpose room look like a Moroccan restaurant. Several children serve as hosts and hostesses or sell a class-made recipe book of Moroccan dishes. The students rotate each day being the cooks, the waiters, or the hosts. Every student has a job. With the charge of about $8.00 per person for the meal, the whole seventh grade and some Lab School faculty go to a Moroccan restaurant in Washington, D.C., and critique the waiters and the food. (Note that children also participate in a Brazilian Restaurant and a Japanese Restaurant later in the year and dine at corresponding ethnic restaurants in Washington, D.C.)

For the second trimester, the great diversity of Brazil is emphasized. Children learn interesting facts about this country. For example, Brazil was the winner of the 2002 World Cup in Football (i.e., soccer). An important topic is the rainforest. To translate the abstract idea of the rainforest into a concrete activity, teachers carry out an activity to help children understand and visualize the four layers of the rainforest. Some students sit or lie on the floor to represent the forest floor. Other students sit in chairs to represent the under story layer or stand to represent the canopy. The last group of students stands on chairs to represent the emergent layer. Follow-up activities include constructing a small three-dimensional paper collage as well as a large three-dimensional bulletin board model of the four layers of the rainforest, including the animals found in the various layers. We have found that students get so upset about the worsening conditions in the Brazilian rainforest that they make posters describing these conditions and collect money to send to Brazil.

During the final trimester, students study Japan. They learn about flower arranging, the ritual for serving tea in a Japanese teahouse, and the drama of Noh plays. In addition, they study the history of World War II leading up to Pearl Harbor and the subsequent internment of Japanese Americans in concentration camps. A field trip to the low-key monument erected in Washington, D.C., to the memory of the internees is not easily forgotten by Humanities students. Current events in present day Japan are always followed, and, whenever possible, the students meet people from Japan and shower them with questions. At the end of the year, students transform their classroom into a Japanese restaurant complete with a Japanese landscape. They sell Japanese recipe books and display origami and Japanese watercolors.

To immerse students in each country, we use journal/diary activities in which each student takes on the role of a character from the country, for example, a scientist, banker, dancer, soldier, Moroccan Berber, Sahara camel trader, Mediterranean merchant, souk storekeeper, Japanese artist, sumo wrestler, or princess. Students are given worksheets with starters such as "Today I . . . " "I can't believe that . . . " and "My family . . . " Then, they complete the phrases with historical and cultural information combined with their own creativity. After the writing is completed, the students design and make a costume, a backdrop, or a prop to go with the character they have chosen. They then present the materials to the class.

We have found that students provide valuable input on the kinds of activities or topics they would like to learn in the Humanities Course. We tell them, "Use your investigative powers to find materials and use these resources to generate ideas. What would you most like to learn about this country?" Teachers encourage students to make up teaching materials, such as games to learn the high points of history, cartoons, dioramas, and even entertaining worksheets. Our students claim they never forget the information they have learned in the Humanities Course because they experienced so much of the life of each country and drew so many pictures in their minds.

DEMOCRACY COURSE

At The Lab School, an eighth-grade course on democracy is taught that is similar to many middle school American history classes. The class, however, begins with a role-playing game in which the teacher plays an autocrat. Students are Citizens who must do what the autocrat says. The game is set up so Citizens are empowered to take action—the goal being that students petition for the teacher's removal and create a democratic class. Students are instructed to respond to the game truthfully within their role as Citizens and are encouraged to communicate with each other. Potential leaders are coached on the most effective leadership strategies. The game is interrupted frequently for reflection and evaluation.

One teacher, Nancy Rowland, has taught the democracy class for 7 years. She starts each year by informing students that they are Citizens of the Nation of Rowland. For a week or so, she plays the role of a cruel dictator (the Queen) who wears a crown and a robe. She posts the Nation of Rowland Laws and places signs around the room to mark the Jail and Morgue. Ms. Rowland's students usually are quiet and a little fearful at first. They watch carefully as the Queen establishes her authority by handing out cruel sentences to unsuspecting Citizens. As the game continues, some Citizens' fear turns into determination. These Citizens form dissident groups that meet secretly during and outside of class. Other Citizens survive by becoming loyalists to the Queen.

Each action by the Queen creates an emotional reaction from the Citizens, and this emotional charge has huge benefits for learning. Students are motivated to do written work without direct instruction to do so. For example, at least one student each year goes home and creates a written declaration to present to the Queen. Because students are actively engaged in the outcome of the game, they remember the lesson for a long time. Years later, they can recall whether they were dissidents or loyalists. Ms. Rowland uses this game as a hook for students to learn new concepts about government.

Students begin by learning about the Founding Fathers, who created the Declaration of Independence and the U.S. Constitution. They then learn about the American Revolution through the struggle between Thomas Jefferson and Alexander Hamilton about the future character of the United States. Next, students study the Civil War. From there, they explore the Industrial Revolution and the beginning of labor unions. Students build projects, interview each other as different characters, visit the Supreme Court, and put on mock trials while wearing judicial robes. The Democracy Course is a great foundation for students who go on to take high school government classes.

SCIENCE COURSE

Science is often taught through art in the middle school. For example, students create mock stained-glass windows as part of their study of earth science and astronomy. Each pane in a large window is covered with a black matte-board frame with tissue paper behind it. Students choose a topic (e.g., stars, galaxies, meteors, planets) and independently research the topic using books and on-line sources. After their research, students create images to represent their topic. The class then decides how to arrange the images on the stained-glass window to simulate the Earth and the Universe.

Students learn about diffusion by participating in a Diffusion Disco. They are confined to a small space in the room. Students are told that they are molecules and should dance to lively disco music. After a few minutes, students are asked to stop and describe how they feel. They say things such as, "I feel hot," "It's too crowded," and "I need more space." Then, the confined space is opened. Students are told that they now have more space. The music and dancing resume. Students spread out and take up more space. They are then asked to react to having still more space. After the activity, the teacher explains that the students behaved the way molecules do during the process of diffusion.

Students also learn through making their own experiments and projects. After learning about diffusion, one student may open up a bottle of perfume in one corner of the room. Its scent is soon detected throughout the classroom. Students discover that when the scent molecules are released and no longer confined in the bottle, they move to an area where there are fewer molecules.

Almost any topic of science lends itself to an art form and a specific role for each student encouraging him or her to probe deep into the subject. Simple machines, such as levers, blocks, and pulleys, have been studied in the Science Course then reproduced with various materials. Students use their simple machines to design a building or create a moving vehicle. Ecology is a subject that students love to explore because of the continuous drama from the formation of the Earth, to the evolution and development of the Earth, to today's problems of pollution and global warming. Along with hands-on experiments, water testing, and temperature recordings, students in small groups make up allegorical dramas accompanied by appropriate original music.

Instead of the science fairs that middle and high schools typically conduct, The Lab School holds a Health Expo. We choose to conduct a Health Fair instead of a science fair because it is more concrete and personal. Students look at their own bodies, their own fitness, and their own nutrition. The Health Fair also provides students with a definition of good health. The event focuses on the body, nutrition, exercise, and experiments that prove that fitness improves health. Students conduct research, interviews, and surveys and present their findings in displays, graphs, and charts using their computer skills.

SPANISH

In order to graduate from high school in Washington, D.C., a student must have 2 years of a foreign language. At The Lab School, we teach Spanish. Because many Lab School students experience so much trouble just speaking English, no less writing it, Spanish can be their nemesis. The goals of The Lab School Spanish program are to build general language and communication skills as well as to broaden students' familiarity with Hispanic culture. Students make handicrafts centered around the Mexican Day of the Dead. They view Spanish art at the National Gallery of Art, watch Spanish movies, and prepare Hispanic foods. They listen to Spanish music and poetry, study Spanish architecture and design, and learn about classic Spanish dances.

Students particularly enjoy their assignment of creating a television show. They videotape themselves and must speak only in Spanish. They may create a program that starts with the weather person, segues into a headline news segment, proceeds to an advertisement, and concludes with a Spanish soap opera. One of the funniest scenes students have produced is a series of car salesmen who attempt to sell their cars in Spanish and become more and more aggressive. Other topics include a cooking show and an art appreciation forum. These hands-on activities are extremely motivating for students.

SCHOOL STORE

Ninth graders run the School Store at The Lab School. Some tenth graders also take part in the store management. Because every year the School Store is under new management, students get to choose its logo and name. They sell food and products such as school shirts, sweatshirts, caps, pencils, notebooks, pads, drink containers, and emblems to put on automobiles. They learn math by operating the business. They must buy products wholesale, then figure out how to sell them retail and still make some profit. Students study methods of selling and learn to making change quickly and accurately. They have to change prices, sometimes doubling the amount on the tag or recalculating inventory. They must keep inventories and make spreadsheets on the computer. They place orders, deal with distributors, and pay bills, which involves check writing and checkbook balancing.

One year, students took themselves so seriously that they designed shirts with logos for their salesmen and developed an advertising brochure of their products. In this particular class, there were four students who had really enjoyed their Academic Clubs in elementary school (true "Clubbies"), and all they wanted to do each day was work in the School Store. We are proud that all four students went on to sales positions after graduation. All of them received college degrees in business management, and one is currently the president of a large manufacturing business in Indiana.

APPRENTICESHIP PROGRAM

The eleventh-grade Lab School curriculum includes an Apprenticeship Program. Approximately 30 students each year attend classes half of the day and work in internships in the Washington, D.C., metropolitan area the other half. The Apprenticeship Program helps students learn positive work habits and taste success, which we hope will lead to future employment. The program is designed to increase career awareness, to encourage students to emulate their employers as adult models, and to motivate students to put more effort into academic studies. Thus, the program also helps students develop skills to enhance their academic work and focus on future goals—both for learning and for the workforce. Students are placed according to their special interests and talents in the following businesses:

- Animal hospitals
- Art schools
- Bookstores
- Boutiques
- Ceramics studios
- Coast Guard
- Commercial businesses
- Computer businesses
- Environmental groups
- Filmmaking studios
- Frame shops
- Furniture-making studios
- Government offices
- Graphic arts studios
- Hospitals
- Jewelry-making studios
- Labor unions
- Libraries
- Magazine publishers
- Magic stores
- Museums
- The National Institutes of Health
- The National Park Service

- Photography shops
- Preschool settings
- Radio stations
- Schools with physical education classes
- Science labs
- The Smithsonian Institution
- Television stations
- Theatre companies
- Zoos

Eleventh-grade students learn to complete job applications, interview for jobs, and self-advocate. They periodically present oral job reports to ensure reflection on their internship experience. They write detailed reports laying out a typical day's schedule, their general activities, their impressions of their bosses and fellow workers, and, finally, what they have gained from their internship experience. Students learn to discuss with someone else what they are good at, what they have difficulty with, what methods work for them, and what methods do not work for them. They develop self-awareness and the ability to talk about themselves in regular conversations, which augurs well for their future in college and in the workforce.

The Apprenticeship Program has helped students avoid pursuing higher education in fields not suited for them. One student wanted to be a nurse from the time she was a little girl. Her internship placed her at a nearby hospital, where she quickly learned that she hated the sight of blood and did not like being around sick people. Nursing was clearly not for her.

To add an apprenticeship or internship program to your school, you don't have to be a career counselor or have a background in this area. Every person who understands the students can help with this kind of program. The Lab School Apprenticeship Program has been run since 1988 by a teacher with her master's degree in special education: learning disabilities and a specialty in reading diagnosis and remediation. This teacher realized how important the Apprenticeship Program was for the overall development of high school students and has trained our students well. She carefully matches jobs to students' interests and talents. Individually, she aims for, and often does find, the appropriate placement for each student every semester. It is a full-time job to seek out the employer and then supervise each of these students carefully (with suggestions for improvement), and she does a wonderful job.

I designed the Apprenticeship Program because I wanted Lab School students to have more experience in the real world, which might serve as a career awareness course and could motivate them to achieve more academically and to emulate their bosses. Also, I knew they would grow socially on the job. What I had not foreseen was how many of our students received paid weekend employment and summer jobs as a result of their experiences in the program.

We culminate the Apprenticeship Program each year with an employer–employee award ceremony. Employers are given certificates thanking them for what they have given to their student employees. This occasion is a wonderful time to celebrate the continued success of The Lab School Apprenticeship Program.

DEADLINE MANAGEMENT COURSE

Seniors at The Lab School often need as many study skills and organization classes as we can give them. I created a Deadline Management Course for seniors going to college. They needed something intriguing to involve them in meeting a very specific time limit. Too often, time-management problems keep gifted children with dyslexia and other learning disabilities from succeeding in, or even graduating from, college. Typically, these students do not plan out their work or allow time for reflection, review, and revision. They are known for turning in their assignments late, if they turn them in at all. Tutors often step in to help such students organize their work, write deadlines on calendars, and write the sequences necessary to finish the work, but these students need more.

The Deadline Management Course gives students a real-life project—an arts booklet, now titled *DC Area Artists,* that is distributed each year on June 1. This project was started in 1988, and, at the time, we gave students the names and telephone numbers of artists we knew. The students' job was to call the artists, explain the project, make an appointment for the whole group to meet with each artist at his or her studio, and create a list of questions to ask the artist. They then photographed the artist and his or her work, wrote up the philosophy of the artist that their questions revealed, listed the shows and galleries that had presented the work of the artist, and got a quotation from the artist. Their teacher helped them to structure the work so that they could meet their deadline.

Students now complete the steps necessary to update the artist interviews from the previous year and add new artists to the booklet. Students are excited when previously featured artists send in new artwork and explain the rationale behind the artwork. Hence, a project that started out as a 15-page pamphlet now is a 170-page booklet that is sold at some museums and galleries in Washington, D.C.

In the first few years, students had to sell advertisements to pay for the printing of the book. Today, they mostly use the income from the museum and gallery sales, so this aspect is no longer part of the course. Nevertheless, students still engage in earnest, frank talks with artists regarding their philosophies, style of work, and painting approaches and techniques. They go on trips to museums and galleries. They also learn basic desktop publishing skills and aspects of book production—from an analysis of the tasks involved to the final printing and distribution. Overall, they learn strategies for short- and long-range planning through this multifaceted senior art project.

RAUSCHENBERG DAY

Since 1994, Robert Rauschenberg, acclaimed Master of Modern Art, has sponsored an Arts and Learning Disabilities Workshop at The Lab School for 30 art teachers from all over the United States. The purpose of the workshop is to teach art teachers more about learning disabilities, as well as to show them how much they already do for children who are experiencing difficulties by offering the art room as a refuge. In the afternoon, Lab School middle and high school students perform a mixed-media dance, drama, and musical production to honor Mr. Rauschenberg. They use the Academic Club Methodology in conceiving this production because they immerse themselves in one topic and present the topic from many different angles.

One year, a reading of the *Ramayana,* a great epic poem of ancient India, led students to become intrigued by the Monkey God, Hanuman, who moved mountains and accomplished marvels in his mythological world. Students made a 9-foot, two-dimensional cutout sculpture of Hanuman out of marine plywood. Then, they took bottle caps and made jeweled belts and a hat for Hanuman, followed by armor made from aluminum sheets. They decided to dedicate it to Mr. Rauschenberg, whom they proclaimed also has "moved mountains."

WHOLE-SCHOOL LEARNING PROJECTS

Since the beginning of The Lab School, we have conducted at least one project a year involving the whole school. In the early years, we created a totem pole. Each class built a section of the totem pole and listened to or read stories about Native Americans of the Northwest. They learned about different tribal dances, the importance of drumming, the use of sand and paint to create decorative arts, and the creation of pottery with intricate designs. They also studied the history, geography, and culture of a variety of Native Americans. Another whole-school project took place when students studied Africa's contributions to the world. Students made tiles that they used to cover the ceiling in the school's dance-drama room with African motifs. They also became fascinated with African textile prints and put them on shirts.

For The Lab School's 25th birthday, students created an 11-foot friendly dragon made of heavy plywood painted kelly green. The dragon has become the school's mascot. The ceremony during which the dragon was deemed school mascot consisted of stories and myths about dragons presented by students and faculty. Then, the high school students carried in the behemoth dragon for placement on campus while the school band trumpeted their march.

For The Lab School's 30th birthday, students made a 10-foot sculpture of Ganesh—the Hindu god of good fortune and remover of all obstacles—out of old pipes and various tractor parts, including fenders for the ears and taillights for the red eyes. This experience lead to the students' interest in India and further discussions about India's past and present, geography, literature, science, development, and government.

For The Lab School's 35th birthday, high school students created a griffin, which they had read about in their literature classes. They designed it on a computer, then made it into a sculpture that hangs on an exterior wall in the courtyard. The griffin is made out of carved foam that looks like metal. While making this project, students learned the history of bas-reliefs and developed artistic skills in carving. Recently, middle and high school students created an 8-foot tall gleaming white Pegasus made out of papier-mâché. They studied ancient horses, drew many types of horses, and finally created Pegasus, a horse with wings that saved Bellerophon from the three-headed monster, Shimera.

Please note that not every child has to be an artist to participate in the whole-school learning project. Just as in an Academic Club, there is a role for every child in whole-school learning projects. Whether the child sands something, conducts research, or generates a story from the project, the goal is the same—total involvement.

All whole-school learning projects use the arts, history, geography, literature, and science. Students of all ages brainstorm, plan, decide, organize, and assign roles. Because of these many projects, the campus of The Lab School is covered with student-made art. The Baltimore Lab is starting to look the same. This artwork not only brings many compliments to the students, but also reminds them of the content they learned in the process. The size and placement of these huge sculptures outdoors excites Lab School students about the possible art experiences they will have indoors. Little do they know that each art project is an interdisciplinary learning experience with a detailed academic agenda!

6

Summer School Academic Clubs

Thematic Adaptations in 6 Weeks

In addition to the academic school year, The Lab School also runs a Summer School. This program has been in place since 1968 and welcomes enrollees who do not attend The Lab School during the school year, some of whom have milder learning disabilities than our academic year students and benefit from the substantive progress they make in this program. The program also accommodates students from inner-city schools on full scholarships and potential Lab School students who want to get a feel for the school during the summer. Only one third of our Summer School students are regular academic year students.

For elementary school students, the program runs from 9 A.M. to 2 P.M. and includes a language arts class, a performing art (e.g., drama, music, dance), a visual art (e.g., woodwork, painting, sculpture, graphic arts), individualized tutoring in groups of three students, and an Academic Club. The Summer School itself has a theme each year that is incorporated into art and language classes as well as the Academic Clubs. Tutoring does not usually follow the theme but instead offers intensive reading, writing, spelling, and math. In addition to the Summer School program, some students attend an after-school program consisting of swimming, gymnastics, various sports, and computer and arts activities.

Students in the higher elementary grades attend Summer School from 9 A.M. to 2 P.M. but participate in an Academic Club; a performing art; and a combination of storytelling, art, and computers that culminates in their producing their own CD-ROM.

Older students attend Summer School from 8:30 A.M. to 12:30 P.M. to allow them to hold jobs and participate in non–school-sponsored activities. Their curriculum follows the theme of the Summer School but concentrates on study skills and classes for credit, such as Spanish and algebra.

The programming in a Summer Academic Club usually includes a story read by the Club Leader that the children then reenact. Club Members also develop a project (e.g., relief map, diorama, puppets, masks, flags). They discuss what they are doing and play diagnostic-prescriptive games that test if they understand what they just did or heard.

LEARNING INFORMATION WITHOUT READING

For those students who can't read or who read poorly, there are no reading demands in these Clubs. Instruction is all visual, concrete, and designed to trigger memories of information and vocabulary. Deep involvement is attained through the students' experiencing this total environmental approach. After a summer of learning in a decorated room, saying passwords, putting on costumes, doing projects, and playing games for review and assessment, students master the information from the Academic Club's period of history. All Academic Clubs require total involvement and thinking skills. If the Club Leader uses the Club's dramatic framework to play a character who is a leader, Club Members will be inspired to also use the dramatic framework to learn. If the Club Leader begins to lecture and loses the sense of drama and fun, most of the time he or she will also lose many of his or her Club Members, who then do not learn the information.

TYPICAL SUMMER SCHOOL THEMES

Having a theme usually inspires all staff to play a part in the summer magic. It brings a little healthy competition, spurring teachers to be their most inventive and creative; students reap huge benefits from this enthusiasm. Research on thematic education has proven that it builds high learning curves. When students learn from interdisciplinary thematic instruction rather than from a traditional single-subject curriculum, they learn better, are more engaged, make more connections among subject areas, and have a more positive attitude toward school and about themselves as learners (Lawton, 1994; Schubert & Melnick, 1997; Yorks & Follo, 1993).

Some common themes of Summer School are Detective Work, Sales Work, Geography, Explorers, and the Environment. The Detective Work theme helps students enrich their critical thinking, language development, and reading readiness as well as explore literature. Academic Clubs associated with this theme include Secret Agents Club, Nature Detectives, Space Detectives, Sherlock Holmes Club, Agatha Christie Club, Spy Central International (SCI), Polynesian Detectives, and Geo-Detectives. The Sales Work theme helps students improve their math and money skills. Students practice estimating and counting and participate in Academic Clubs such as Storekeepers Club, Lab Pet Salon, Fashion Boutique, Carnival Club, Restaurant Club, and Commercial Enterprise Club. The Geography theme helps students learn about continents, countries, and water bodies and about mapping skills. Associated Academic Clubs include the Cruise Club, Travel Agents Inc., Pirates of the Seven Seas, Mediterranean Café Club, Treasure Island Club, The Aristocrats Travel Club, Magic Carpet Club, Seven Wonders of the World Club, and A Monumental Summer at The Lab School (emphasizing monuments in Washington, D.C.).

The Explorers theme allows students to study history, geography, science, and literature. The various Academic Clubs include The African Harambee Club, Polar Expeditionaries Club, Oregon Trail Club, Covered Wagon Club, Wild West Club, Marco Polo Club, Space Station Club, Space Voyagers Club, Pyramid Sun Club, and The Lost Cities Club. The Environment theme teaches students to protect the land, water, and endangered species. Science is especially emphasized. Academic Clubs include Smokey the Bear Nature Club, Rainforest Club, Park Rangers Club, Forest Rangers Inc., American Indian Club, Jacques Cousteau Underwater Club, Endangered Species Club, Oceanographers Club, Meteorologist Club, Canal Boatman Club, and Secret Garden Club. Some other interesting Academic Clubs related to other Summer School themes are the Mark Twain Club, Railroad Engineers Club, King Arthur and the Round Table Club, Alchemists Club, The Chocolate Town Club, The City of the Future Club, The Revolutionaries Club, and The Charles Dickens Club.

TRAINING OF TEACHERS

When a group of new teachers joins the Summer School, they are trained to be Club Leaders through a series of workshops. One intensive workshop concentrates on visual concrete thinking to spur staff to create ways to teach math, geography, and science through visual methods. Then, the Academic Club Leaders have to take that knowledge and turn it into an Academic Club and a week's worth of highly programmed activities. Sometimes the topic under study is even more specific, such as Dr. Jacques Cousteau's work, which could readily be turned into the Underwater Club. First-aid techniques can easily be turned into a 6-week Paramedics Club. Studying the material and turning it into visual, concrete activities becomes second nature to Academic Club Leaders, which holds them in good stead in any teaching they do afterwards.

Planning and preparing for a Summer Academic Club is an arduous task because the Academic Club Leader must think through the strengths and interests of all children and create activities in which the children can excel. It may mean that 12 youngsters are in three groups with the teacher and two college students guiding each group. Sometimes it means pairs of students work on activities, or each one works alone. Students may work in smaller groups or one large group, depending on the activity. For example, in the Secret Agents Club, three students may be working on translating a code while six students are earning their tactile badge by feeling inside a closed box with one hand and identifying mysterious objects within. Two other students may be completing their auditory badge by identifying sounds they are hearing on a tape. One student may be drawing clues on index cards for a treasure hunt. Everybody is totally involved and productive; each Secret Agent is being supervised and is in the process of earning a badge.

Summer School Clubs require the same process of planning as the regular year Academic Clubs. The Academic Club Leader must read a great deal on his or her subject, not just from books but from other sources. The Club Leader must become acquainted with the artifacts associated with the Academic Club. For instance, the Secret Agents Club Leader might take a tour of the FBI or the Spy Museum in Washington, D.C., and look for gadgets that could be adapted. The Storekeeper Club Leader needs to become adept with a calculator or cash register. The Oregon Trail Club Leader must learn all about buffaloes—how they served the explorers and how the explorers harmed them. The Leader of the Polar Expeditionaries has to learn all he can about penguins and seals, stages of ice formation, and how travelers move across ice. The Carnival Club Leader should visit carnivals, read about them, see them on film, and learn to use the megaphone to help draw "customers" in.

Despite the research involved, Summer School is a lot easier for teachers to plan because it is 25–30 days long versus the 175- to 188-day school year. Teachers usually explore one concept each week. For example, the Cruise Club can explore seven continents in 6 weeks by putting Australia and Antarctica together. The Sherlock Holmes Club can solve six big mysteries in 6 weeks. The Marco Polo Club can travel from Italy to Cathay and back to Italy in 6 weeks. The Endangered Species Club can learn about one endangered species each week in different continents, bringing geography and history skills into play. Although Summer School classes are larger than typical Lab School classes (12 versus 8–10 children), students tend to have less severe learning disabilities. In addition, the Summer School has at least one college student per Club to lend a hand.

THE ROLE OF COLLEGE STUDENTS

College students from American University and other universities assist during Summer School. They gain college credit for serving as Group Leaders to the elementary school students. Most of these students are undergraduates studying elementary education and/or psychology. They are selected through an application and interview process. Internships are also offered to The Lab School alumni, college students from all over the nation with learning disabilities themselves, college-age children of former staff members, and some graduate students who have heard of The Lab School and want to get involved. Summer School interns are not paid, but those who help with swimming, athletics, or other after-school activities are. Training for interns is 2–3 days. They meet with Club Leaders, prepare materials for classes, and read about the Academic Club's subject matter.

Summer School students travel from classroom to classroom and have different teachers throughout the day. The children have no homerooms, either, so they need an anchor. Interns serve as the anchor and are assigned 12 students each. They are the first ones at The Lab School in the mornings to greet the students in their group. Each group is represented by a color, for instance the Green Group, and the intern tries to come up with a name, such as the Green Giants, the Green Dragons, or the Green Grasshoppers.

Each Academic Club may have one or two interns who are assigned roles. In the Secret Agents Club, the Club Leader is Captain, and the interns are Lieutenants. Interns are Assistant Managers in the Storekeepers Club. In the Cruise Club, they are the Purser and the Social Director working for the captain; in the Polar Expeditionaries Club, they are the Zoologist and the Meteorologist who assist the leader of the Scientific Expedition. Interns are taught to assume their dramatic roles with enthusiasm and support the Academic Club Leader. Often, they fill out forms (see Figure 2) that analyze why specific activities worked during the Academic Club meeting.

CARNIVAL CLUB

The Carnival Club has been popular in Summer School. It lends itself easily to elementary and middle school students. An adapted form with many more challenges built in works with high school students. Designing a carnival booth takes great planning skills. Children with learning disabilities and attention-deficit/hyperactivity disorder (ADHD) and children who are at risk for academic failure tend to be neurologically immature, disorganized, and impulsive. Planning is rarely their strength. Often, the Carnival Club breaks down into smaller groups in which students can brainstorm about what booth their group will make. Twelve children in the group each establish a game, a ride, or an activity that others will do. Again, the teacher is the Head of the Carnival, and each student has his or her own booth for other students to try out their luck. They can use Polaroid photographs to create their employee tags that hang from chains around their necks. Carnival games include the following: Together, the group can stuff a huge bottle full of bubble gum pieces to estimate the number of bubble gum pieces in the jar. A scale can be used to weigh people after they have guessed how much they will weigh with a heavy

Name of club: _____ Date : _____

Objectives to teach:

_____

_____

_____

Activities:

_____

_____

_____

Materials used:

_____

_____

_____

Vocabulary learned:

_____

_____

_____

Effectiveness of activities in meeting objectives:

_____

_____

_____

What did not work:

_____

_____

_____

Figure 2. Academic Club activities evaluation form. Copyright © 1968 by Sally L. Smith.

rod in their hands. (Note: No child is ever forced to be weighed!) Each booth needs prizes, so together Club Members can make dolls, toy animals, and games. Signs have to be written or painted to demonstrate how to enter the Carnival and proceed through it. Music has to be chosen to set the proper atmosphere. Entertainment in the form of a singing group, clowns, or dancers might liven up the Carnival. Banners and posters can be made advertising the Carnival.

A logo has to be created to interest visitors to come in and spend their money at the Carnival. The logo is designed by the students, and they may choose to tie-dye shirts or wear black shirts and white pants as uniforms. Refreshments also have to be made. Although cookies and lemonade often suffice, students must keep track of the ingredients they need and what the raw materials cost so that they can set appropriate prices. They thus learn the concept of profit and loss. Gross profit and net profit become part of their vocabulary. Fractions, decimals, and percentages must be dealt with, and calculators and computers must be utilized. Carnival workers also learn to give correct change for admission and refreshments.

Perhaps they will create a huge Ferris wheel with Legos and place little animals in the seats. The object is to guess which animals will land at the top near the arrow. Another booth can involve a hammer and a way to measure how hard the hammer hits a scale; reaching a certain height guarantees a prize. Disguises fill another booth where the customer has to make him- or herself unrecognizable or copies one of six models. Three balls are provided at another booth, and one of them has to land in the clown's mouth or in a hole in the board. Another booth might involve shooting marbles along a certain path to enter a space reserved for them.

Many procedures and rules have to be devised. How do people enter the Carnival? Do they have to buy tickets? If so, how will tickets be made? What if customers cause disruptions? What is to be done if an employee steals from the Carnival? One Carnival can be planned with simple games for children in kindergarten to third grade. Another Carnival can be designed for older children in fourth to sixth grade who have more dexterity. Perhaps these students can use a fishing pole to fish out six different items or use dice and poker chips to reach certain combinations that bring prizes. Middle school students develop more complex carnivals.

STOREKEEPERS CLUB

The Storekeepers Club is great for second graders who experience great difficulty in sorting information, categorizing, and doing math because it enables them to work in an enjoyable way on these areas of difficulty. The Club Leader is Store Manager, and the Club Members are Employees. The first day, they make identification cards with their photos, height, weight, and names. A turnstile is built for Club Members to enter The Lab Store. A password to enter could be *consumer*. Students can learn this password the first day by clapping out each syllable and whispering it into the Club Leader's ear. They can each put the password into a sentence at dismissal (e.g., I am a consumer when I buy things at a store). For the next few days, Club Members can bring in empty cereal boxes, cans, and egg cartons to have more products in addition to the ones the Club Leader already has collected. To add to the products, Club Members make fruits, vegetables, meats, fish, breads, and sweets out of papier-mâché, paint them, then place them in the various categories of the store.

Club Members also find out the derivation of the word *store*, discuss the difference between department store, grocery store, drugstore, boutique, and such enterprises as Giant, Safeway, and Food Lion. They design a logo for their store and put the logo on store aprons that they make. The next week, Club Members can have a sale and learn such words as *profit* and *loss*. They must add items up and make change. The third week, there could be a robbery that takes place in the store, and Club Members can study the effects it has on profit and loss, on their property, and on their morale. The fourth week, students can acquire a drugstore and add all appropriate items to the sales list. During the fifth week, Club Members can make advertisements for their store to be placed all over the building; they can tape radio announcements and take digital photos of their produce and make ads from their computers. The last week can be Super Sale week, with heavy emphasis on the store's profits and loss, Club Members' understanding of numbers, and the creation of charts to show the amount of money they made.

Throughout the Summer Academic Club, students hear stories about stores, or books about stores and purchasing items are read to them. They can visit stores, see photographs of stores, and create diagrams of different stores. They also look at newspapers and magazines that advertise items to be purchased. In one Storekeepers Club, Club Members formed a union. In another, they designed a special discount plan for employees to purchase food, and in another Club, they set up a little Day Care Center. Another Storekeepers Club elected a special executive committee to decide which kind of products they should sell at the store. There are many paths to take. It all depends on the talents, knowledge, and interests of the teacher and the specific strengths, interests, and ages of the children in that class.

AMERICAN INDIAN CLUB

Outside the American Indian Club room, the third graders put on headbands and enter a Tepee in single file through a narrow gap between hanging blankets. Princess Eagle-Eye, the Club Leader, welcomes each Indian inside with a tap on her drum when the password, *heritage*, has been whispered correctly.

Inside the Tepee, a huge mural, painted by Lab School children, depicts Indians hunting, tracking, cooking, building, and doing other activities in a very lively manner. A large display table shows objects made by real Native Americans and similar artifacts made by Lab School children in their American Indian Club. There are photographs of Native Americans, prints, and a chart of trail signs that use sticks and stones as markers.

Princess Eagle-Eye invites 12 Club Members to find their correct place in a circle on the floor by matching a coded card with a simple code of dots and dashes that marks each place. Once seated, the Members were given the first Rule of the Tribe: sit quietly. A Meditation Table is provided in a corner, where any Indian who finds the rule too difficult to follow can go until he or she feels able to rejoin the group. Anthony tries out the system by pretending to throw a tantrum and is kindly but firmly led to the Meditation Table, where he rapidly regains his ability to sit quietly.

Two more Rules of the Tribe—listen carefully and look sharply—are taught and immediately put to use as the Indians learn to translate the visual code of dots and dashes into taps and scratches on a drum. Several games were played using the code—sometimes writing it, sometimes playing it on the drum, and other times saying the words *dot* and *dash* aloud. All of the Indians become highly proficient, and all receive feathers to tuck in their headbands as rewards. The Members then choose names for themselves by matching colors and objects. Red Feather, White Arrow, Black Eagle, and the rest make their own symbols to wear and to hang with their correct colors on the Tribal Roster hung on the wall in the shape of a buffalo hide.

A last Rule of the Tribe—speak clearly—is put into force with the telling of stories while sitting in a circle. The story takes shape as each Indian adds a new incident based on the picture card he holds—a brave, a bear, a river, a snake—and the last incident brings the story to a satisfactory conclusion. By shuffling and redistributing the cards, a completely different story emerges from the same ingredients, to the great amusement of the tribe. This is a fine exercise in part–whole relationships. All of the participants learn a rhythmic toe-and-heel dance step that evolves into a Native American dance, taking them all around the room. There, individual tables with games, projects, handicrafts, and activities to reinforce reading readiness are set up for them to try.

Other fun activities include puzzles and a buffalo hunt game as well as opportunities to try simplified forms of weaving, beadwork, and sand painting, with examples of actual Native American work and photographs of Native Americans performing these arts for inspiration. One very successful craft project is to make a pouch of artificial fur that can hold gold nuggets or stones that serve as rewards for helpfulness and attentiveness. The discovery of the drawstring can be a fascinating experience.

Tables can also include herbs to smell, textured breads to taste, grains to touch, and vegetable dyes to experiment with. Club Members can make designs with bright markers and play games with Native American themes that require sharp eyes, close attention, and organizational skills. Club Members can also make drums that they decorate, play, and take home. All of the tables give participants direct experience and individualized learning.

TRAVEL AGENTS CLUB

As our world becomes smaller due to the speed of transportation, communication, and the Internet, it is important that we excite our youngsters about other countries and teach them to appreciate different customs and traditions. The Travel Agents Club does that with ease. A summer unit for fourth through eighth graders in the Travel Agents Club is set up with half of the classroom filled with maps and posters that entice the viewer to visit beautiful beaches, climb majestic snowy mountains, dive into turquoise water for sunken gold treasure, revel in a masked carnival, or go deep into Africa on a safari to see the royalty of animals. The other half of the room looks like an airplane with chairs with seat belts lined up for immediate departure. The Club Leader is Head of the Travel Company. Club Members are Travel Agents who send people on trips. The 6-week summer program is their training period.

The first day, Travel Agents make their own passports to be stamped wherever they travel. They have identification badges that they wear showing which part of the world is their specialty. Agent Frank, for example, specializes in France, and he has the Eiffel Tower on his badge. Agent Ariel is an expert on England, so Big Ben is featured on her badge. Agent Claudia has Angkor Wat on her badge because Cambodia is her specialty, whereas Agent Fareed has the Great Wall of China on his badge. No Agent specializes in Brazil, but after a pretend trip to Rio de Janeiro, one of them will return as a specialist.

All Travel Agents and their boss go into the pretend airplane where each takes a carefully assigned seat that has a series of maps showing how to fly to Brazil. When possible, a short film is shown on board the flight. Either an appropriate short story or a poem is also shared with the travelers. They look at the countries, the ocean, and the cities they fly over. When they land, they each are given a souvenir of something important in Brazil. They each have to identify their token and draw it or trace it on to their Brazilian Travel Folder. Next, they have to use Brazilian money to figure out how much money they have in American dollars and cents, and they are each given a fake credit card as well. Off they go to see photos of important sites to visit. Baskets of products are there to lure them to buy. On the return flight, they check to see how much money they spent. Often, they go into credit card debt because they don't visually see their spending as they can when spending cash. After the trip, they put all their material together in their Brazilian scrapbook and get ready for their next trip to Iceland.

Some groups may only visit six sites in 6 weeks while others may tour seven or eight sites in the same time period. On trips, Travel Agents learn about the country, its nearby neighbors, its oceans, its landmarks, its major cities, its major features, its primary products, and a little about its culture. Their scrapbook reminds them of what they have learned. Each time they land in a new place, music of the country is played.

The Travel Agents Club gives students fascinating experiences. It relates subject matter to their lives and relates cause to effect and planning to action. Ten-year-old Fareed commented, "I will never forget Brazil because I loved the music, the masked pageant there, the rainforest, the Amazon River, the Anaconda snakes, and the colors of the country. I want to really visit it now. My second favorite was Cambodia because that Angkor Wat is so amazing."

BROADCASTERS CLUB

Nine-year-old Reon's favorite Summer Academic Club is the Broadcasters Club. He thought it was really cool to pretend to be a famous broadcaster like Dan Rather, Tom Brokaw, Peter Jennings, or Jim Lehrer. Amy and Laverne wanted to be famous lady broadcasters like Diane Sawyer, Katie Couric, and Cokie Roberts. Burton and his friend Ian wanted to make up the advertisements for the Broadcasters Club, while Tommy and Tim wanted to cover sports. They thought it was pretty funny that Reginald wanted to do news from Wall Street, and Mary Allen, Shannon, and Erin were eager to do a soap opera. Otis and Jon wanted to host a call in-talk show.

The teacher, whose dramatic cover was Oprah Winfrey, ran her studios with very clear rules. People listened to one another, helped each other, and never humiliated or teased others. Negative behavior was not tolerated. On the contrary, helpfulness and cooperation were rewarded with coupons to use in the school store. The setting of the Academic Club was a broadcast studio with control panels, lights, cameras, a table with chairs for guests, and extra screens to use for films, slides, CD-ROMs, and other visual presentations. This Club has been successful with upper elementary and middle school students.

DETECTIVE CLUBS

The Secret Agents Club, a form of Detective Club, is a big draw among children younger than third grade. They like being known by numbers only. They like earning badges—a badge for discriminating all kinds of pictures and syllables from one another; a badge for touching things unseen and distinguishing them correctly; a badge for how discriminating one smell from another; a badge for differentiating one sound from another. In this Academic Club, students do reading readiness work, sort information, and use their senses to tell one thing from another. To solve crimes, they have to decode secret messages. Agents try to fool each other with disguises. They listen to stories and have to create the endings to these stories. They also look at photographs or pictures and have to put them in a particular sequence to give them meaning.

The Club Leader, Captain Wolfe, is in charge, and the Captain's discipline is law. Some Club Leaders have preferred to be Agent 007, the Chief Agent. As long as the Club Leader has a good deal of authority, it does not matter. The decorations may vary, also. Some rooms look like libraries or Laundromats to deceive the public. Others look like police stations. Club Members use their magnifying glasses to study fingerprints or footprints. They look at crime scenes set up by the Club Leader and find the important clues. They listen to clues on tape and postulate what happened. They break secret codes. Every step of the way, they problem-solve.

A similar club, a DC Detectives Club for 8- to 10-year-olds, made sure its detectives did the same activities as the Secret Agents, but Club Members also came to know many of Washington's landmarks, such as the Washington Monument, the Lincoln Memorial, the Jefferson Memorial, the National Gallery of Art, the Smithsonian Museums, the National Cathedral, the White House, the Supreme Court, and the Capitol. All sorts of crimes took place at these landmarks, and the DC Detectives had to solve them. They had a replica of a metro train in their room and used their fare cards to visit the sites.

The Agatha Christie Club, set in England, has a tea room filled with cheery window boxes filled with painted flowers. Agatha sat in her rocking chair and read Club Members stories like "Murder on the Orient Express." Club Members then acted out the stories and analyzed them. While sipping tea, they had to put together clues to a mystery.

The Interpol Club's crimes take place on the seven different continents. Detective work can focus on the environment with Detecting Endangered Species, Nature Detectives, Geo-Detectives, or the Pollution Trackers Club. Students interested in ecology enjoy being Park Rangers, Conservationists, Protectors of Clean Water, and participants in the Smokey the Bear Nature Club. In the icy, white, freezing cold Polar Expeditionaries Club room, the Explorers have to predict when it is safe for them to travel by boat and when it is not. The Oregon Trail Club Members must figure out when it is safe for them to travel by covered wagon. They not only predict the weather but also analyze which unfriendly animals and tribes may block their way. They plan for the future and prevent disasters.

THE END OF THE SUMMER

At the end of The Lab School 6-week summer program, parents are invited to visit the program. They see dance, drama, and music performances and art or woodwork exhibits. When they come to the Academic Club, they are given clues to guess the password to come in; then, parents are asked to play some of the Academic Club games for which the students already know the answers. Thus, Club Members dazzle their parents with the amount of knowledge and sophisticated information they have learned in a short time. Projects are on display and can be taken home at the end of the day. What may have looked like child's play to many parents impresses them with the academic depths that came from that play. A number of Summer School students return yearly. These students are referred to as "Clubbies" because they just love this style of teaching and feel so successful in learning.

7

Using Props, Songs, and Teacher-Made Games

Props, songs, and teacher-made games are vital aspects of the Academic Club Methodology because they offer vehicles to help students organize space and time. Children with learning disabilities, attention-deficit/hyperactivity disorder (ADHD), and language and memory problems frequently have trouble with their internal clocks and compasses. These students learn to organize time, direction, and spatial orientation through Academic Clubs.

Because difficulty with time and spatial orientation are hidden dimensions of learning disabilities, they often cause students more difficulties in daily living than the inability to read and write. Students frequently become lost, even when finding their own classrooms, and they rarely are organized enough to get out the door on time, which makes them constantly late for the next class. Often, these behaviors appear to be purposeful and defiant, but they are simply the nature of learning disabilities and ADHD.

Space and time are organizing systems that are involved with every task, every performance, and every aspect of life. Poor organization not only results in forgetting to bring home work and missing deadlines for papers but also in trouble establishing priorities (e.g., What is most important to study? What's less important? What is the main point?). Inability to distinguish priorities contributes to poor memory.

When students cannot learn from listening, when they are nonreaders or painstakingly slow readers who lose meaning of the content, when they are afraid that they can't learn or will fail again, other avenues are needed. Academic Club decorations, props, songs, and diagnostic-prescriptive games are crucial learning tools. They not only help students organize, but they also help them pay attention, focus on the subject at hand, and remember material. Objects and pictures, bright colors, miniature figurines, rhythms, drumbeats, card games, and board games help students learn information, remember it, and use it. Academic Club materials battle students' distractibility, poor attention span, impulsivity, poor memory, and disorganization; they open new routes to learning.

LEARNING SEQUENCES AND ORGANIZATION THROUGH PROPS

Because students with learning disabilities often are confused about the parts of a subject that make up the whole, Club Leaders use boxes to teach a set of facts. In the Knights and Ladies Club, a small box may be named the City Box with a picture of London in it. Then, the City Box is placed into a larger Country Box, which contains the map of England, and both boxes go into a bigger box called the Continent Box, in this case, Europe. The same idea of boxes can be used in the Industrialists Club, with four boxes representing city, state, nation, and continent. After students place these boxes inside one another a few times, they seem to understand the relationships clearly.

Similarly, creating plot boards helps students conceptualize the sequence of events in a story. One summer, the Agatha Christie Club created plot boards for "English Tea Room." Using foam core board that was precut and scored by the Club Leader, Club Members bent the board into a shape that was flat to represent the introduction, then sloped to represent the rising action. After reaching the climax, the board dropped off sharply for the conclusion (see Figure 3).

Push pins were inserted at the beginning of the introduction, at the beginning of the rising action, and at the climax. A string was wound around these push pins to represent the story. At the conclusion, the string was left dangling and then tied in a knot to show students that the conclusion ties loose ends of the story together. Preprinted labels with the important terms *introduction, setting, characters, rising action, climax,* and *conclusion* were appropriately affixed.

Making these plot boards was just the beginning of the learning experience. After each story that the characters lived through, the Club Leader gave every Member a sentence about the story. Club Members decided where on the plot board the sentence would go and used a push pin to stick the sentence to the appropriate spot on the plot board.

Academic Clubs use special seating to help students locate themselves in space. Cave Club Members sit on mats that contain certain picture symbols. Gods Club Members each have a column with their symbol on it. In some Academic Clubs, pieces of colored tape are placed on the floor to delineate the space reserved for a particular Club Member. The Industrialists Club has as-

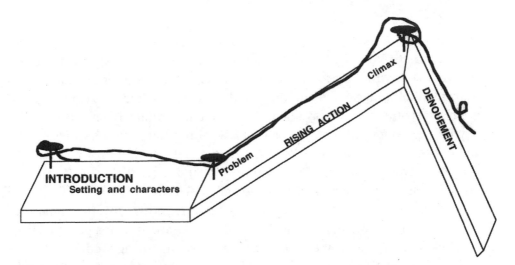

Figure 3.   A plot board used to evaluate the sequence of story events. Designed by Amy Aden.

signed seating at the corporate table; each Industrialist has a piece of wood with his or her name burned on it. The Club Leader's job is to make sure the props and decorations are employed to teach specific skills and reinforce certain information.

Using Props to Teach Philosophy Concretely

As mentioned previously, the Philosophers Club proved to be too abstract for 11- and 12-year-olds with language learning disabilities. It was abandoned after 2 years in favor of the more concrete Museum Club. Nevertheless, the Philosophers Club Leader (Socrates) discovered a lot through his efforts to represent abstract ideas with Academic Club props that would aid students in memorization and understanding. For example, each Philosopher was given a concrete symbol to represent his or her abstract philosophies. The symbols were located in a Tavern with wooden tables and chairs where Club Members could drink fruit juice or water.

René Descartes wore a cloth billboard with a question mark signifying the fact that he questioned everything, even his own existence. This question was finally resolved with the idea, "I think, therefore I am." Voltaire carried a huge paper chain as a reminder of his belief that people had the right to break the chains of their own mental and political bondage. Galileo clutched a big pendulum as a reminder of his experimental investigation of natural laws that enlarged human understanding of the universe. John Locke held a blank slate demonstrating that life experience can make a human bad or good. He believed that babies are born neutral, as expressed in the saying "The mind is a blank piece of paper."

Isaac Newton carried a huge apple as the object that spurred him to discover the law of gravity. David Hume, who believed in a two-pronged approach, carried a huge fork with two prongs—one prong represented all of the truths that come from reasoning, and the other prong represented matters of fact. Immanuel Kant carried an umbrella that depicted large starry heavens to remind everyone that he was filled with awe and wonder when he saw the starry heavens above him and the moral law within him. Jean-Jacques Rousseau believed that people were born naturally good and that only civilization made them bad. He wore a large white toga and carried a black bag with money, houses, machinery, and other so-called evils in it.

Each Philosopher's period in history was clearly shown on a pictorial time line on the wall. His or her geographical place was marked with a personal flag and symbol. Each Philosopher had a birthday party featuring food from his or her country. Isaac Newton offered tea and cucumber sandwiches from England. Voltaire made chocolate mousse from France. Galileo cooked up spaghetti. Descartes, who lived in Holland, brought in Dutch Gouda cheese, and Hume from Scotland baked shortbread cookies. Kant, who came from Germany, made sausages. Fondue was served by Rousseau, who came from Switzerland. The students recalled their symbols and the food they brought in, which helped them remember each philosopher's basic theories. From there, they learned how these philosophies affected the American Constitution.

The amount of learning that the Philosophers Club Members experienced is explained by California neurobiologist Dr. Marian Diamond. Her research showed that the sights and sounds of enriched school environments cause dendrites to form neural pathways, which she calls "Magic Trees of the Mind" because they branch out like tiny trees. Her data demonstrate that the curious mind, stimulated to further inquiry, makes the central cortex thicker and, thus, the brain more developed and available for learning. Certainly, the Philosophers Club helped build many dendrites!

THE RELATIONSHIP OF PLAY TO PROPS, SONGS, AND GAMES

Some scholars worry about the amount of pretend play and general play that takes place in Academic Clubs. The Academic Club Methodology supports the belief that children learn best through play because play demands thinking and total involvement. Play is children's work as well as their recreation. According to Jean Piaget, much of what adults call "play" is really the activity of intelligence. Discriminating one thing from another, categorizing the material, then integrating several things at once are all vital components of play.

Consider the pretend play that takes place in the Industrialists Club. Club Members play with trains in order to learn geography. Their trains visit Guggenheim's smelting mines, Vanderbilt's ships, and Ford's car factories. Club Members study the building of railroads and Rockefeller's actions, including his reasons for decisions and where major events took place.

The root of play is sorting out the environment. Developmentally young children tend to deal first with color, then shape, and finally size. Through play, children confirm what they know about the world. They pretend to be Mommy, Daddy, or the teacher, and they recreate a family meal or a school activity. Preschoolers imitate what they see, hear, and feel. They begin with what they know, then—like artists—they reshape what they know, fiddle with it, try something new, make mistakes, try again, and use new combinations.

Play is also diagnostic. A child whose play ends with fires, explosions, or volcanoes gives the message that he or she is volatile. In contrast, another child will be kind, good, and peaceful during play. A child who constructs only the same block building over and over, never deviating, may be afraid to take risks. He or she may be a perfectionist or have obsessive-compulsive disorder.

ACADEMIC CLUBS BUILD MASTERY

Americans seem to have less and less patience for children's play. Schools often cut music, eurythmics (a combination of music, rhythm, and dance exercises), painting, and drama classes in an effort to save money, but the skills learned in these classes are the foundations on which academic abilities are built. In addition, adults often deprive children of play in an attempt to rush them to acquire skills. They schedule youngsters every afternoon for piano lessons, ballet, tap dancing, physical education, tutoring, religious education, or other assorted activities. As a result, these children frequently do not know how to spend time alone, how to play by themselves, or how to manage free time.

Exceptional learners need more time to play than other children because they have difficulty perceiving, processing, and retrieving information. Their diminished neurological maturity and organization, in addition to memory problems and poor attention spans, make play essential. Many exceptional learners need to learn how to play because they have considerable language difficulties, motor problems, and sequencing issues. They must be given numerous opportunities to learn specific academic material through play.

The big pleasure in play is mastery. Children may put things together to look pretty. They may build something that looks familiar or that stands up, moves or whirrs when you pull it, or makes a pleasing noise. The child controls what he or she does. The child experiments—What happens if I put bigger blocks on top of little ones? When the blocks fall down, the child reverses the order of the blocks and feels successful. Putting a puzzle together so that all of the pieces fit also gives children the feeling of mastery.

Play is active; it uses head and hands and feet. It involves looking, listening, touching, and feeling. Play is so engrossing to preschoolers that they often talk to themselves (e.g., "Now do it this way") and carry on long conversations with themselves. Choices and decisions made at simple levels are endemic to play. Likewise, choices and decisions must be made constantly in Academic Clubs (e.g., What kinds of hats did Renaissance artists wear? How can we make them?). When building a large castle in the Knights and Ladies Club, Club Members strategize ways to make the castle look medieval with crenulations. Play is all-involving, not passive. An observer can see a boy in the Knights and Ladies Club almost obsessed with the Legos with which he will build a castle. The boy looks at his creation in awe of his own prowess and often with excitement that he created a masterpiece.

Making Connections

Children with learning disabilities frequently experience difficulty making connections. Thankfully, play leads children toward making connections. Children are engaged in creating games, fantasizing, acting out exciting dramas, and figuring out new ways to do things (e.g., a new way to climb up the steps of the slide). They engage in trial and error. They try to create tall buildings with their dominoes or keep a balloon up when it needs air. Play is a creative activity through which children make connections to what they know and use those connections to make new ones. Some cultural anthropologists have studied play in animals and found that the more complex the animal, the more the animal plays.

Through play in Academic Clubs, children develop an ability to represent their world, relationships they observe, and relationships that might exist. They also explore the unknown, experiment, and problem-solve. For example, in one Industrialists Club, Club Members played a teacher-made game called Free Enterprise. Each student moved a game piece that represented his or her business around the board after correctly answering a question. Half of the questions reflected information about connecting individual Industrialists to the Industrialist era. The goal of the game was to own all assets by taking over one company at a time. The game emphasized strategy, timing, and abstract thinking. Students had to relate information, think ahead, and plan accordingly. This game was a favorite activity of Industrialists Club Members, and playing the game helped Members build huge storehouses of information about the Industrialist era.

Academic Club Play Demands Reasoning

Play has a reflective quality. Children look at what they have created with blocks and question themselves about what would happen if they tried to attach some smaller blocks to the middle section. The reflective nature and self-questioning of a creative person contrasts with a person who mechanically follows instructions and doesn't think things through. Reflection requires the containment of impulsivity, which is particularly important with the students with ADHD.

Another aspect of play is an opportunity to break the rules. If a child has been taught to paint with red, blue, and yellow paint, he or she might dare to mix the colors to see what happens. The child dares to do something he or she has never done and has not seen anybody else do before. Play promotes daring and questioning. Children want to learn things for themselves and see why things are done a certain way. This mental activity keeps children involved in their learning.

BIGGER PROJECTS, THEN SMALLER ONES

Projects for younger children are often big and use sturdy materials because younger children do not have the eye–hand coordination or visual-motor skills necessary to create delicate miniatures. The 6-year-olds in the Cave Club build huge representations of animals that lived in the Old Stone Age and New Stone Age. The 7- and 8-year-olds in the Greek Gods Club use trays to make huge maps of Greece out of molding clay. The Knights and Ladies make big gargoyles. Older children have the ability to make smaller objects, and certain students may have the skill to make miniatures. Club Leaders determine from initial projects which children work well with their hands and which students experience difficulty. Projects are then planned with the children's abilities in mind.

Simple, everyday materials are used in Academic Clubs not only to fire imaginations but also to save money. The Clubs demand a wealth of talent and a paucity of materials to buy. Found objects do well for most Academic Club projects and everyday classroom materials are used, such as construction paper, crayons, and clay, but more often markers, Sculpt a mold, papier-mâché, and leftover fabrics are the materials of choice for Club Members.

SONGS TO REVIEW MATERIAL

Many adults learned the alphabet by singing the alphabet song. Some recall learning left and right as well as parts of the body from The Hokey Pokey. Songs have a wonderful ability to help students learn and remember information. Club Leaders develop songs to teach new concepts, present new vocabulary, or review material. Students with poor memories remember the material because they sing it, act it out, point to pictures as they sing, and do certain movements related to the content. In this way, complex information is learned by students with poor language, learning disabilities, and ADHD.

To help her students learn about early man, Cave Club Leader Amanda Wolfe created a song to the tune of the Beatles' "Lucy in the Sky with Diamonds" called "Lucy is an Australopithecus." The words are as follows:

Picture yourself in Hadar, Ethiopia,
with hominine Lucy and her prehistoric friends
Someone invites you—you answer "Terrific!
Let's tour human evolution"

There will be five homonines we will see
Shall we begin with the first?
Look for the girl with opposable thumbs
And she's gone . . .
Lucy is an au-stra-lo-pith-e-cus
She's not a panine
Lucy is an au-stra-lo-pith-e-cus
She's a homonine
Lucy is an au-stra-lo-pith-e-cus
She's bipedal
Ah ah

Follow her down to Latoeli Tanzania
where footprints were found in volcanic ash
Lucy is smiling at Homo habilis in a savanna so incredibly hot
Lucy is an au-stra-lo-pith-e-cus
She's not a panine
Lucy is an au-stra-lo-pith-e-cus
She's a homonine
Lucy is an au-stra-lo-pith-e-cus
She's bipedal
Ah ah

Picture yourself anywhere in the world
Homo sapiens sapiens no more a nomad
He painted scenes in Lascaux and Altimira
It's the man who tamed wild animals
Lucy is an au-stra-lo-pith-e-cus
She's not a panine

Lucy is an au-stra-lo-pith-e-cus
She's a homonine
Lucy is an au-stra-lo-pith-e-cus
She's bipedal
Ah ah

Cradle of mankind appears on the shore
a place called Olduvai Gorge
Look for the man with tools in his hands and he's gone . . .
Lucy is an au-stra-lo-pith-e-cus
She's not a panine
Lucy is an au-stra-lo-pith-e-cus
She's a homonine
Lucy is an au-stra-lo-pith-e-cus
She's bipedal
Ah ah

Picture yourself a few million years later
when Homo erectus traveled out of Africa
Suddenly someone is holding a firestick
the man who standing upright
Homo sapiens lived in the Ice Age
He hunted woolly mammoths
Look for the man who had rituals in his clan and he's gone.

Club Members love to sing this song, and they learn a wealth of information in the process. Students tell us they still remember this song many years later.

GAMES

Games are also used at The Lab School of Washington to introduce, reinforce, and review content and to assess knowledge. Adult concepts broken down into concrete activities allow children who can't read or who read poorly to receive a classical education. The Bayeux Tapestry, Dante's *Inferno,* and the philosophies that led up to the American Revolution are not generally the topics studied by elementary school children and particularly those with moderate to severe learning disabilities. These are highly sophisticated topics filled with huge amounts of information, yet Lab School students succeed in incorporating this information into their knowledge banks through games.

Very young children like to play Lotto. The 6-year-olds in the Smokey the Bear Environmental Club play Smokey the Bear Lotto. They look carefully at cards picturing Smokey the Bear and match the cards with corresponding spaces on their Lotto boards. After Club Members cover all of their Lotto spaces, they say, "Lotto" or "Environment Okay." The game becomes more difficult when the cards show Smokey in various positions. Six-year-olds in the Storekeepers Club can play Vegetable Lotto, Meat Lotto, Dairy Food Lotto, and Wheat Lotto. As you can see, Lotto can be adapted to any Club and to any subject matter.

Club Members of all ages seem to enjoy Bingo. The first player who has a vertical, horizontal, or diagonal line of spaces covered with counters is the winner. Usually, Bingo is played with numbers, but it can be played with endangered animals in the Environmental Club. The Greek Gods Club can play Greek Gods Bingo, where each space has a picture of a famous God. For example, the caller says, "King of the Gods," and the players have to put a counter on Zeus's square. The caller yells, "God of the Sun," and players find Apollo. The Messenger God corresponds to Mercury, and so forth.

In the DC Detectives Club, Club Members solved mysteries that took place at famous DC Monuments or places. During their Bingo games, the cards featured pictures of the Capitol, Washington Monument, Jefferson Memorial, Lincoln Memorial, Vietnam Wall, Smithsonian Castle, FDR Memorial, Union Station, Korean War Memorial, and White House. The Baltimore Detectives Club had a similar game that featured places unique to their city.

Continent Bingo is a fairly sophisticated geography review game for middle and high school students. Teachers make several large Bingo cards divided into seven columns, each with a different color. The columns are labeled with one of the seven continents. A basket holds a large number of small square cards showing famous landmarks, animals, or natural features from around the world, such as the Eiffel Tower, the Taj Mahal, the Sydney Opera House, the Pyramids, the Empire State Building, a king penguin, a kangaroo, a giraffe, a llama, a tiger, the South Pole, Mount Everest, the Andes Mountains, and the Rockies. Each player picks a card and places it in the correct column on his or her Continent Bingo board. The first player to get three in a row (middle school) or four in a row (high school) wins the game. Continent Bingo can be simplified or made more sophisticated as desired.

When they hear about the use of games in teaching, many educators tend to take a negative view that it is watered-down education. In fact, games are not watered down but a vehicle through which highly sophisticated concepts are introduced. Games are concrete and visual, so students can use their senses to explore abstract material. Students who do not learn well in traditional settings—listening to lectures; reading; writing; and taking multiple-choice, matching, fill-in-the-blank, and essay exams—can learn classical works and high-level material through games.

At The Lab School and Baltimore Lab, the use of games raises the bar and introduces and reinforces the knowledge of classical works and high-level sophisticated material. For example, Gina Van Weddingen, the Gods Club Leader in Washington, D.C., since 1997, created a game to help students understand the voyages of Odysseus. She designed it so half the class can be the Athena Team, which moves Odysseus and his ship to the various islands, while the other half of the class forms the Poseidon Team, which uses clever moves to send Odysseus back to a previous island and disrupt his journey. This game, which has a large backdrop of the Walls of Troy and decorated clothespins with shields, is used to tell the stories of *The Iliad* and *The Odyssey.* Following is a description of the game and how it is played.

The Odyssey Game is a tool for introducing content, reviewing specific main ideas and sequences, and assessing individual and group mastery of facts in its specific content area. The game consists of a game board, maps of the ancient Greek World to hold "tokens of the voyage," ships to represent Odysseus (i.e., the Athena Team), a large Poseidon, and tokens that represent the various adventures that Odysseus encountered on his long voyage back to Ithaca. The game may be played two ways. Option One is that individual students take turns, beginning at the four corners of the board, visiting each adventure to obtain a token, and finally returning to their "home." Question cards and activity cards, along with rolls of the die, determine the winner (i.e., the first to return home with all tokens attained).

Option Two, the more *interesting* way to play the game, calls for two teams (e.g., four students on each team). One team (the Athena Team represented by a ship) starts at the corner of the board nearest the Island of the Cyclops. The other team (the Poseidon Team represented by the Poseidon piece) waits in the center of the board. The foregone conclusion of the game is that Odysseus will return home. The *fun* of this version is how difficult the Poseidon Team can make the journey for Odysseus and his crew. Being immortal, Poseidon's team can move backward as well as forward and can return to the sea to cut off Odysseus. When the Poseidon piece lands on the ship, the Athena Team is sent back to revisit the last location. Along the way, Athena cards help Odysseus.

Each team must correctly answer relevant questions before they move. The Club Leader controls the questions, so they can be targeted to the specific needs of individuals or groups and changed as needed. Because the outcome of this version of the game is already known, winning and losing become irrelevant. Strategy, teamwork, and mastery of content become most important. Along the way, the students still get to accumulate tokens of each adventure (e.g., a plastic eyeball for the Island of the Cyclops), which serve as strong visual cues for the main ideas of the adventure. The path traveled on the game board reinforces the sequence of the story, and the two teams reflect the actual sides taken by the immortals in *The Iliad* and *The Odyssey.*

Each Club Leader creates games to teach the specific facts and information he or she wants Club Members to carry with them. Evidence of what students know and don't know can be extremely diagnostic. What students don't know is revealed in the games, and the prescriptive response is to teach them the material in a different manner than before, perhaps using different senses. Maybe they need to learn the information through tactile stimulation (touching) or kinesthetically (through body activity).

Board Games Created by Graduate Students

I have been in charge of the special education degree program at American University since 1976, and one of the assignments in the M.A. Program in Special Education: Learning Disabilities and in my class called Methods of Teaching the Learning Disabled (LD II) is to produce a board game that teaches very specific content, reinforces or reviews it, and emphasizes thinking skills and the acquisition of knowledge. By observing the way a child plays these games, the teacher can learn the child's strengths, weak areas, knowledge mastered, and information and material that needs to be retaught. What a teacher can diagnose from one of these games provides a prescription of activities to improve a child's skills.

Graduate students enjoy the idea of producing a board game until they attempt to construct one. They then realize it is exceedingly difficult to make one that accomplishes all academic objectives and, at the same time, is fun and interesting to the students. To begin with, the graduate students have to be very clear on the content they wish to include. Then, they must be sure it is presented in a clear concise manner so the game players understand it. The game must be colorful. It helps to have surprises in it; some students have found that by making the game three dimensional (with mountains/bridges/underground caves) they can present more information. There has to be a spinner or dice. Usually each game includes at least two packs of cards (one of information, one of chance), and there are little objects to move—the more intriguing, the better.

Some graduate students become so involved with design that they do not do a particularly good job on presenting content. Others are so serious about content that they do not present it in a pleasing manner. All graduate students must try out their games on children with learning disabilities of a certain age and with particular trouble learning the subject of the games. Graduate students must listen to the critiques of the children (e.g., It's boring. It doesn't give me enough chances. You need another pack of cards that are simply luck cards. You need something like losing a turn because your car broke down or you had to go to jail. You need to give us a token, a sticker, or money when we manage to get over the worst hurdles of the game). Usually the children know how to improve the games, make them more exciting, and add more risk factors. Graduate students are guided to follow the children's suggestions and continue to listen until the children ask to play "that game you made," meaning they like it. Then, the game-makers need to observe different children playing the game so they can assess what the children know and where they need help.

For example, a simple board game about cavemen can identify the children's knowledge of what took place in the Old Stone Age (what animals existed then, what inventions had been made) and what happened in the New Stone Age (what animals surfaced, which inventions came into being at that time). Although most of the games demand skill, the children like games that are a little bit dependent on luck. So, most board games have spaces that say "Go back 2 spaces," "Go to the bridge," "Go forward 3 spaces," or "Rest for one turn."

The game has to be set up so that the procedures are abundantly clear. For example, a series of pictures of hunters and nomads could be appropriate to locate the Old Stone Age on the board. Pictures of domesticated animals, farming, and lake villages would locate the New Stone Age. Then, there might be a photo of a supersonic jet, which would allow 6-year-olds to boast that they can't be tricked and to laugh about how silly it is to see a jet in the games. They know that the Old Stone Age and New Stone Age had nothing like that!

A game like Clue may serve as a model for one of the Detective Clubs or a game like Monopoly might be adapted for the Industrialists Club. Games such as Stratego, Parcheesi, and Backgammon may give the game-maker ideas, but many games should be played and reviewed before trying out the best format to teach specific academic objectives to a particular age group.

Sample Academic Club Games

One of the most abstract concepts in the eighth-grade Democracy class seems to be the economy. One teacher at The Lab School finds role-playing works well to explain this concept, but props are needed as well. She explained, "Economic problems that existed under the Articles of Confederation and that led to the Constitutional Convention are taught using a trading game. Each student represents one of the original 13 states. He or she has population pieces, gold pieces, currency, and a product to trade such as iron, pork, or tobacco. The products are represented by baked clay pieces made into objects such as horseshoes, pigs, or tobacco leaves. Students must trade products with other players, but they must travel across neighboring states to do so. Because there was little unity under the Articles, students are left to make their own rules about whom to trade with, whom to allow through their state, and how much to tax those who pass through. Students must also deal with the different values for each currency. Playing cards are used to introduce other factors such as natural disasters, trade with foreign nations, and the lack of help from the weak central government. Students are fully engaged because they are invested in the outcome of the game."

Noel Bicknell, a Renaissance Club Leader, developed a diagnostic-prescriptive game called Buon Fresco. The game is played on a square board with 36 squares around the edges (see Figure 4). There is a start square on the board but no end. The different icons on each square instruct players to draw question cards or take other actions. The board is colorfully decorated with examples of Giotto's work. Inside the boards are stacks of question cards ready to draw. Token cups with small red hats (apprentice symbol) and rain clouds (damp weather symbol) made of modeling clay sit in the center of the board.

There are three stacks of question cards, of different levels of difficulty, each containing 20 cards. Questions are designed to force the making of connections; it is like cognitive cueing. Teams use game pieces with Renaissance themes such as a gold florin, small hat, and mortar and pestle. Large foam dice are used to determine how many squares a team moves each turn. In addition to the main board, each team receives an empty 5" x 7" picture frame and 40 puzzle pieces with which to build the four-level Fresco painting puzzle.

The object of the game is that the first team of artists to complete their Fresco puzzle by answering questions correctly wins the game. The team with the highest role of the die goes first, and board play is clockwise in rotation. Students follow the instructions on the board and then read a question card from the correct pile. The number of apprentices a team has and the current weather conditions determine which question pile to select from. The more apprentices a team has, the harder the questions become. Some cards have special instructions or valuable tools. Students either follow the instructions or save the card for future use, whichever the card says. More than one team can be in a space at once.

Adding Apprentice and Damp Weather squares increases by one the number of Fresco tiles a team can add during a turn. Losing Apprentice or Dry Weather squares decreases by one the number of Fresco tiles a team can add to their Fresco. If a team lands on an Add Apprentice or Weather square, team members should keep track with special tokens from the cups on the board. If a team lands on Pope Visit, Earthquake, or War squares, the team loses a turn and one tile unless team members have the correct protection. Protection cards go back into the deck after every use. Landing on the Festival square means the team loses a turn, but team members are allowed to stand and dance around the table.

Teams can talk over their answer before giving a final answer, but the team member who gives the final answer must rotate among teammates. Blurting out answers when it is not the team member's turn causes a loss of one turn for the team. When a team has completed the Fresco puzzle, team members shout "Buon Fresco!" to win the game.

As you can see, games used in the Academic Clubs are scholarly and extraordinarily effective. The diagnostic-prescriptive games serve as a transition to more traditional ways of learning content. Former students have reported that they remembered specific games they played in their Academic Clubs when they studied difficult textbook material in high school and college. Similarly, props and songs are an important part of the Academic Club Methodology. They encourage children to play, which aids their understanding and memo-

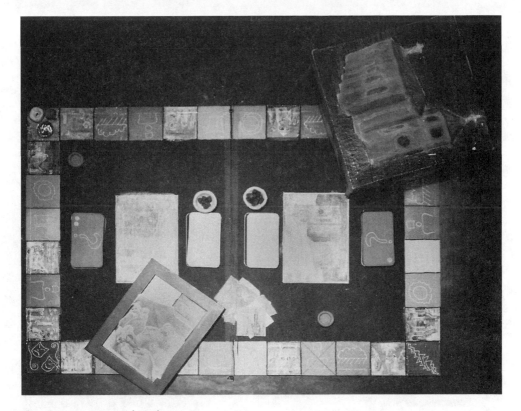

Figure 4.   Buon Fresco board game.

rization of information. Through props, songs, and games, students with severe learning disabilities and ADHD have experienced great academic success.

Try the game I created to see if it reinforces for you the important features of the Academic Club Methodology (see Figure 5). How much have you learned?

Figure 5. The Academic Club Methodology game to test how much you have learned in this book. Copyright © 2003 by Sally L. Smith.

8

How to Assess Students Using the Academic Club Methodology

When we think of testing or assessment, we think of quantitative evaluation. Measuring if test scores have gone up or down or stayed the same is simple. It is less simple to measure a student's reasoning and ability to compare ideas, take in information, apply facts, and slot information into original, new forms. Many children with learning disabilities have poor attention spans, moderate to severe language difficulties, and very weak rote memory. They cannot repeat back what has just been said to them. Not surprising, these children test poorly on standardized assessments because they need extra time to do more associative thinking and to retrieve information through strategies they have devised over the years. Many teachers do not realize that there are alternative ways to assess these nontraditional learners. The Academic Club Methodology assesses these students through means that allow them to truly present what they have learned.

At The Lab School, a Supervisor of Academic Clubs keeps track of the academic content of classes and checks on the way this content is being assessed. Club Leaders are given specific academic content and certain values that they are accountable for teaching their students. They do not work from textbooks. They do not use any published criteria. They do, however, use original sources and a variety of books and other media. Club Leaders immerse themselves in the subject of the Academic Club and develop units of study to be carried out in the order that makes sense to them.

There is no one way to conduct an Academic Club. In fact, there are so many different ways to teach the same material that Club Leaders who have taught the same Academic Club for several years take the initiative to highlight different aspects of the topic and produce new exercises and projects every year. They hold on to their curiosity, acquire new knowledge, and feel the excitement of seeking new avenues of teaching and testing what has been taught.

PIAGET'S INFLUENCE

The Academic Club Methodology is, to some extent, based on Jean Piaget's model of concrete learning. Piaget believed that "the task of the teacher is to figure out what the learner already knows and how he reasons in order to ask the right question at the right time so that the learner can build on his own knowledge" (Piaget, as cited in Schwebel & Raph, 1973, p. 203). He believed in active learning or discovery with concrete materials. The teacher functions as a guide, a demonstrator, or a facilitator who brings helpful materials into focus and empowers the child to discover knowledge. Piaget believed that a child's mistakes were diagnostic. He urged educators to always ask a child to explain his or her thinking. For example, if a child adds 27 + 17 and comes up with the answer of 71 instead of 44, then the child may demonstrate that he or she did the math correctly, but wrote down the 1 and carried the 4, instead of writing down the 4 and carrying the 1.

Club Leaders are taught to examine children's mistakes. In the Renaissance Club, after students have completed their fresco project, each student is verbally questioned on what he or she found difficult in the project. Students are asked which job they would have wanted in the actual Renaissance and why. The Club Leader, Lorenzo de Medici, asks them to reflect on what would happen if they taught a younger child the project. What advice or warning would they give the younger child? Club Members often do very well with this kind of questioning, even though they may have difficulty being questioned about names, locations, and dates.

Built into the Methodology is constant accountability through visual materials, objects, projects, songs, and games that are diagnostic prescriptive. In the Egytian Gods Club, students remember the word *shaduf* because they constructed this irrigation tool out of sticks. They proudly wear the *scarabs* they have created. The Nile River runs down the middle of their classroom, just as it runs through the middle of Egypt, so they don't forget the word *Nile*. They call their Club Leader *Cleopatra*, so that name, too, becomes part of their knowledge. The *Rosetta Stone* is part of their classroom design. By seeing this important piece of ancient history every day, students remember it, along with the word *hieroglyphics* (because they have written in hieroglyphics). Students must use the vocabulary daily; if they forget a word, they are cued by the Club Leader to recall what they have constructed, touched, or said.

Club Members are also taught to greet every visitor with, "Welcome to the Cave [or other] Club. What's the password? We'll give you some clues." Watching the visitors struggle does please Club Members, but the point of this routine is for students to learn and demonstrate how to give clues and devise strategies to help themselves and others remember the password.

Club Leaders keep written cards or notes with a profile of each student. They are given sheets asking them to log in the strengths, interests, and weak areas of each of their students (see Figure 6). Later, they are asked to note which methods of teaching work effectively for the students and which do not. They are given one section on the chart, called Questions to Explore, that they can keep checking over the course of an academic year, regarding a child or a topic. A Questions to Explore section might include "Is this child's very weak memory due to ADHD, language problems, or poor associative thinking? Does he need more picture clues, gestures, or movements to help him remember? Verbal repetition does not work."

Evaluation materials that are designed by the teacher are built into the daily curriculum. A number of Academic Club activities involve the child's whole body or the shifting of his or her body in order to learn directions such as north, south, east, or west. Trained in keen observation, Club Leaders can assess gross motor skills and any adaptations that have to be made in the Academic Club. Their keen listening skills pick up on language maturity, articulation, language flow, and word retrieval ability.

ASSESSING MATURITY

Another area that is closely monitored in the Academic Club is each child's approach to a task: how the child organizes his or her work, materials, and self. The level of each child's behavioral and emotional maturity is noted. Maturity can be readily seen in the Academic Club setting because of the amount of activity learning taking place in small groups. Two or three youngsters working together clearly show how socialized they are. Another form of maturity that is continually observed is a child's tendency to do only one thing at a time. A number of Club Leaders have told me that they cannot get over how many of their students cannot do two or more things at once. For example, some Knights and Ladies Club members cannot stir a pot and speak at the same time. They can either do one action or the other.

Flexibility of thinking is also a measure of maturity. Rigid thinking is an indication of immaturity. For example, a Club Member may say, "I can't use

Child's name: _____   Name of club: _____

Date of birth: _____   Child's role: _____

Child's strengths	Child's interests	Child's weak areas

Methods that work	Methods that don't work	Questions to explore

Figure 6.   Academic Club Member assessment form.

peanuts to represent the small farmers in this African town we are making because farmers plant peanuts and eat them." Another may say, "The tallest Greek
God is the oldest" or indicate that a nickel is worth more than a dime because
it is bigger, which is typical thinking of 5- to 6-year-olds, not 8- to 10-year-olds.

ASSESSING REASONING SKILLS

Reasoning is continually assessed by Club Leaders. After reenacting the Battle
of Hastings, Lord Don asks his Knights and Ladies, "What if Harold had won
instead of William the Conqueror? Tell me how history would have been different." Lorenzo de Medici asks how the Gates of Paradise would look if Brunelleschi had won the competition instead of Ghiberti. In the Museum Club,
the Director of the Museum asks Club Members, "If you had lived in Minoan
times, would the lives of boys and girls be very different? What about in Greek
times?" The Director also asks how the Muslims, the Hebrews, and the Hindus
were alike and how they were different. The Chairman of the Board in the Industrialists Club asks the Industrialists to think through how the Industrial
Revolution would have been different if the South had won the Civil War.

Children with severe learning disabilities who have failed in a number of
school environments jump with alacrity to answer these questions that demand a depth of critical thinking. They love to put themselves in the place of
their characters, so they don't feel intimidated or think that they are being
tested when they explain their characters' lives. They readily engage in syllo-
gistic reasoning. They think through cause-and-effect relationships and combine knowledge with imagination.

In-depth projects also serve as a means for children to demonstrate their
reasoning skills. In the Polar Explorers Club, students serve as the Crew of
Roald Amundsen, the first explorer to reach the South Pole. After learning
about the Arctic and Antarctic environments, the Crew decide what to bring
on the 4-year expedition. They make models of the ship and dog sleds complete with miniature supplies they would need. Club Members then verbally
describe their models to the group. By listening to the presentation and inspecting the student's physical preparations for the imagined journey, the Club
Leader can instantly see which students have *analyzed* the necessities of the
arctic environment, *reasoned* the impact on human and dog, and *applied* this
information in selecting the correct supplies to bring. The finished projects are
displayed in the classroom as a visual reminder of learned information and
brought out for review later in the program.

In the Secret Garden Club, students study botany, listen to the book *The
Secret Garden,* and grow their own vegetable garden. Each student invents a
new flower made of paper, wood, and other materials. Students are required
to make the flowers anatomically complete by creating anther, filament pistil,

stigma, and stamens. Beyond this basic structure, students are required to design how their particular flower will be pollinated. They apply their knowledge of the many ways pollination takes place and pick a system for their invented plant. Completed flowers are then presented to a peer partner and then to the larger group and teacher. After that, a younger group of children and the student's parents listen to the presentation. Throughout the process, Club Members add more information to their presentations, correct errors, and compare and contrast their flowers with their peers' creations.

In Summer 2003, following the theme of Summer in the City, The Lab School had a City of the Future Club. The students, led by their Mayor on a planet in the sky, built a city with transportation services, waste disposal, communication systems, and human resources. The 10- and 11-year-old students thought through basic human needs and imagined the most sophisticated communication and transportation inventions possible. How could the Club Leader not evaluate the quality and depth of thinking or the independence of thinking demonstrated in this Academic Club?

KNOWING WHAT'S BEING TESTED

There are times when a child is labeled as having problems in reading comprehension, when in fact he or she is unable to decode the words fast enough to hold onto the meaning. Similarly, if a student with auditory and language problems is read a word problem in math, the results of the test may in no way reflect his or her knowledge of math. A geography student who cannot draw the continent forms of Africa and South America may be experiencing visual-motor problems, not problems with geography.

In an article in *Education Week* (Manzo, 2003) on scholars recommending ways to better teach history, E.D. Hirsch, Jr., President of Core Knowledge Foundation based in Charlottesville, Virginia, cited research showing that reading comprehension problems can be traced primarily to students having little or no background knowledge of subject area content, rather than just poor reading skills. In the Spring 2003 issue of *American Educator*, Hirsch said that he disagrees with common practices in elementary schools that eliminate or cut time from social studies, science, and the arts to allow for more math and reading instruction.

Hirsch said, "Reading comprehension depends on privileged knowledge that comes from learning about history and science and other areas . . . . If we really want them to read (proficiently) you've got to teach them content." Ways to assess content have to be varied for children who cannot read, cannot express themselves well, or are learning English as a second language. The Academic Club Methodology assesses content knowledge through its daily activities.

RESULTS OF LAB SCHOOL STUDENTS' IMPROVEMENT

The Lab School measures reading skills, writing skills, math skills, and the acquisition of content for all students. Benchmark testing every year determines the rate of progress for each child. Children compete against their own past performance, not the performance of others.

The Lab School gathered 5 years of student scores on the Woodcock Johnson Psycho-Educational Battery: Tests of Achievement. Data from 515 Lab School students was analyzed for progress over time in basic academic skills as well as academic applications. The Head of Psychological Services Dr. Luanne Adams and Quantitative Analyst Roya Rassai found significant increases over time in the reading and writing abilities of Lab School students (see Adams, Rassai, Shottenbauer, & Iseman, 2004).

Evidence on the long-term educational impact of the Academic Club Methodology emerged in the analyses of middle and high school students at The Lab School who had participated in Academic Clubs in their early years of schooling versus those who had not. The statistics demonstrated that students who had participated in Academic Clubs had significantly higher scores on the Broad Knowledge Cluster and, specifically, in all three content areas (i.e., science, social studies, and humanities) as well as in their reading vocabulary. Thus, Academic Clubs do indeed lay the foundation for a lifetime of learning.

What is particularly significant about these findings is that children who needed special education at an early age and who experienced Academic Clubs seemed to have more severe learning disabilities than those who were able to manage regular classes until middle or high school, and, still, they achieved significantly higher scores. The initial assessments document that the Academic Club Methodology intensively teaches academic content, vocabulary, and critical thinking. Further research and assessment of the Academic Club Methodology are now taking place.

DRAWBACKS TO STATE ASSESSMENTS

The constant pressure of legislators to raise the bar for all children and force much more testing tends to produce a one-size-fits-all approach to teaching and assessment. When standardized testing becomes this important, teachers stop educating children and spend much of their time teaching to the tests. Many practices designed to prepare students to score well on state assessments are not sound educational practices, and students' opportunities to think on a higher level diminish. Rote memorization often becomes the basis of the score sheet, but many students with learning disabilities have weak powers of memorization or very little rote memory. Their performance on tests helps determine the efficacy of a whole school and the salary increases of their teachers. Textbooks are being bought with an eye to raising test scores so chances are that fourth graders will be using the math textbook put out by the publisher of the math test. Something is wrong with this system.

Because America's school boards are so anxious to see test scores rise in math and reading, teachers tend to neglect the humanities and sciences and to eliminate the arts and physical education. In an article in *The Washington Post* about a plan to raise test scores, (May 25, 2003), a senior research fellow at the New America Foundation and a former School Board Member, J.H. Snider, stated,

> *There are two ways of raising educational test scores for students . . . the real way and the fake way . . . No one in his right mind can be against raising test scores . . . The concern is over how it's done . . . There are many ways to abuse a system of test based accountability. The most widely reported is "teaching to the test" . . . Only a small fraction of subjects are actually tested. And only a small fraction of these—reading and math—are high profile, high-stakes tests . . . Starting next year 50 percent of class time in middle schools will be devoted to just two tested subjects—math and reading—up from 33 percent two years ago . . . tested subjects should not be allowed to cannibalize the untested ones without public awareness and debate. (2003, p. B7)*

Unfortunately, many people equate good test scores with good education. In the 1990s, newspapers began publishing score-based ranking of schools, and many people believed that schools with high-ranking students were successful and that the others were failures. Low-scoring schools were singled out for extra help, changes of principals, inducements to improve, and penalties for not improving.

The faculty at negatively ranked schools felt unfairly blamed when they had a preponderance of students who spoke English as a second or third language or students from impoverished families whose parents may have experienced only a few years of education themselves. Some teachers had classes that were far less accomplished than last year's classes and therefore tested at a lower level. Many teachers complain today that they have been turned into drill masters, inspiring no one, including themselves. Commercial publishers have produced a plethora of test-focused materials that they say are guaranteed to raise test scores. Test Score Fever has become so virulent that during the 1999–2000 school year, 52 educators from the New York City Public Schools were charged with cheating on student tests (Popham, 2001).

Although tests *can* help teachers make sensible instructional decisions and *can* help teachers give grades, there are other ways to assess learning. Consider a student's degree of interest or passion to be in a class. Club Members tend to have almost perfect attendance and very little lateness. They cry or protest vigorously when removed from an Academic Club for some other event. Traditional state assessments overlook children's zest for learning.

Tests do not always have to be paper-and-pencil exercises. Projects using art or crafts that students inaugurate and describe inform teachers of the levels of information they understand. Student-composed songs or dances also demonstrate knowledge. Games that require providing specific information in order to move ahead are excellent gauges of knowledge. When the students make up their own games for others to play, content can be rated. Not only must we learn to treasure diversity of learning styles but also to appreciate the diverse ways of measuring the acquisition of information.

9

Start Your
Own Academic Club

Here's How!

So, you want to start your own Academic Club. The planning and preparation may seem overwhelming. A good way to begin thinking about starting a Club is to choose a subject that fascinates you, the teacher. Another way is to be convinced that this is the topic needed for a particular group of children you are teaching. In the case of the latter, then you have to put a spin on it that ignites your interest as well. If you decide the youngsters really need a Storekeepers Club because they have to work intensively on their categorization and classification skills and their understanding of money, then it might interest you more if you made it a CD and Video Shop, an Antique Shop, or a Toy Store.

Talking with other staff is helpful when choosing the subject. Many people come up with ideas that, upon perusal, are too hard to wrap under the umbrella of the dramatic framework. Sometimes, the idea seems glamorous but cannot be pursued in depth for a whole year or even for a 6-week summer program. Often, the ideas are too broad or too difficult to break down into manageable chunks. You should keep looking until you find a topic that feels comfortable to you, is appropriate for your students' age group, and appeals to and excites your students. The same topic has to fascinate you because your energy and enthusiasm are contagious. You always have to keep in mind the special needs of your students when choosing subject matter. Don't worry. You *can* find a topic that meets all of these criteria!

Excellent ways to come up with ideas for Academic Club themes are:

1. Listen to what children talk about—their interests, the television shows and movies they watch, the games they play, and the books they like. The popularity of Harry Potter could be translated into a Club format.

2. Study the newspaper for contemporary subjects, such as the exploration of Mars and other space-related subjects.

3. Assess what television has to offer. For example, National Geographic's exploration into jungles or deserts may produce some ideas for you. You can peruse the History Channel to learn about the contributions of each of the Founding Fathers to the U.S. Constitution. A detective show may inspire you to create a Club in which students look at clues, analyze characters, and consider different options to pursue.

4. Great literature lends itself beautifully to Clubs. For example, *Moby Dick* can be turned into a 6-week Club. Authors such as Charles Dickens and Mark Twain have enough masterpieces to explore during a year-long Club.

DECIDE WHAT TO TEACH

Once you choose a topic, then you need to decide what you want to teach. Break the topic down into its component parts so that you can teach it step by step. If the Academic Club focuses on developing reading skills, first list all of the readiness skills that children must have in order to read, then systematically work these skills into your plans or activities.

If your goal is to teach the history, geography, and civics of one specific country (e.g., France) through your Academic Club, then list the basic vocabulary and concepts that you want the children to learn. You can add to this list throughout the year. For geography, you might want to first show students where France is located in Western Europe and label the countries surrounding France: Belgium, Luxembourg, Germany, Switzerland, Italy, and Spain. You can explain that France is five-sided, like a pentagon. You may also want to pursue more geographic details, such as seas, mountains, and rivers.

Some concepts that might be drawn from French history are the Age of Reason exemplified by Rousseau and Voltaire, the French Revolution, and Napoleon. France's role in the first and second World Wars and its leadership in the new European Union could be studied, also.

The culture of France would lend itself to all sorts of exciting projects and activities, starting with French gastronomy, wines, produce, and famous chefs. Paris, one of the centers of European culture, could be the focal point of study. Architecture from ancient castles, cathedrals, and palaces to the postmodern Pompideau Centre in Paris offers another area of study. In addition, many English words derive from the French language.

If you tackle the subject of the history of trade in the world, you could start with trading activities in the Academic Club, then proceed to topic-related information, such as the fact that trade was the reason that Christopher Columbus discovered America. Some Club Leaders prefer to begin with major facts they want the children to learn and develop broader concepts from the basic information. For example, a historical fact is that Columbus discovered America while looking for spices. This *fact* is a good starting point to begin to discuss the concepts of *trade, discovery,* and *transportation.* The teacher could then create a Traders Club.

The teacher may select the dramatic framework of Pilgrims setting up a trading system with the Native Americans in the 1600s. The children could be divided into the roles of Puritans, with big white collars, tall hats, and buckled shoes, and American Indians, with beaded jewelry, fringed garments, and eagle feathers in their hair. Log cabins and tepees could provide a dramatic setting. The Puritans and Native American tribes could exchange metal axes and cloth for corn and turkey.

FIND AN APPEALING DRAMATIC FRAMEWORK

Children must be involved in an Academic Club. The dramatic framework must capture their imagination, excitement, and enthusiasm. Fascination with their Academic Clubs leads Club Members to want to read books, if they can, on the subject matter. Consider a framework that will enable Club Members to practice skills through meaningful activities. What children need to know can be taught through what children like to do, want to do, and can do. Math has been taught in captivating ways through the Storekeepers Club and the Carnival Club. A whole range of readiness, thinking, and academic skills have been taught to children playing roles of detectives or rangers.

The Marco Polo Club might intrigue the children, particularly when they learn that they have to be brave, strong, and clever in order to be a member. Marco Polo, a young man from Venice, crossed into Asia in about 1270, remained there for 25 years with his uncle (a trader), and experienced astonishing adventures on the way. He ended up in the court of Kublai Khan, the Mongol Emperor of China. Marco Polo found China to be more advanced in many areas than Europe. The teaching agenda for the Marco Polo Club focuses on the geography of Asia, exploration, inventions, and empires. Fascinating spin-offs include Marco Polo's bringing pasta to Europe, the importance of salt, the use of paper money, and more.

IMMERSE YOURSELF IN THE TOPIC

Club Leaders need to immerse themselves in material about the Academic Club. Your own interests and enthusiasms are contagious; let them be your guide in approaching the topic. Use the resources you have available to experience the topic.

For example, the Marco Polo Club Leader would read books by travelers who followed Marco Polo's route; read Coleridge's poem "Kublai Khan"; handle artifacts such as brocades and jade bowls; and listen to Asian and early

Renaissance Italian music. The Club Leader would also search the Internet for aspects of Marco Polo's sojourn in China (e.g., his discovery of the use of fireworks, paper, pasta, paper money, and coal mining). Ancient and modern maps can be compared in charting Marco Polo's overland journey to the Orient and his 8-month return by ship. The Club Leader would find out as much as possible about the mythic city of Xanadu—thought to have existed in Northwestern China—so that part of the Club room could represent the Emperor's palace in Xanadu. The Club Leader would also visit museums with collections of Yuan (Mongol) Dynasty artifacts and 13th-century Persian miniatures.

DESIGN YOUR CHARACTER AS AN AUTHORITY FIGURE

Club Leaders must have an authoritative role in the Academic Club. Their characters must be powerful or in charge of the Club Members. However, find a role that you feel comfortable with and one that is not condescending to students. For example, in an Egyptian Gods Club, you would not want to be Pharaoh because he is an absolute authority and, as monarch, a dictator who is condescending to his subjects. Instead, you might choose to be Vizier, Chief Advisor to the Pharaoh, who remains a powerful presence offstage. If you are running an Academic Club on ancient Greece, a good leadership role would be Socrates, who taught by asking wise questions. In an African Market Club, you may choose the role of Nana, the matriarch of the market place.

Some Club Leaders are uncomfortable playing authoritative roles of the opposite gender. If you feel this way, find a role that is suitable to your gender. If you are a female running a Pirates Club, find material about the few female pirates (e.g., Mary Read) rather than identifying with a male pirate. Choice of roles, however, is based on what you feel comfortable with. A male teacher might feel more comfortable than a female acting the role of Marco Polo, but a confident woman could do it as well. Your belief in, and comfort with, your role in the Academic Club will allow Club Members to believe in their roles, too.

FIND BELIEVABLE ROLES FOR
STUDENTS THAT WILL HELP THEM LEARN

For an Academic Club to succeed, each Club Member must be excited by his or her role and be committed to it. Club Members must be able to identify with a specific character involved in the topic (e.g., Michelangelo in the Renaissance Club). As mentioned previously, pretending to be someone else and taking on a character role allows Club Members to dare to try and to dare to risk failure, which they would not do if they were not protected by a dramatic role. By "becoming" another person (usually a heroic figure), children are often willing to try certain things, such as deciphering codes (basic reading) or writing in a newspaper, which they would never volunteer to do in a traditional classroom.

Being Secret Agents, with all of the associated reading readiness activities, has helped many children learn to read. The Secret Agents decode messages, sound out letters, combine symbols and signs, and earn badges for discriminating one sound from another and one symbol from another. In other words, as Secret Agent 007 or 005, they work even harder to concentrate on decoding and encoding as well as comprehension, which is what reading is all about.

Egyptian Gods love to decode hieroglyphics and leave messages for their teachers and parents in hieroglyphics. Being Zeus, King of the Gods, encourages learning as much as possible about ancient Greece; playing the role of rich J.P. Morgan activates intense interest in the Age of American Industrialism and the stock market.

In the Marco Polo Club, each Club Member is a famous trader from a different part of the medieval world, such as Indira from India, Rustam from Persia, Olga from Siberia, Farida from Lebanon, Hassan from Egypt, Benjamin from Babylon, Silvia from Samarkand, Milton from Mongolia, Carusa from the Caspian Sea, Vladimir from the Volga, Wafa from Arabia, Slaithong from Thailand, Sita from Sri Lanka (formerly Ceylon), Sarvat from Turkistan, and Arturo from Afghanistan. Each Trader who joins Marco Polo's adventures has one or two unique products to trade from his or her country. They all become wealthy in the end, regardless of whether they return home or stay with Marco Polo.

Because the Club Leader assigns a name and a country to each child, the Leader should naturally assign a country that a child demonstrates a particular interest in or connection with. With poor readers, the Club Leader must also devise mnemonic devices for helping Club Members remember such names as *Turkistan* (e.g., children make the shape of a turkey head with one hand and then *stand* up quickly putting together turke + stan). Club Members cut out their countries from a map and color them. If there is a computer in the room, Members can find the large geographic area where their country's language is spoken.

CREATE INEXPENSIVE PROPS

A few props made of ordinary, inexpensive materials can create striking visual effects and can transform your classroom into an environment that invites the teaching of the topic. You should decide on the décor and start to put it up to create a specific atmosphere from the very beginning. Club Members help to complete and embellish the scene. With a parachute (from an Army-Navy surplus store) on the ceiling and floor to ceiling columns (cut from plain brown butcher paper) pasted on the wall, you can create a veritable Mount Olympus for a Greek Gods Club. With some old sheets (dyed red and tacked to the wall) and folding chairs from someone's basement (covered with velvet and spray painted with gold leaf), you can create a plush railroad car for the American Industrialists Club. Rely on your own strengths and talents in decorating or find friends to help you in areas where they are skillful and you are not. Don't let your lack of extraordinary artistic talent keep you from doing an Academic Club!

In a large public school classroom, curtains or screens can be used to portray the background the Club Leader wants. Students can be chosen as Academic Club Stage Managers, who set the scene before the Marco Polo Club begins. They can hang the gold-framed picture in the Xanadu part of the room; put the screens and curtains in place; arrange the chairs, cushions, and wall hangings; and put the Marco Polo Club poster or design on the door.

With the Marco Polo Club, part of the room can be devoted to the overland journey to China and another part can be a boat that holds everyone as they go from place to place on their return to Venice, with Marco Polo at the helm. A special area represents a pavilion in Xanadu, with bright, striped wall hangings; cushions on the floor to sit on; and a large, gold-framed portrait of the Emperor Kublai Khan on the wall. Background scenes can be painted on the wall or pagodas can be drawn on a curtain.

ESTABLISH CLUB-APPROPRIATE CODES OF BEHAVIOR

An appropriate code of behavior becomes the discipline of your Club. For example, Secret Agents have "agent discipline" (i.e., they have to have tight security, use their eyes and ears actively, and rarely use their mouths), whereas Renaissance Councillors have "Council discipline" (i.e., the council decides what constitutes inappropriate behavior and the consequences of inappropriate actions). In the Marco Polo Club, the Academic Club Leader is Marco Polo. Student assistants serve as Uncle Nicolo and Marco Polo's father. Marco Polo is the authority in the room and on the boat. The Emperor, Kublai Khan, who is a potent off-stage personality, issues decrees, which must be part of the story, woven into the action in Cathay. His gold-framed picture hangs in Xanadu. When the traders see the gilded picture, they immediately kow-tow, squat, bow their heads, and put their hands over their heads until their hands touch.

FOSTER A SENSE OF MEMBERSHIP

Establish immediately a sense of membership and belonging in the club: Each child needs to feel important as part of this close-knit group. Start with the door to the room you will be working in; decorate it to reinforce the theme of the Academic Club and to highlight the idea of membership. A bright red and orange sign with balloons bordering it beckons Club Members to the Carnival Club, whereas a sign of "Employees' Entry Only—Show Your Pass, Please" reinforces the Storekeepers Club Members' sense of belonging. A black and white railroad crossing marks the entry to the Industrialists Club and lists the names of its exclusive members.

For a number of Academic Clubs, first day activities should be devoted to making identification cards (e.g., elaborate ones with Polaroid pictures of the child and his or her height and eye color), badges, arm bands, and amulets—in short, any visual token that symbolizes belonging to the Club. It is equally important for the teacher to develop a secret password that has meaning to the Club, such as *espionage* for the Secret Agents Club or *heritage* for the Museum Club.

All of these activities can be programmed to teach specific skills. For example, the password provides a fine opportunity to teach vocabulary (e.g., *consumer* can be the Storekeeper's Club password) and finding a word that rhymes with *sound* can be a password for the Broadcasters Club. Memorizing a phrase of a great revolutionary can bring entry to the Revolutionaries Club. *Literature* would be one password for the Charles Dickens Club. Club Leaders sometimes make at least one change to the password each week to increase children's vocabulary.

Bodily kinesthetic clues are sometimes used to aid memorization. As described previously, in the Renaissance Club the password was *contrapposto* meaning "the weight-shift stance," describing the pose a of statue like "David." Students remembered it by swinging their hips right and left and shifting their weight back and forth in time with each syllable. In the Cavemen Club, the members wiggled the fingers of their hands saying the password *Homo habilis*.

CREATE AN ENTRY RITUAL AND SEATING ARRANGEMENT

When students enter their club, they must perform a formal and Club-appropriate entry ritual. Pirates walk the balance-beam plank (which is good for coordination) and give the password. Storekeepers go through a home-made turnstile and give their password. Greek Gods give their password, pull themselves up straight, and head for their individual columns, whereas Renaissance Councillors give their password and walk with dignity toward the mat decorated with the symbol of their city-state or to the portrait that represents their artwork. The African Harambee Club Members enter by identifying themselves and the country they represent (e.g., I am Kirk of Kenya). Then, they find their countries on the large map and walk in ritualistic fashion to the straw mat that has their name on it.

The appropriate "entering behavior" to a club helps to focus Club Members' attention on the subject, screen out distractions, and set the tone for learning. It lures children's attention to the subject at hand and is particularly necessary for distractible children with short attention spans.

INVENT REGULAR ROUTINES
AND RITUALS TO ENHANCE LEARNING

Children with learning disorders have great difficulty learning sequences, so Club Leaders should invent regular routines and rituals to enhance learning. A regular, sequential ritual in the Secret Agents Club, for example, is to take turns calling the roll. Freedom Fighters Club Members, who are trying to improve their coordination, have to turn a somersault and walk, following a rhythmic beat, through a mini-maze (which contains small obstacles) to enter their hideout.

The Marco Polo Club needs a ritual that involves some movement to accommodate the restlessness of children with attention-deficit/hyperactivity disorder (ADHD) and fits with the Club's adventures. This task might be accomplished as Club Members recite in unison, "From Venice to Cathay, we're on our way," while making vigorous arm gestures, stomping first right, then left, and ending with a hand clap. Club Members also need a prescribed way of leaving Xanadu: paying proper respect to the Emperor. The traders might bow deeply toward the portrait of Emperor Kublai Khan on the wall and recite "Kublai Khan, Grandson of Genghis Khan, we hail your mighty civilization." A Club Leader needs to devise his or her own phrases emphasizing what is most important to remember in the curriculum.

ANY MATERIAL CAN BE TAUGHT IN A CLUB

What is taught in a traditional classroom can be taught in another way in an Academic Club as long as the teacher introduces the necessary content through a dramatic cover. The Marco Polo Club, for example, will teach students about Italy and China and the long trek Marco Polo made across land and back by sea. Students will learn about the rich civilization in China and the many foods, objects, and ideas Marco Polo brought to Italy that influenced Western civilization. Club Members will learn that the Mongols of Central Asia had the largest empire the world has ever known, stretching from the Pacific to Poland. Ways of life and government in China and Italy are contrasted. The excitement, perils, and importance of exploration are studied.

You have to decide the main points you want your students to leave with. A plan like the following helps you to create curriculum.

Marco Polo Club

Objective 1: To work on position in space and directionality.

Activity 1: Marco Polo dramatizes time on the ship. When he says "all traders north, all traders south, all traders east, and all traders west," the children turn in those directions and salute the flag of Venice.

Objective 2: To compare Venice with China.

Activity 2: Make a game contrasting the Church and the Doge of Venice as great powers with the Emperor's rule though the Mandarins in China.

ADJUST THE CLUB'S PACE AS NEEDED

Plan to change the pace in your Academic Club about three to four times an hour. Because children with learning disabilities, ADHD, and language problems tend to have short attention spans and trouble listening, following directions, and verbalizing, class periods have to be broken up into chunks of time. For example, read to the children or hold a discussion. Then, reenact the material. Later, have a physical activity, a game, or a craft project. Halfway through the year, you can add a twist to the Club in order to teach new information. For example, in the Marco Polo Club, Marco Polo could get Kublai Khan's permission to accompany a Mongol princess on her sea journey to Persia to marry a great Prince. Marco Polo decides to invite his fellow Traders (the Club Members) to come along in their boat. This make-believe journey around the coast of Asia offers great opportunities for more geography. The boat will touch several countries that are "home" to various traders such as Kampuchea (now Cambodia), Thailand, Sumatra, Burma, India, and finally Persia, where the old Prince has died, allowing the princess to marry his handsome son. This actually happened! Progress of the journey can be followed on a big map using colored push pins. Diagnostic-prescriptive games can be played for each country or group of countries visited.

USE GAMES

Games are used to reinforce academic work or to teach specific information. You can adapt commercial games to meet your academic needs or make up your own games. A real test both of your own knowledge and your perception of what a child needs to know is whether you can make up a game that tests knowledge but is fun to play.

In the Marco Polo Club, the Club Leader may create the Marco Polo Traders Game, which includes various maps and goods. Students win if they roll the dice correctly or land in a certain lucky spot. Skill cards (i.e., geography, history, civics questions to answer) and Luck Cards (i.e., move forward 3 spaces) are involved. There is also an area where a player can be captured and lose two turns. The objective of the game is to be able to keep all your riches and go home or join Marco Polo's new travels.

PROGRAM FOR DIVERSITY

When you plan your Academic Club, build on your own strengths and talents. Do the same for each child in your Club as much as possible. Follow your students' interests, seek out their strengths, and build on their knowledge. As much as possible, program for diversity, prize the uniqueness of each student, and demonstrate to students how much better the product or the situation is when there are many different solutions. The Marco Polo Club, for example, has a diverse group of Traders. All Traders add to the strength of the group, and the variety of exotic sites that Club Members explore offer opportunities and flexibility for new projects.

USE ALL OF THE ARTS

All of the arts come into play in an Academic Club. Whether the goal is to teach reading readiness, arithmetic skills, history, geography, or civics, the Academic Club relies on drama as its primary tool. Drama helps to screen out distractions and achieve focus; artwork and crafts sustain the focus and reinforce information learned. The body and all of the senses come alive in an Academic Club and are used to learn basic concepts. Music and rhythm and sometimes dance, sculpture, architecture, films, and filmmaking are all employed to teach the subject matter of the Academic Club. Drama also provides the method of discipline. Art defines the historical period or whatever setting suits the subject of the Club. Art forms not only introduce information and reinforce skills, but they also are employed as diagnostic aides to test what a child has learned.

- *Architecture*—Club Members can see pictures of houses, palaces, temples, and structures.

- *Weaving*—Rugs and mats may be woven by Club Members.

- *Ceramics*—Club Members can learn about jars or plates made of ceramics.

- *Puppetry*—Club Members can study puppets, jesters, and musicians as popular forms of entertainment.

- *Printmaking*—Club Members can hand-print fabrics

- *Scroll paintings*—Club Members can use different paints.

- *Paper making*—A fun art project is for Club Members to follow a recipe developed in 105 A.D. to make paper.

- *Mask making*—Papier-mâché can be used by Club Members to create masks.

- *Calligraphy*—Club Members can learn the ancient art of calligraphy with special pens, brushes, and ink.

- *Cartooning*—Making fun of an adventure through drawing is a good activity for Club Members.

- *Carpet art*—Club Members can take rug remnants and put them together to depict a scene.

FINAL ADVICE

If you do your research thoroughly—go to original sources; interview knowl-edgeable people; and study photographs, art books, and travel books—then you will be filled with ideas for your Academic Club. This chapter is meant to be a guide, not a recipe book. You should not follow each and every detail. The Academic Club Methodology is designed to inspire teachers to pull together, break information down into manageable chunks, and turn that material into hands-on visual and motor activities to inspire children with special needs to learn effectively. The process of creating your own Academic Club will help you become a better teacher. Starting with a 6-week Academic Club may be a good first step because it is easier to plan and organize than a year-long Club. You will be amazed at how much you will learn in that time and what sophis-ticated knowledge your Club Members will acquire. You can do it! If neces-sary, The Lab School Academic Club Advisory Service can help facilitate your planning process (see p. 205).

10

Conversations with Club Leaders

Club Leaders have taught Academic Clubs since 1966, when I first designed the Academic Club Methodology. Most of the Club Leaders have been artists interested in history, teachers interested in history and the arts, and history buffs fascinated by the use of art. A large number of Club Leaders were graduate students majoring in Special Education: Learning Disabilities at American University in Washington, D.C., who were fascinated by teaching through the arts, had a passionate interest in history, and believed that children with special needs learned best from hands-on, experiential education. Occasionally, a reading specialist or classroom teacher became a Club Leader as well.

Since 1967, I have conducted Club Leader group meetings every other week to share teacher-made materials and inspire the making of diagnostic-prescriptive games or other means of assessment. The Club Leaders stimulate one another's interest in history and research, express a desire to track down the roots of words or names, and share enthusiasm to adapt ideas presented by others. Club Leaders also help each other decorate their rooms and determine how to make frescoes, mosaics, and wall paintings.

They share ideas on how to keep behavior management within the dramatic framework of the Academic Club. For example, in the Egyptian Gods Club, one Club Member, in the role of Anubis, was apparently hoarding objects instead of trading them. The Club Leader as Cleopatra was frustrated. Other Leaders suggested that she give everybody an object and ask for it back. After thoroughly complimenting the hoarder for returning the object, Cleopatra could ask Anubis to start another sequence on trading and praise him lavishly.

Another Club Leader had difficulty with a bright student who kept saying "I know, I know" whenever the Leader asked a question. Other Club Leaders advised that he give this student one area of expertise to share with the group each day. The student would have to keep his hand down and be quiet when his area was not being discussed. That way, other students could have a chance to answer questions.

Another Leader experienced difficulty with students who did not want to leave the Academic Club and made the rest of the students late to the next class. The other Academic Club Leaders suggested the use of three cards: one red card, meaning stop what you are doing; one yellow card, meaning prepare to leave; and one green card, meaning time to leave now. This suggestion worked well because it was visual. Many children with learning disabilities have auditory and language problems as well as trouble stopping projects and moving on. They hear so much reminding (and nagging) that it helps to offer them visual reminders.

Diagnosing particular difficulties in Academic Club learning is another function of the group, along with problem solving as a group and coming up with new ideas to try. For example, a student who cannot seem to learn the password may need to clap it out or may need to move in a certain way or point to a part of the body (point to knee to help remember Neanderthal).

Hearing from the other Club Leaders helps teachers dare to try new methods. This chapter contains conversations with Club Leaders for this reason. These outstanding teachers individualize their group lessons, present material through different senses, and use an experiential approach that is followed by discussion. You will learn something from each of these extraordinary educators.

AMANDA WOLFE

B.A. Psychology; M.A. Special Education: Learning Disabilities; 9 years as a Club Leader

Academic Clubs taught: Secret Agents Club, Cave Club, and Dinosaur Club (for 5- to 6-year-olds)

1.   What makes you enjoy being a Club Leader?

I enjoy being a Club Leader because the teaching principles of an Academic Club are so effective with children. The goals are easily achieved based on the structure and the multisensory approach where the student gets to participate as a character of history (see it, be it, and do it). This works especially with children with a learning disability. Being immersed in the atmosphere of a Club allows children to lower their defenses and become more available to receiving and processing information. It is a guaranteed success for a student on so many levels.

2. Describe the Academic Club activity that you are most proud of.

My most creative activity was designed for the Cave Club. This Club explores the evolution of man through five developmental stages of humans. The first human, or hominid, is Australopithecus (aw-stray-low-PITH-ih-kus). One of the most famous was nicknamed Lucy. She was an *Australopithecus afarensis* found in Hadar, Ethiopia, Africa in 1974 by Donald Johanson. The excavation team working at the site was listening to the Beatles song "Lucy in the Sky with Diamonds," which resulted in her nickname. I took the background music to the song and developed lyrics and movements with curriculum-related material. The song is entitled "Lucy is an Australopithecus" (see Chapter 7) and covers all five stages of evolution learned in the Club.

3. What abstract concept did you translate into concrete practical activities?

I introduce the idea of time by using a timeline in six parts: earth began; first plants; first animals; dinosaurs; first mammals; and humans. I present this material several different ways, for instance, on cards that are placed sequentially left to right and top to bottom. I also use multicolored crates stacked together to resemble stairs. The most effective and multisensory activity is using the staircase, the building, and the school grounds. In this scenario, the difference between each of the six parts of the timeline is emphasized. This is not done to memorize a specific number, but to understand the difference visually and/or kinesthetically between 4 billion years ago and a million years ago. Spots along the course are chosen to represent each space on the timeline, and the children are walked through the course backward and forward. They are also given photo cards of the spots where they stopped and are asked to sequence those cards.

4. What materials or situation have you set up to produce exciting thinking?

When the students evolve into *Homo sapiens neanderthalensis,* we go on a woolly mammoth hunt. This occurs at the conclusion of the unit when the students have listened to stories, made specific tool kits, and reenacted daily Neanderthal activities. In preparation for this hunt, the students must design a plan of attack as well as an alternate plan. With the playground as their staging area, students use manipulatives (human models, scenery, and a toy mammoth) to describe and present individual ideas. As a clan, they decide which two plans to use and make a list of all the materials they will need to be successful in the hunt. The students also make a list of the uses of the woolly mammoth: food, shelter, clothing, tools, fuel, and so forth. After completing all of the steps, practicing their techniques, and wondering who will play the part of the Mammoth, the students are surprised to learn the Wise Elder is dressed up as *Mammuthus primigenus* (the woolly mammoth). The whole process is exciting to watch as students come up with practical and creative strategies for capturing this Ice Age beast. The students naturally fall into roles of leadership, mediation, and compliance. Their cooperation for the common goal is inspiring from a teaching standpoint.

5.   How have you translated the Academic Club Methodology to other teaching you have done?

Several of the Club techniques are applicable in my elementary science classes, for instance, the use of the password to help learn and retain difficult scientific terms. For the majority of vocabulary, I include a kinesthetic component to assist in the retrieval of the word. The use of drama can be very compelling as well. When teaching about the human body and its immune system, I designed a 7-minute skit, which helped to explain the different types of cells and their roles. The students produced the skit entitled "Cell Wars," mimicking the theme of the movie *Star Wars*. The skit opens with cells patrolling a particular wall of the immune system. An antigen springs forth piercing the wall of cells (balloons). It continues with messages being sent through different colored flags to other cells. Those cells respond and attack and kill the antigen.

6.   What do the students seem to enjoy most about their Academic Clubs?

The students seem to enjoy the sense of belonging to something so exciting and special. The dramatic aspect of being someone else, being anonymous, is very rewarding. Students can experience learning without traditional judgment. Depending on how the particular Club is structured, it is very easy to assess whether the student has made gains; however, the student never has to experience the negative aspects of "testing" and failure. If they make a mistake, it is all right because the atmosphere is set up so that a "mistake" can be turned around in several ways. For example, in the Cave Club, we study the history of ancient hominids. This is based on archeological findings. Anthropologists do a considerable amount of guesswork about these humans' daily life. Therefore, if we are replicating an object and the student's replication isn't like everyone else's, the reason for the difference is built into the activity. It is in this atmosphere and through their character roles that students delight in making the cognitive connections from the past to the present.

7.   What's the most important advice to give a new Club Leader?

In the Academic Club setting, drama is a key feature. As a teacher, there is a fine line when role-playing. You must set yourself up in an authoritative role—one that cannot be questioned. This doesn't mean you have to be overly austere in your teaching methods; rather, set firm boundaries. Believe it or not, this makes it comfortable for students. If the students have a clear understanding of what your role and their roles are, you as a teacher achieve a more effective response. An Academic Club is not "playtime"; it is a structured, dynamic, cleverly disguised academic program with dramatic license.

CARRIE HILLEGASS

B.A. Special Education; M.A. Special Education: Learning Disabilities; 6 years as a Summer Club Leader, 3 years as an academic-year Club Leader

Academic Clubs Taught: Cruise Club, Space Station Club, Space Club, Magic Club, Cave Club, and Secret Agents Club

1.   What makes you enjoy being a Club Leader?

The role of a Club Leader is so exciting. Not only do you transform the actual room you are teaching in from a stale "traditional" classroom into an ancient cave or a cruise ship or a magician's chambers, but you also "become" a new person. The students and the teacher leave their original identities at the door. It is as if you are passing through a time warp into the future or into the past.

As the Leader of the Cave Club, I became the Wise Elder, and the students became cave boys and girls with names such as Gum Ba. This ability to completely immerse yourself into the time period or the topic you are studying had a significant impact on the student's ability to become "risk-free" learners. The students' desires to try, to enjoy, and to succeed learning difficult matter was directly correlated to the comfort they felt in the created learning environment. Therefore, students who had "failed" in a regular learning environment felt successful and were successful through the methods used in teaching Academic Clubs. Every time I saw one of their successes, which was often, it made me realize how much I enjoyed being a Club Leader.

2.   Describe the Academic Club activity that you are most proud of.

The Academic Club Methodology is so effective because it makes the teacher stray from the traditional lesson plans of direct teaching and lean toward engrossing the children in the subject matter through multisensory projects. Therefore, as a teacher I could not stand in the front of the classroom and talk about the Lascaux Caves discovered in France and expect the students to remember them. Instead, I would expect the students to use the term *Lascaux Cave* as a password to enter the cave. Once inside the cave, they would don their cave costumes, become cave boys and girls, and actually recreate the Lascaux Cave paintings on the walls of their cave. This type of project learning empowered the students by enhancing their memory skills as well as their conceptual learning abilities.

An activity that I am most proud of was developed during the summer that I taught Space Club. During that summer, it just so happened that the Shoemaker Levy 9, a comet composed of 20 fragments, was actually pelting Jupiter. The students were working on the solar system at the time. We, of course, used the *Shoemaker Levy 9* as our password, but to make sure the multisensory lesson was used, the children actually became the comet that day. We had a huge yellow ball, which became Jupiter, and the children ran through "space" and collided with "Jupiter" as the comet did in space. This was using their kinesthetic intelligence as well as visual and auditory skills. It was so exciting that children 5–7 years of age knew more about this current "space" event than their parents did.

3.   What abstract concept did you translate into concrete practical activities?

Keeping the concept of making the abstract concrete was particularly important when teaching Cave Club and Space Club. The Cave Club examines the entire time period from after the dinosaurs to the genus of *Homo sapiens*. Not only does this whole Club take place in the past, which is an abstract concept, but it also covers millions of years of evolution. This is difficult for 5- and 6-year-olds to grasp. One approach to show-ing the cave students the past was to have them stand erect in the "present" face for-ward and then walk backward down the stairs to reinforce the concept that the past was backwards in time. As we went from time period to time period, we would re-trace our steps (walking backwards of course) until we ended up in the time period of Australopithecus. This was an activity we did periodically throughout the entire school year. By the end of the year, as we became Australopithecus, we had walked almost in the street because we had to walk so far to cover the time periods.

4.   What materials or situation have you set up to produce exciting thinking?

Teaching and reinforcing concepts is particularly exciting when it is done in a game format. I created several games throughout my years as a Club Leader. We always did a wrap-up Jeopardy game at the end of each Summer Club. We invited the parents so that they could see how much their children knew!

As the Wise Elder in the Cave Club, I created a game that the children played each time we "evolved" into a new species; we went from *Australopithecus* to *Homo sapiens*.

In the Space Club, a student game prompted me to do extended lessons on a topic we had only touched on. I had only briefly discussed the Big Bang theory, and after one game, we spent more time discussing and, of course, role-playing the "bang." One student exclaimed, "If only we were in Space Club all day, we could cover everything!" Of course, that was music to my ears!

5.   How have you translated the Academic Club Methodology to other teaching you have done?

When I was a classroom teacher and a tutor, I used the Club way of thinking to en-hance my ability to teach reading, math, and language arts. As I planned lessons each evening, I found that personalizing material, bringing information back to the body, and multisensory approaches worked best. These ideas should not be exclusive to children with learning disabilities.

Personalizing information for a student is critical to improve their ability to retain the concept and then apply the skills. For example, I was teaching a student who had a significant reading problem. She had tremendous difficulty remembering the conso-nant digraphs such as "sh," "ch," and "th." After attempting the strategies in current remedial reading programs, I found that this student needed more. After we related the digraphs to her best friends, "ch" = Charlton, "sh" = Ashley by making sound cards with their pictures and posting them on her desk, she was able to use them con-sistently when decoding words with these sounds.

I also found that it was particularly important to relate sounds back to the body when teaching reading to students who were struggling with learning the "code" of our al-phabet. For example, when teaching the short "e" sound, say "e" elbow and touch the elbow.

I heavily relied on the Academic Club Methodology of making lessons multisensory in learning. When I was teaching prepositions to my students, we did not memorize lists. Instead, we made cards with the written word and a picture. We took these cards out to the playground and created an obstacle course. The children would stand "under" something or "next to" something. This way of using the kinesthetic learning channel as well as the auditory and visual channels was particularly effective. We used that same concept in math when learning addition and subtraction. We used a big number line and the stairs to walk forward and backward; this allowed the children to feel the problems with their bodies.

6.   What do the students enjoy most about their Academic Clubs?

The concept of Academic Clubs is so ingenious. The students love it on so many levels. The use of a password to enter the Club shows them that they belong to something very special and secret. They feel important and, therefore, develop an attachment to seeing their Club succeed, which ultimately allows them to succeed. This sense of ownership has a profound impact on the learning that naturally happens through the effective use of the Academic Club Methodology. Not only do they become important Club Members, but they also get to take on a new identity, which empowers the student who is often reluctant to take risks. The ability to become a risk-taker in the learning process manifests itself in many successes. The student who is so afraid because of prior failures is able to blossom in a way that would otherwise be impossible. The Club Members become successful in many ways: taking risks, exhibiting model behavior, learning exciting and sophisticated material, and building pride in themselves.

7.   What's the most important advice to give a new Club Leader?

The most important advice to give any teacher—but particularly a new Academic Club teacher—is that planning is the key to success. It is critical for new Club Leaders to become extremely well versed in the subject matter they will be teaching. This requires a lot of dedication and a lot of time. Unless you know the subject matter inside and out, it is very difficult to plan creative lessons that will make the topic concrete and understandable.

In a Club, there is never a day when you can stand in front of the class and read from a textbook. The teacher must invent projects that either develop a new idea or that reinforce a concept previously taught. These projects create the forum in which the students can use all of their individual learning styles and unique talents. It will amaze any teacher, new or old, the in-depth thinking, learning, and retention that takes place through the Academic Club Methodology.

Being a Club Leader is one of the most rewarding jobs any teacher could ever hold! Challenge yourself, challenge the students, and watch the learning begin!

GINA VAN WEDDINGEN

B.A. Philosophy; M.A. Special Education: Learning Disabilities; 7 years as a Club Leader

Academic Clubs taught: Gods Club, Pirates Club, Space Voyagers Club, Rangers Club, Science Giants Club, Sherlock Holmes and the Space Detectives Club, Oregon Trail Club, and The Lost Cities Club

1. What makes you enjoy being an Academic Club Leader?

It's 5 minutes until 10 o'clock, and Cleopatra is almost ready to receive her guests. The seating is organized around the circular hearth in the center of the column-lined room. Her throne is cleared of books and project items. Materials to hammer out the bronze belt buckle (crafted by Hephaestus for his wife, Aphrodite's, Golden Girdle) wait in organized piles near her throne. All that remains is for her to robe herself as the Macedonian queen of Egypt, the last of the Pharaohs, and to receive the young visitors who will enter into the past with her . . .

Does this sound like fun? Does it seem more like an actress preparing for a play than a teacher awaiting her class? Right on both counts! Being a Club Leader is very much like being involved in an improvisational theater group, for which I provide the script (after careful and extensive research—this is an historical play after all). I am also the producer, director, prop master, set designer, and wardrobe chief, in addition to being an actor in the unfolding stories. However, the stars of the show are the 8- and 9-year-old students with learning disabilities who will remember a difficult, content-laden password so that they can take their place on stage and become an integral part of the stories (histories) I tell.

Stories need characters. These characters, through their interaction with one another, in the context of their time and in the authenticity of their setting, propel the action and make it understandable. Each child becomes a specific character, who is related in some way to all the other characters in the stories. Luckily, in Gods Club, the characters tend to be siblings or children of Re, Zeus, or Jupiter, so the family relationships make it easier for the students to become invested in each other's characters. When the students really care about what they are studying, amazing results can occur.

Being a Club Leader is primarily about transmitting vast amounts of information to students in as many ways as possible so that each of them will be able to access the information. Students are at The Lab School because they have had trouble acquiring information in traditional ways, so my prime directive is to create visual, auditory, and kinesthetic ways to bring my beloved content alive. In order to accomplish this task, I need to think divergently whenever possible. The silly jingle, to the tune of "Head, Shoulders, Knees, and Toes," can become a way to remember the parts of a Greek column and its capital. I can even add a dance step and hand movements to make it more fun and easier to remember. I can use art, puppetry, drama, or anything else that demonstrates the content I try to teach. My options are almost limitless, and I am encouraged to experiment and take risks.

Of course, in order to properly use the Academic Club Methodology, I must wrap my students in a cloak of authenticity. My room must draw them into the content I will be sharing with them, but they must be willing participants in the process. I absolutely love researching artifacts (since I cover the ancient civilizations of Egypt, Greece, and Rome, I get *really cool* artifacts!) and then recreating them for the students to actually use in class. The children are able to absorb an amazing amount of details because they are engaged in *play* as they're learning about canopic jars or the concept of surplus food and its value to developing civilizations. Vocabulary and abstract concepts are presented in context.

There is a lot of work involved in getting a Club going, but the rewards come as I begin to teach each morning. Our kids *do not* want to miss Club. They look forward to saying their password and joining me in another time and another place. And who could resist getting paid to be Cleopatra!

2. Describe the Academic Club activity that you are most proud of.

Games are one of the most under-utilized tools in a teacher's arsenal. I personally believe that virtually anything can be either introduced, reviewed, reinforced, or assessed through a game. These games can be as simple as Tic-Tac-Toe or quiz-types, or they can become elegant, beautifully crafted treasures that tell your children how much you care about them by the thought and effort they display.

Although I have made many games during my time at The Lab School, the game of which I am most proud is *Odyssey* (described in Chapter 7), which I use to teach the voyages of Odysseus. I especially like it because each team can, in some sense, win the game. It is designed so that one team, the Athena Team, moves Odysseus and his ship to the various islands while the Poseidon Team controls a large Poseidon, who, through strategic moves, is able to send Odysseus back to a previous island. Because the end of Odysseus' story is so exciting, the students do not care that Odysseus has won and Poseidon has been thwarted. Every year, the kids cheer at the end of the game, and they really remember the story, which makes me very happy.

This game is used in conjunction with a large backdrop of the Walls of Troy, complete with puppets, a Greek *trireme,* a Trojan Horse, and warrior action figures (decorated clothespins with shields), which I use to tell *The Iliad* and *The Odyssey.* The characters include both gods and mortals, and I introduce Aeneas, who will sail from the burning ruins of Troy to become the mythical founder of Rome, in our final unit. Together, the game and puppet set manages to sum up a large quantity of information in a tidy package, makes it fun, and draws many important connections for the young students.

3. What abstract concept did you translate into concrete practical activities?

As Captain Vee in the Star Voyagers Club, I needed to teach the very abstract concept of gravity. Because gravity is a force, albeit an invisible one, I tried to make it visible and concrete by using two ropes and a scale.

I try to use the student's world and the student's body whenever possible to help make concepts personal and meaningful to the student, so first, I weighed each of them and had them record their weight. They were able to see how much they weighed in "regular" gravity. Next, I explained to them that gravity was a force that pulled their bodies toward the earth, sort of like this rope (which I ask one student to hold). I pulled on the rope and let him feel the "gravity," then I asked him to get on the scale and see how much he weighed when the "pull of gravity" increased. We discussed how some planets have a bigger mass, so they have more gravity, and I demonstrated this using a huge yellow towing rope (I love to do the weighing with the tow rope!). Next, I set the scale down very far and let them weigh themselves on the moon or Mercury, where the pull of gravity would be less. Then, I ask them if they had changed shape, gotten fat or thin, or changed in any other way. They usually always under-stood the concept of gravity as an invisible pull (and not as a change to themselves) because they had experienced it through the string and rope. The abstract concept was made concrete by making it visual and by relating it back to the students, where it would be meaningful.

Another science concept that is very difficult for even older students to grasp is the con-cept that air is made up of many different particles and molecules which are too small to see but which, nevertheless, swirl together like a salad to form our atmosphere. To help them see the components of our atmosphere, in the proper proportions, the stu-dents made "atmospheric salad" using multicolored packing peanuts (the biodegrad-able kind that stick together when slightly moist). We made lots of nitrogen molecules, sticking together two green peanuts for the two-atom bond and made sure we had four nitrogens for every oxygen (double yellow for O_2). Water vapor, carbon dioxide, trace elements, pollen, carbon monoxide, and pollution were all accounted for and were added to the salad bowl, then tossed well. Some students were able to remember the components by color, and some finally understood the difference between oxygen (we pretended to breathe these molecules in) and carbon dioxide (we pretended to exhale those molecules, which was great fun and became predictably silly).

4. What materials or situation that you set up produced some very exciting thinking?

One of my favorite surprise outcomes to an activity occurred during the Rangers Club in Summer School. Our "location" was a ranger station in a national park, in the middle of the wilderness. After giving the password, the rangers entered the room and silently walked around, intently looking for what was new or what had been moved. Each day a new, small, camouflaged creature would appear or would change loca-tion. The children had to learn to control their reactions to discovering the new ani-mal or its new location and were to quietly join Ranger Gina at the fire once they had made their daily discovery. If one or two rangers were having a particularly hard time finding the creature, the other rangers could give them hints ("Go north, now west. Look higher").

When I began the activity, I had no idea how important it would become to the students. They were able to sequence the animals in the order in which they had appeared, and later they wanted to try it in reverse order. During the last week of Summer School, I asked the children to share the strategies they used to locate and remember the animals. Many of the rangers were able to reflect on their own strategies and on how these strategies had evolved and improved during the 6-week period. Some claimed they had never developed a strategy, but had chosen another child to follow until his expression gave away the location (which turned out to be an effective strategy in its own way). Hearing the children think about their own thinking was very exciting, for them as well as for me.

5. How have you translated the Academic Club Methodology to other teaching you have done?

During the regular school year, I teach science as well as Club. I have found it particularly useful to incorporate many of the Club techniques in my science classes, to constantly make the abstract concepts visual and concrete to the children. I use a password to focus the children before they enter the classroom. This password often involves using their hands or their whole bodies to act out the concept their lips are speaking. The use of passwords can be very diagnostic, with regard to identifying long-term memory problems, on-demand retrieval, or occupational therapy issues. However, their main benefit comes to the students as a boldface, underlined, italicized main idea indicator, which they will hear from each student in line, sometimes for 2 weeks.

For example, as I write this paragraph, I am teaching the difference between our earth's rotation and its revolution around the sun and how these motions create our days, seasons, and years. When the students give the password *rotate,* they create an "axis" by putting a finger on top of their head. Next, they tilt their bodies backward or forward at what they judge to be a 24 degree angle and start to spin. It's fun, and it reinforces one of the concepts I'm trying to teach.

Other influences from the Academic Club Methodology have included changing the way we do our Science Fairs. The Lower School Science Department puts on a Science Museum instead of a Fair. Our museum allows the students to study a topic in depth (in a way similar to a traditional science fair project) while keeping the emphasis on making the topic visually understandable. Last year, the students turned the science wing into a giant human body. You entered through the mouth (double doors) after walking down the red carpet (tongue, complete with display of taste buds and how they function). Once inside the mouth, a brain with firing synapses pulsed above you, while pullable teeth and free graham crackers (to help locate your salivary glands) were displayed. The entire digestive system was represented on one wall, while a side room contained a walk-through four-chambered heart and lungs. Visitors to this room followed the path of blood through the complete circuit, taking oxygenated blood from the lungs, depositing it in one of the extremities, and returning back via the heart to be exhaled. Another room contained a student-made video of the immune system, using a *Star Wars* theme that creatively personalized and made concrete a very complicated topic. Teaching science this way is very labor intensive, but it is rewarding beyond anything you can imagine.

6.   What do the students seem to enjoy most about their Academic Clubs?

Without a doubt, the thing the students enjoy the most (in my experience) is the sense of fun and freedom you develop in the Clubs. The students get to alter their identities. "Being" someone else allows them to take risks they might not ordinarily take or to engage in activities that their regular selves might think were "uncool." A shy, almost electively mute student, who was almost unable to speak in class due to his overwhelming difficulties with organizing language, was able to demonstrate his understanding of the Pandora's Box story during our hilarious reenactment of it. This student added laugh lines spontaneously because "Apollo" was doing the acting; he was not doing it.

My all-time favorite Summer Club has been the Pirates Club in which I was Blackbeard (in full pirate regalia, plus accent). We walked a plank to get onboard the Queen Ann's Revenge, got scurvy, went on raids for citrus fruit, and indulged in humorous elaborate rituals each morning to learn another set of phrases with double meanings (my favorite was "hit the deck"). For 50 minutes, they were proud and free pirates, and there was no formal reading or written math involved.

Besides being fun, Club teaches the students a lot of information. Often, it is rather sophisticated information presented in a very simple form. Our students with learning disabilities LOVE knowing this kind of stuff! One student became an expert at writing in hieroglyphics and achieved fame in her Brownies troop with this ability that none of her "regular" friends possessed. Another student, who had huge memory and articulation problems, was easily able to lead our Director on a tour of his room, showing her "the caduceus, my attribute of power." Using these vocabulary words appropriately came naturally to him because they had been learned in context, not as a lesson but as a normal part of his day. Needless to say, this young man felt justifiably proud of himself.

Finally, our students love their projects because they always have a purpose. When we study mummification, we create an entire mummy kit with everything the students need to conduct this most important of Egyptian ceremonies. In the process of creating the pieces, the students learn the mummification process. They learn the whole by assembling and playing with the parts. Then, they get to take the kit home and show off for their friends and relatives. When the students learn Roman numerals, they do it in the context of "Roman School," which is part of a 3-day "Day in the Life of a Roman Child" unit. The children "wake up" in a darkened room, eat bread and honey, and hurry off to school, where "Socrates, the Greek school master," teaches them on wax (modeling clay) tablets. They write with a stylus and erase using their fingers. So much more interesting than pencil and paper!

7. What's the most important advice you would give to a new Academic Club Leader?

I would offer five basic suggestions to a new Academic Club Leader. These are:

- Do your research thoroughly, before you do anything else.

- Believe in your character, and amass the props to help you.

- Think divergently, using all your talents.

- Don't be afraid to ask for help.

- Have fun, and don't be afraid to get a little silly.

Do your research thoroughly, before you do anything else. As a teacher, you are in the business of helping students to connect the dots, to erect schema, to fill in the blanks that can be daunting to anyone with part-to-whole concept problems. It is no good if you yourself have not connected the dots. When you thoroughly know your subject; you can focus the students on the main ideas; you can choose passwords, which summarize a concept well; and you can effectively plan your curriculum. In addition, if you are starting from scratch, you will have to plan and execute your room design and primary props. Not doing your research first is like setting out on a journey without money, gas, or a road map. Start early, take notes, make sketches, be prepared. It is more important than anything else.

Believe in your character, and amass the props to help you. As you are doing your research, you will encounter historical personalities who epitomize the time and place that you are studying. At some point, one of these will strike a chord within you (or else, one will become so obvious that you will have no choice but to choose him or her). Focus part of your study to relate as much as possible to the effect that character had on events or on how that character was affected by events. Learn as many personal idiosyncrasies about your character as possible, and incorporate them into your portrayal. If, for example, you are portraying Albert Einstein, and you discover that he hated socks, make sure you never wear socks (and make sure you tell the students why. Kids eat these details up). Go to thrift shops, yard sales, and dollar stores for costumes and props. If you can sew, you're set! If you can paint, you're really set!

Think divergently, using all your talents. There is no one right way to do a Club, as we have all found out. Each Club Leader brings his or her wealth of experiences, talents and techniques to the task. If you have "inherited" a Club, you might want to spend the first year using the existing curriculum, keeping the projects intact, until you find your own way. If you are starting from scratch, then you have the opportunity to create a fresh experience. Do not be afraid to use what you know best to enhance a solid curriculum. If all the other Club teachers are great artists, and you happen to excel in music, then by all means, create songs the students will love to sing that teach content in a different way. Then find someone who can help you with the art, which brings me to . . .

Don't be afraid to ask for help. When people find out what you are attempting, you will be surprised at the interest you will generate. Items will emerge from attics and basements, and colleagues will exhibit long-hidden talents, in the short-term start-up of a Club room. You may find a history buff who just happens to have the complete history of whatever you're working on right on his library shelf, gathering dust. Let people know what you're doing, and take all the help you can get!

Have fun, and don't be afraid to get a little silly. Once you've done your research, found your character, organized your activities, and gotten your room together, the curtain opens, and the play begins! Since this is as much improvisational theater as it is carefully scripted drama, anything can happen (and usually does). Once you're out there "on stage," ideas will creep into your mind that are so spontaneous that you may doubt their validity. For example, in our study of Egypt, we discuss the early burial monuments, called *mastabas.* Later, as we learn about the Step Pyramid, we find that it is basically six mastabas, in decreasing size, stacked on top of each other, creating a stairway for the pharaoh Djoser to ascend to the sun after his death. As I was demonstrating this, the song "One potato, two potato, three potato, four" came into my mind. I immediately realized I could use this to help the children remember 1) the word "mastaba" and 2) how many levels that Step Pyramid contains. I changed the words to: "One mastaba, two mastaba, three mastaba, four. Five mastaba, six mastaba, And there are no more." The students loved it and asked to sing it. We used our hands to stack the levels and had fun. If you're having fun, your kids probably are, too! That usually means they're learning.

URSULA MARCUM

B.A. Theater; M.F.A. Art; 3 years as a Club Leader

Academic Clubs taught: Gods Club (at the Baltimore Lab)

1.   What makes you enjoy being a Club Leader?

The most fulfilling thing about being a Club Leader is watching the children become enthusiastic about the material. Because the students in the Club classroom are involved in such a multisensory way, they become invested in their own learning. Seeing the students take off with an idea or concept never fails to excite me. I also enjoy my own continuing education in the subject areas of Ancient Egypt, Greece, and Rome, and I am constantly on the lookout for new resources.

2.   Describe the Academic Club activity that you are most proud of.

Something I created for Gods Club of which I am proud is the "Trojan War in a Box." With some assistance from my students, I created all of the main characters in the story of the Trojan War by making clothespin dolls. When we are studying Homer's *Odyssey,* I read small portions of the epic poem, but in addition, I tell the myth using the dolls, which I use like puppets. Along with the dolls, I crafted some miniature props and sets, and I begin the story with the Golden Apple and end with the Trojan Horse. The students can then use the puppets to retell the story, which is great fun for them and an excellent assessment tool for me.

3. What abstract concept did you translate into concrete practical activities?

In my first year as a Club Leader, bartering for goods in Ancient Egypt seemed to be a concept that most of the students easily understood. However, anytime I asked how an Ancient Egyptian procured something he needed, they would continue to say "money," or "gold," or "He bought it!" So, I made the Go to Market game. A very simple concept, really. I took a game they already knew—Go Fish—and altered the cards and the rules somewhat. First, using blank flash cards, I made a playing card deck. There were number cards and face cards, four of each, but no suits. I drew pictures of common Egyptian goods that were traded in the markets, such as papyrus, linen, and honey. I assigned lower numbers to more common goods, and the higher face cards were linked with rare items to help students understand the relative worth of the materials. Because they were familiar with Go Fish, they knew that they had to ask another player for a specific card. But in the Go to Market game, they had to trade a card in order to get a card (or cards) from the player. Not only did they become familiar with Egyptian goods, they quickly understood how bartering worked and that Ancient Egyptians did not use money to obtain them.

4. What materials or situation have you set up to produce exciting thinking?

Role-play helps students. It is a great way to get kids to begin to explore new ideas. In the course of studying three ancient cultures, many questions arise regarding who was in charge. Children are interested to know who was in power, how they got there, and how it worked. We did a role-play that explored monarchy, democracy, and a republic. Having individual children act out the roles of these different leaders and giving orders to the others students as they played the "citizens" made for a fascinating class. A classroom discussion ensued about the merits and disadvantages of each system. The children also took an active part as "directors" and gave advice to the student who was acting out the leadership role at the time.

5. How have you adapted the Academic Club Methodology to other teaching you have done?

Being a Club Leader has greatly influenced the way I teach my art classes. As the students build their core knowledge in the Club classroom, they are most excited when they can make connections to things they have already learned or have experienced personally. In art, I try to make comparisons to previous projects or artists discussed in class. More important, I try to provide supporting context for materials, methods, or artists. For example, if we are working with clay, we'll discuss where clay comes from first. During the course of the project, the students will have a chance to experiment with different methods and describe what method worked best for their piece. Finally, we may look at different styles by other artists—kids and grownups alike. Being a Club Leader has also taught me the importance of thematic learning. If I spend a whole year in my art classroom exploring ecosystems, the students are going to come away with a richer experience than if I teach individual projects that are in no way related to one another.

6. What do the students seem to enjoy most about their Academic Clubs?

The students become very involved in the myths and stories of these ancient cultures. They are fascinated by the escapades of the gods, goddesses, heroes, and heroines and often provide sound effects and character interpretation during the storytelling. The children take their costumes and assigned god or goddess roles very seriously.

7. What's the most important advice to give a new Club Leader?

Don't be afraid to say, "I don't know." This shows the students two important things. First, it assures them that it is okay if a person does not have all the answers. Also, it opens up opportunities to introduce your students to information-gathering techniques. If I don't know the answer to a query, I write it down on my "Find Out" list. Sometimes, I'll enlist the help of the children to help me look through books or at images to find the answer. On other occasions, I'll track down the answer myself and then share not only the information with the class but also the resources I used to find it. Don't be hard on yourself if you can't find the answer or could not answer the question in the first place. Remember that you are in the lifelong process of learning, too.

DONALD A. VICKS

B.A. Early Childhood Development; M.A. Special Education: Learning Disabilities; 21 years as a Club Leader

Academic Clubs taught: Knights and Ladies Club, Industrialists Club, Indian Club, Mark Twain Club, The Aristocrats Club, Carnival Club, Spy Central International Club, Oceanographers Club, Meteorologists Club, Railroad Club, Park Rangers Club, Canal Boatman Club, Sherlock Holmes Club, Frontier Club, King Arthur and the Round Table Club, Outer Space Club, Magic Carpet Club, Wild West Club.

1. What makes you enjoy being an Academic Club Leader?

I enjoy the challenge of setting up my room to establish the environment that reflects the period we are studying. I also enjoy researching the content and connecting the abstract concepts to the concrete activities and projects.

My teaching approach recognizes that all children can succeed in learning at some level; my challenge is to gauge where a student can begin and to design a program that will proceed from one achievable goal to the next. This individualized approach is the most successful when goals are well planned and the lessons are implemented in a highly structured way. This allows me the freedom to take an active role in my students' learning process and to build subsequent lessons based on what they have successfully learned. I also believe very strongly in positive reinforcement. A student's positive and appropriate behavior should be recognized and rewarded. In my Knights and Ladies Club, students earn token valuables representative of the Middle Ages, such as medallions, precious stones, and "rings of magic." Focusing on appropriate behavior not only reinforces a student's desire to achieve and learn but also reinforces his or her feeling of accomplishment and, more importantly, of self-worth.

2. Describe the Academic Club activity that you are most proud of.

One activity that I presented to Knights and Ladies Club that combines the historical information with creative "hands-on experience" was a lesson on the Bayeux Tapestry. My first step is to research and acquire information from several resources for a plan of implementation so that the content would be exciting and motivating to a 10-year-old. I want my students to attend to the task for the required time frame and to leave wanting to know more information. To accomplish this, the class is presented a challenge. The students are asked to compare a present event to a past one, to make the past seem real.

My challenge is to set up a situation where one student promises two other students the same thing. For example, one classmate promised another student a ticket to go see a popular movie after school if he could use the student's computer game at lunch. Later the same day, the same student with the single ticket offered it to a second student if that person would give him a free homework pass. That afternoon, the student with the ticket leaves early to go home. The challenge is, which student gets the movie ticket? The discussion that follows is interesting and heavily debated, but is eventually stopped and past events are now introduced.

In England, King Edward the Confessor had done something similar. He gave England to both Harold (a Saxon) and to Duke William (a Norman). The results ended in a famous war (Battle of 1066, the Battle of Hastings, the Norman Conquest) that lasted just one day. The class had a mock battle, half being Norman (under Duke William) and the other half was Saxon (under King Harold), and the result was found on the Bayeux Tapestry. I use a replica of the Tapestry that is 31 feet long to show important events that took place, such as Edward the Confessor in Westminster promising the crown to Harold then later to William when he captured Harold. Also included on the tapestry is a scene in which Duke William sees Halley's Comet, crosses the English Channel, and meets Harold at the Battle of Hastings. Harold dies with an arrow in the eye. The students look for facts and get very excited as they find those events.

At this time, the actual length of the real tapestry is told—231 feet. I bring out two rolls of toilet paper and suggest we measure to see how long it really is. To keep the students attentive, I use humor whenever possible, and I suggest we use my foot to measure out the toilet paper because my foot is 12 inches—making me a good ruler!

A frequent comment afterward is, "Oh, I get it—a ruler you measure with and a ruler that is like Lord Don."

The final step of the activity is to have each student make a 3-foot replica of the Tapestry on a linen strip, including a beginning (Edward promising England to both men then his death), a middle (Duke William seeing Halley's Comet then crossing the English Channel), and an end (Battle of Hastings, including King Harold getting shot in the eye). The class ends with a discussion of similarities and differences between the results of the two situations: one from the past (Edward the Confessor with Harold and William) and the present (the person with the one ticket who promised it to two friends).

3.   What abstract concept did you translate into concrete practical activities?

The concept of guilt and innocence can be hard for some students to grasp. In Knights and Ladies Club, we compared the Ordeal by Fire to the later trial system, which was introduced by King Henry II. Under the Ordeal system, a person was subjected to a physical event. If a physical reaction was visible, they were guilty. If none was present, they were innocent. To demonstrate this, I set up a mock fire in the center of the room, placed a brick in the fire, and then grabbed it. I bandaged my hands, and then turned off the lights (to show the passage of a night). When the lights went on, the students unwrapped my hands and saw "blisters," which I had put on with red ink before class. When the class saw the blisters, they yelled out, "You're guilty!"

Later, we discussed the probability of someone being able to pick up a hot brick and not get blisters. The students quickly responded that everyone would get blisters, and the system wasn't fair because no one could ever be innocent. They could see that Henry's trial by jury system was fairer.

4.   What materials or situation that you set up produced some very exciting thinking?

In Industrialists Club, while we were studying Henry Ford, the students were reenacting the moving assembly line that Ford invented. The students were divided into four categories with an equal number of students in each group: painting, constructing, inspecting, and shipping. As the students worked together on the moving assembly line, some activities, like the chassis building, took a lot longer than the other divisions. Several students realized that they should reallocate their human resources to increase productivity. They realized they needed fewer inspectors and more chassis builders.

The initial reaction among the chassis workers was relief because they had trouble maintaining the fast pace of the other divisions. Once the students' jobs were reassigned, they could see that "equal" is not necessarily "better." Sometimes, in order to achieve "quality," which is most important, people or things are not divided equally.

5. How have you translated the Academic Club Methodology to other teaching you have done?

Another Academic Club approach works extremely well in my geography classes to teach abstract concepts in a concrete way. While teaching geography, many students have difficulty understanding the concept of what the differences are between a city, state, country, or continent. I had the idea for a visual representation of the proportions of a city to a continent. I used different size boxes to represent a city (smallest box), which was placed into a larger box labeled "state," which was placed in a "country" box, then placed into the largest box called "continent" (see Chapter 2). Later, students made their own set of boxes and several suggestions were made about the next step—making smaller boxes for "town", then a smaller one inside labeled "neighborhoods" or making larger boxes for "Earth," then "planets," and "universe."

6. What do the students seem to enjoy most about their Academic Clubs?

Students seem to enjoy the period costumes, role-playing, constructing models of historical sites, and recreating works of art that represent important historic events and ideas. Playing academic review games to show how much historical information they have retained is also fun for the students. I use board games (Castle Conquest, in which you move through a medieval countryside answering questions), card games (Medieval Hierarchy, which is played like war and teaches the feudal system), and visual discrimination games (Live or Die, a hunting game in which the students must match the footprint to the animal and track it down).

7. What's the most important advice you would give to new Academic Club Leader?

For a new Academic Club Leader I would emphasize that students learn in a variety of ways. The first step in helping the students is to make sure that concepts have been presented through many different modalities. If a child continues to have difficulty, consider breaking down the task or activity into manageable parts. Being a Club Leader has been extremely rewarding because I have been able to experience the results of the Academic Club Methodology of teaching.

NOEL BICKNELL

B.A. Coordinated Studies with focus on Urban Studies/Visual Arts; M.A. Special Education: Learning Disabilities; 5 years as a Club Leader

Academic Clubs taught: Renaissance Club, The City of the Future Club, Polar Expeditionaries Club

1. What makes you enjoy being an Academic Club Leader?

The Academic Club Methodology is a celebration of a child's intellectual strengths. This makes the Academic Club an oasis in the student's day—a place that allows the child to exhale and enjoy academic success on her own terms. The greatest joy is seeing children gain new knowledge, make connections, and discover how to learn on their own terms.

But the question is telling, too. There is a central expectation for Club Leaders to enjoy the art of teaching. This sort of teaching is meant to be fun by design. It is the central variable in the formula. The joy of curiosity—investigating, reflecting, discovering, researching, experimenting, creating—it is what creates lifelong learners. You cannot tell someone to be curious. You have to model curiosity and nurture it in the student. The state of curiosity is purely intrinsic. If I'm in the middle of a project and I'm feeling no joy, that's my first warning sign that the project needs an overhaul. If I'm bored, frustrated, distracted, or otherwise joyless, it's pretty much guaranteed my students are, too. It's time to haul out plan B, C, or D.

2.   Describe the Academic Club activity that you are most proud of.

The fresco-painting unit has been a great success. Students study the early Renaissance fresco artist Giotto while painting a large fresco using the same techniques used in the Renaissance—gathering pigments, grinding pigments into paint, preparing the wall surface, drawing a cartoon, transferring the image by pouncing, working in day sections, mixing colors, and so forth. All the while, they are actively discussing which technique worked best, how Giotto organized his assistants, what to do next, what's working, what failed, and how we know if we're finished.

This is the first major project or commission of the year so it makes for a great vehicle to teach the culture and economics of the Renaissance life such as guild structure, organization of city-states, and geography of Europe. Study of Giotto's frescos is also an excellent way to introduce humanism—simply by looking at the emotion-filled faces in his frescoes the students can see the increased importance of earthly human experience. Along with the project, I use a custom-designed board game that reviews the facts of the unit and encourages the making of historical connections.

With this group of students, it is just not enough to describe a particular process and expect them to understand, remember, and make future connections. For these students to learn, they need to partake in the process. Every year, I'm surprised by the new solutions the students find during the fresco project. Providing the intellectual space for divergent thinking really pays off when teaching atypical thinkers.

3.   What abstract concept did you translate into concrete practical activities?

During the first week of class, the students of the Renaissance Club each make their own guild hat, which they wear throughout the year while in this Club. This is a symbol of their knowledge and status as expert artists as well as Renaissance fashion. Using needle and thread, each student measures, cuts, and sews a felt hat custom sized to his or her head.

This project first started out as a diagnostic tool for me to see which students had weak eye–hand or attention skills. But while making the hats, I realized that I could teach the students how to use π (2 x radius x 3.14 = circumference) when they are cutting their material. They needed to cut the sidepiece of fabric so that it matched the circular top piece of the hat. They could use the formula for π to save time and make a better-looking hat. I told them that there was a relationship between the circumference of their heads and the diameter of the circle on the top that remained the same no matter whose head we measured. We tested it out and found that 3.14 worked for everyone in the room. I also researched the history of π and taught them how π was invented, lost, and rediscovered throughout history. I taught them that as far as we know Egyptians were the first people to use π in mathematics. This, in turn, provided an opportunity to introduce how many lost ideas rediscovered in the Renaissance returned to Europe via Arabic culture.

This example also illustrates the importance of starting with quality projects and creating connections to abstract concepts rather than working from abstract to concrete. Get students engaged and curious with an authentic process and only then build in the abstract concepts with authentic connections. This is the reason why most canned story problems in math class never make the connection with students—the story problems are reversed engineered to fit the abstract concept being taught. By contrast, a dramatic framework allows me to work from the other direction. The theme of the Club makes my students want to make a great guild hat. The difficulty of correctly measuring the different pieces of cloth for the hat makes the students look for an easier way. When I show them how to use π, suddenly π is the *easy solution* they've been looking for—not a *difficult problem* to be solved. Using π in this context makes sense to them.

4. **What materials or situation that you set up produced some very exciting thinking?**

For every major project we complete in the Renaissance Club, I have the students reflect by brainstorming all the steps they completed to get to the final product. I write down all the steps they can think of in the order that they give regardless of sequence. Then, I ask each student to draw a picture of one of the steps on a card. Once all the steps are drawn, I give the stack of cards to the group and them cooperatively sort out the correct sequence from beginning to end. They are all very invested because they want their own ideas or drawing to be placed in correct order. Standing back, watching them figure out this puzzle—listening to them sort out what came first, next, and last—is very informing and produces the best language use by the group of any activity.

5. **How have you translated the Academic Club Methodology to other teaching you have done?**

I also teach general music to students with learning disabilities. For part of the year, I change my music class into Jazz Club. Each student becomes a famous jazz musician, and I become the consummate jazz leader, Duke Ellington. We study the biography of each musician, listen to jazz, identify common musical forms used in jazz, and learn to improvise over the blues progression. We talk about the times in which jazz grew up, the migration of African Americans from the rural south into the northern cities, and the civil rights movement. I use passwords to build the vocabulary and review key facts and connections. I have students wear hats from the 1940s and 1950s. One could also create a similar Club based on classical musicians.

6. What do the students seem to enjoy most about their Academic Clubs?

I think students enjoy the expert knowledge they master about an era or subject. The detailed biographical information they learn about their assumed characters gives many of them their first taste of subject mastery—I'm thinking here of the Gods Club. These students come to my Club 2 years later still knowing all the Greek and Roman gods and myths cold. They're able to spot Greek and Roman symbols and references in Renaissance art in a glance. This understanding of expert knowledge is the foundation for interest in future learning and lifelong learning in general. There is joy in being an expert, no matter what age we are.

7. What's the most important advice you could give to a new Academic Club Leader?

Devour the history of your time period or your subject. Read both primary texts about your subject and the very general, watered-down versions, too. Both will inform you on how deep to go into a subject. More important is to maintain the dramatic framework of the Club. Children have amazingly flexible and fertile imaginations. You don't have to be a master thespian to bring drama to a classroom, but you do have to be willing to put yourself out there and risk being a fool in front of children. Take being a fool seriously! When we ask children to try learning again after many of them have failed, we are asking them to take enormous emotional risks. The more you can model educational risk-taking, curiosity, and lifelong learning, the greater the chance your students will join you.

KELLY McVEARRY

B.A. English Literature and Studio Art; M.A. Special Education: Learning Disabilities; 4 years as a Club Leader

Academic Clubs taught: Renaissance Councillors

1. What makes you enjoy being a Club Leader?

Is there any other job that allows you to wear a bejeweled purple cape to work? The Academic Club Methodology subverts the commonplace terms "teacher" and "student"—and the drudgery they connote—by establishing dramatic roles that transport you to another world, another era. In Renaissance Club, for example, every day began when Ghiberti's *Gates of Paradise* parted and I, posing in costume as Lorenzo di Medici, emerged to greet students with a smile and flamboyant "Buon giorno!" The students, waiting in line outside of these gilded "bronze" doors, reciprocate with equal aplomb: "Buon giorno, il Magnifico!" In the hallway, a student might be a hyperactive 10-year-old who masks his reading struggles or who can't seem to memorize his multiplication tables; inside the Club, he is transformed. He becomes Michelangelo, the brilliant body builder of the Renaissance who can sculpt marble as though it were butter; the scientist who dissects corpses to understand the architecture of human life; and the poet who questions his society in verse. By the end of the year, "Michelangelo" possesses deep understanding of how "his" ideas and the ideas of his illustrious cohort—classmates Leonardo da Vinci, Brunelleschi, Giotto, and so forth— influenced civilization.

In an Academic Club, every day is as exciting as a field trip day, and I believe that the cornerstone for this excitement is the unconventional, dramatic learning relationships that are established for Club Leader and students. By letting "teacher" and "student" assume identities of famous people, they work side by side as "experts" who recreate the landmarks and masterpieces that illustrate history books . . . the history books that most students read rather than experience. Despite the open climate of inquiry, freedom to make decisions, and what may at times appear to be hectic shuffling of materials in a Club, creative fervor and order prevail. Authority remains intact because it, too, is dramatic, for it derives from history (Lorenzo de Medici is the wealthiest man in the world and, thus, has the power to commission you to create a great work of art) and that era's context (i.e., we must comport ourselves like a Renaissance humanist), rather than schoolmarmish "rules."

Being a Club Leader lets you treat a room with four walls like a theater set, rather than a classroom. When you construct a learning environment that simulates the era, region, or place you are studying, you achieve two goals critical for the kind of learning that endures: 1) a "classroom" becomes a tantalizing place where children *want* to be, rather than *have to* be; and 2) classroom design reinforces the class content. As the Club Leader for Renaissance Club, for instance, I designed a classroom that would mentally transport students to 15th-century Florence, Italy, where the Italian Renaissance was born. Lattice hangs from the ceiling, wrapped in grape vines and dangling plastic grapes, like a sunny vineyard. A mural of the Duomo Santa Maria del Fiore covers one wall, adjacent to a large linear perspective mural composed by a student. In one corner is the student-engineered model of the Palazzo Vecchio.

When visitors stop by, the Club Leader can ask students questions that provide an opportunity for them to show off how much they have learned. Open-ended questions often reveal sophisticated answers: "What is so special about that building you guys constructed?" One student might say, "The Palazzo Vecchio is like our own U.S. Capitol in some ways—the architecture might look different, but the Palazzo Vecchio was a center of legislation during the Renaissance because it is where elected councilors assembled to vote on issues that affect the citizens of Florence." And another student will, no doubt, interject commentary that this departs from the governance practiced by the monarchs who prevailed in the previous era, the Middle Ages, which the students experienced in Knights and Ladies Club, the Club they experience before Renaissance Club.

2. Describe the Academic Club activity that you are most proud of.

There is no way I can choose one. Impossible!!!! I have identified and outlined four.

Theme 1: In the Footsteps of Michelangelo: Rendering the David, Understanding Humanism

- **Project:** Sculpting Michelangelo's David, using authentic chisels and rasps, from a block of simulated marble that the student makes him- or herself

- **Costume:** Newspaper hats, as still worn in Carrara

- **Relevant literature:** Vasari's *Lives of the Artists*; Michelangelo's poetry; *David and Goliath* (Bennett edition); Irving Stone's *The Agony and the Ecstasy* (segments); Stanza from Dante's *Inferno*: On Carrara and the white marble embedded in the Alps

- **Language and concepts:** Humanism; Contrapposto; Di polvere di marmo (covered with marble dust)

- **Other media:** Film: *The Agony and the Ecstasy,* first half

Theme 2: In the Footsteps of Curiosity: Leonardo's Ornithopter and Galileo's Moons and Prison

- **Project:** Life-size model of an ornithopter

- **Costume:** Red "humanist hat"

- **Relevant literature:** Peter Sis's *Starry Messenger*; Leonardo's Codices, especially the *Codex Leicester*; *The Washington Post* article on Sotheby's auction/Bill Gates's purchase of Codex Leicester; Galileo's journals; Inventions of Leonardo

- **Language and concepts:** Ornithopter; Ornithologist; Codex; Mass versus volume; Simple machines (taught with Leonardo's sketches)

- **Other media:** Film: *National Gallery video on Leonardo's youth;* Movie: first 10 minutes of *Hudson Hawk;* Alan Alda educational film: *Science Italian Style: Fixing the Leaning Tower of Pisa;* Music: Indigo Girls' *Galileo*

Theme 3: 87 Feet High and On Your Back: Patronage, Popes, and Michelangelo's Capella Sistina

- **Project:** Receiving a commission from Pope Julius II and replicating a panel from the ceiling of the Sistine Chapel while on scaffolding

- **Costume:** Red "humanist hat"

- **Relevant literature:** Michelangelo's sonnet about Pope Julius II; Michelangelo's sonnet about his back pains and the "goiter on his neck"; Vasari's *Lives of the Artists*; Cennino Cennini's *Craftsman's Handbook* (1437); Segments of Irving Stone's *The Agony and the Ecstasy*

- **Language and concepts:** Patronage; Commission; Cartone ("car-tone-ay"); Pounce

- **Other media:** Film: *Persegeti's restoration video*; National Geographic Magazine's *Sistine Chapel Restoration Issue*; Film: Second half of *The Agony and the Ecstasy*

Theme 4: Down the River with Dante Alighieri: Contemporary Values, a Trip Through His Inferno, and How the Tuscan Dialect Became the National Language . . . "Italian"

- **Project:** Tactile, "Portable" Inferno Red Hat

- **Relevant literature:** Dante's *Inferno*, Musa Translation; Biography from Dante's home in Florence

- **Language and concepts:** Contrapasso; Incunable; Vernacular; Fiction versus non-fiction; Lake Cocytus and inhabitants; Guelphs and Ghibellines (Democrats and Republicans . . . sort of); The Football Stadium Metaphor

- **Other media:** Audio recording of Dante's *Inferno*

3.   What abstract concept did you translate into concrete, practical activities?

I will never forget my first true challenge as a Club Leader: How can I teach the concept of Humanism—the concept on which the Italian Renaissance pivots—in a way that promotes deep, fluent understanding? I knew that I needed to convert this abstract idea into concrete terms, but I also predicted that I would need multiple concrete examples so that I could really communicate with *each learner.*

The vehicle I chose to teach this concept was making a sculpture, in simulated marble, of Michelangelo's *David.* The password *contrapposto* was a starting point: in order to enter the Club room during this unit, students said this word while shaking their hips, shifting their weight back and forth, in time with each syllable. This fancy word was easier to learn when each sound was paired with a body movement. The word's meaning—that is, "the weight-shift stance" that describes the pose of sculptures like the *David* which embody man as physically and mentally powerful—is taught through body movement, for you are shifting your weight, acting out the word's definition, as you say each syllable. The David's contraposto stance was natural and confident, a physical example of humanism. But this was merely a starting point . . .

Even a special behavior management system was developed to teach this concept. On one wall in the Club room, the heading of a poster read: "Don't be Savonarola'd!" Laminated cartoon drawings of paintings burning in bonfires are velcroed under this ominous heading. The symbols served as both a nonverbal behavior management system and a reinforcement of a critical event and theme from the Italian Renaissance. As a humanist, you are indeed opposed to censorship, and you are amazed that the religious zealot Savonarola convinced Botticelli, among others, to cast some of his paintings into these fires in the Florentine streets because they glorified man and mythological figures rather than God and religious figures. You know Savonarola merely filled the leadership vacuum left by Lorenzo de Medici's untimely death in

1492; more importantly, you know that Savonarola's zealotry was short-lived, for he died by his own device, burned at the stake in the public square before the Palazzo Vecchio. As a humanist, you dread censorship; your behavior is exemplary because you do not want to receive one of these tokens and be *Savanarola'd*.

4. What materials or situation have you set up to produce exciting thinking?

Authentic methods and materials contribute to recreation of history promoted by the Academic Club Methodology. In Renaissance Club, for example, through a window, the view was once a brick wall. Students transformed it into a fresco using the exact same methods as Giotto: by applying plaster to the wall with a trowel, making paint by grinding pigment and adding egg whites, and transferring your cartoon—*cartone* (car-tone-ay)—by pouncing this full-size line drawing, poked with holes that make a connect-the-dots drawing with pouches of charcoal dust. Then, you learn to be an art sleuth and scholar: You look at a slide of one of Giotto's frescoes, and you count each section—sections that look like puzzle pieces as demarcated by plaster ridges. "These are *journada lines*," you learn, "and a *journada* means one day's worth of work. You had to apply the paint to wet plaster, so you could only apply as much plaster as you could paint that day, before the plaster dries. So, if I count 27 puzzle pieces, I know it took about 27 days for Giotto to make the fresco."

By acting out the emotion in the people Giotto portrayed in "Lamentation of Christ," students learned about much more than the fresco painting process—they learned that emotion marked the departure from the somber art of the Middle Ages. The work is physically hard and mentally sophisticated; indeed, it is college-level content. Does this engage the 10-year-olds? Yes! They were so engaged that they became activists. A month after the fresco was completed, an earthquake ravaged Assisi, Italy, and on the cover of *The New York Times* was a color photograph of a crumbled fresco face, pieced together on the ground, painted centuries before by Giotto. The students were outraged and initiated a poster campaign and bake sale to raise money to send to Italy for the restoration fund!

6. What do students seem to enjoy most about their Academic Clubs?

Inclusiveness: Physically entering a Club classroom gives students a sense of inclusion, of being "in," and the ritualistic framework of the Academic Clubs reinforces this sense of belonging. For instance, in Renaissance Club, the first task is to *get into costume*—students place red hats like the hats worn by many Florentine scholars on their heads. Then, students assume their places around a gilded and marble table as *members of Lorenzo's council*. In unison and with loud enthusiasm, students *chant an "opening ritual"* that begins each day: "From the darkness of the Middle Ages, comes the light of the Renaissance to bring the Modern World!" These rituals also serve as focusing agents, signaling to the child that it is time to channel one's energy into the activity of the day, whether it is sculpting Michelangelo's David or painting the ceiling of the Sistine Chapel.

Academic games: Teacher-made games played a significant role in Renaissance Club, and each unit had its own game designed to present or review the unit's information while developing a more general academic skill. For instance, a simple game like "Linear Perspective Tic-Tac-Toe" taught the difficult skill of articulating directions (horizontal, diagonal, vertical) that is essential to mastering the drawing technique of linear perspective. "Duomo" and "Codex"—illustrated bingo-like games—taught the complicated vocabulary of Renaissance architecture and Leonardo's machine parts, respectively, while it also developed graphing skills. One particularly interactive game was the "Sotheby's Art Auction" game. By requiring the students to categorize masterpieces in terms of art form (sculpture, painting, drawing, or sculpture), medium (e.g., oil on canvas, stone), and time period (before, during, or after the Renaissance), it enabled the students to discuss art using sophisticated, systematic language. In addition to developing these expressive language skills, this game honed their deductive reasoning skills: art was auctioned from all historical periods, so to correctly categorize the work, students had to apply their knowledge of Pre-Renaissance and Renaissance materials, techniques, and subject matter to each item for auction.

7. What's the most important advice to give a new Club Leader?

- Construct a *classroom environment* that simulates another world—truly pretend that you are a set designer for theater production, consult with artistic friends, and—though this may sound horribly practical—invest in a staple gun, a glue gun, and a jigsaw (electric powertool), and make 4' x 8' sheets of plywood your friend.

- Design *teacher-made games* that make mastery of Club content fun, offer diagnostic clues about student comprehension to teachers, and cultivate critical thinking skills. Investing time and creativity in these games is essential!

- Don't be afraid to be silly. When you use drama as a vehicle for learning, it endures! You must get into character as a Club Leader (e.g., Lorenzo de Medici) so that students will also get into character.

- Using authentic and novel materials to learn content. Art makes a scaffold that allows deep comprehension of the subject you are teaching.

- Immerse yourself in your Club theme—learn to research well and seek out original, landmark documents from the era you are teaching. Do not rely on watered-down textbook information or children's books. Children like being treated like adults, and your job is to distill what is essential from sophisticated information.

GRAHAM HOUGHTON

B.A. Fine Arts; M.A. Special Education: Learning Disabilities; 4 years as a Club Leader

Academic Clubs taught: Museum Club, Industrialists Club, Alchemists Club

1. What makes you enjoy being an Academic Club Leader?

From the first moment the child enters the Club Room (through the wonderful, theme-oriented doorway) he feels like he is part of—and belongs to—some special place. As the Club Leader, I build on that feeling of ownership. Incorporating art, drama, energy, and concrete hands-on projects, the Club really addresses—and teaches to—the child's strengths. Personally, being a Club Leader has been the most creative and rewarding employment to date.

2. Describe the Academic Club activity that you are most proud of.

This may sound like a cop-out coming from the Museum Club Leader, but creating a Museum of objects that were assembled by students 10- and 11-years-old and represented time and the major civilizations dating from the Old Stone Age is something I am proud of. Each unit stood by its own, and, collectively, the Museum was an academic showcase of the accomplishments of students with learning disabilities who felt incredibly able when they saw the expressions of those who visited the Club—adult and child alike.

3. What abstract concept did you translate into concrete practical activities?

The most abstract concept addressed in Museum Club is time. Thousands of years are covered in a 181-day school year. The students' work is compared and contrasted to work from the previous unit during Critiques. Students see the development and evolution of housing, monuments, structures, governments, religion, culture, economy, and so forth over time. Students compare the early shelters and cave dwellings to Mesopotamian mud and straw dwellings. Then, the Egyptians build with stone. Greeks use stone and marble, and domiciles become elaborate and practical. The Romans use concrete to make aqueducts and domes. Elaborate cathedrals replace temples in the Middle Ages, and the Duomo is an architectural wonder. Each unit centers around an important structure that will later appear in the art history texts used in college. I know I never had even a basic grasp of time and its many civilizations until college . . . and I had what is considered an excellent education.

4. What materials or situation that you set up produced some very exciting thinking?

I had tried an activity in which students did cave paintings on rocks approximately 8″ x 5″. The students painted with sticks and their hands. They used only yellow, red, and black paint. The benefit of the lesson was that they could each take something home, but cave paintings are large, and they were ceremonial—a real experience. So, we cleared a wall, lit some incense, lit some candles, dimmed the lights, and made a "real" 7′ x 8′ cave painting. It had a much more significant impact on the class. Curators sprayed paint, used sticks (burned the ends and drew like charcoal), and put their handprints on as signatures. The images were animals and the stick-figure hunters in the foreground. What's great about it, too, is that cave paintings are not particularly sophisticated, so even the less-talented Curators could make exciting contributions to the work. It stayed up all year. The students retained the magic and symbolism.

5. **How have you translated the Academic Club Methodology to other teaching you have done?**

Generally, creating some level of ownership in the class can be crucial. Also, I continue to make board games to teach concepts and content that is otherwise "boring" and paper and pencil oriented. Passwords are fun. In short, learning needs to be fun, concrete, hands-on, dramatic, and visual.

6. **What do the students seem to enjoy most about their Academic Clubs?**

Students most enjoy projects, the membership, the structure, the creativity, the drama, the imagination, the multimedia, the positive behavior management, sharing their successes with visitors, and ultimately, the amount that they *learn*.

7. **What's the most important advice you would give to a new Academic Club Leader?**

Have fun, try new ideas, and take cues from the students. Make it real and exciting. It's got to be a magical place . . . like a tree fort or something. My experience has been that children's eyes light up when the teacher has made a game and uses art. Don't conform. Take full advantage of the opportunity to bring experiential learning into the classroom.

SARAH LOWENBERG

B.A. Fine Arts; M.A. Special Education: Learning Disabilities; 2 years as a Club Leader

Academic Clubs taught: Museum Club, Peggy Guggenheim's Venice Art Club

1. **What makes you enjoy being an Academic Club Leader?**

As the Director of The Lab School Museum Club, I sit in my work room waiting for "my staff to arrive." I have called them all to this meeting to discuss our next assignment, to put together an exhibit on the ancient civilizations of Mesopotamia. "My staff," who are my students, are all experts in their fields, on loan from various museums throughout Washington, D.C. They include the curator from the Corcoran Gallery of Art, the exhibit designer from the American History Museum, the preparator from the Arthur M. Sackler Gallery, and many others. They will use their expertise to recreate artifacts, research historical facts, design the exhibit space, and produce educational materials in preparation for the opening of the exhibit. There's a lot of work to be done, but what a lot of fun to be had at the same time!

For children with learning disabilities, the Academic Club Methodology is the perfect vehicle for learning historical content. By using many different creative methods from recreating fresco painting found in the Minoan Palace of Knosses, to building replicas of ceramic votive fragiles from the Mesopotamian city of Ur, to rebuilding and painting a section of the beautiful glazed brick Ishtar Gate of Babylon, the students are acquiring important vocabulary, artistic skills, and historical content through visual, auditory, and kinesthetic methods that are both stimulating and fun. They become completely immersed in their roles as museum experts and take very seriously their duties and the deadlines for getting their exhibit completed by the much antic-ipated opening date.

As an artist, my joy comes from not only teaching the art techniques to my students but seeing these methods of expression become vehicles for the children to learn content that might otherwise be impossible to learn through traditional ways.

By the time "my staff" and I have completed our first exhibit, the exhibit designers have planned where each artifact will be placed, the exhibit artists have painted the props and background scenery, the archivist will have researched the history behind the pieces, the development coordinator will have produced informational brochures to hand out to our visitors, and the curator will have coordinated everyone's efforts to ensure that the exhibit is a success.

As this exhibit comes to a close, we begin planning and researching our next excit-ing assignment—an exhibit about the five main religions throughout our world. From there, we will move on to create an exhibit about ancient China and last, but not least, finish the year with an exhibit of the adventures and discoveries of some of the world's most famous explorers.

2.   Describe the Academic Club activity that you are most proud of.

As part of our Mesopotamian Exhibit, which involved the ancient Minoan civilization from the island of Crete, "my staff" and I recreated a beautiful fresco discovered at the palace of Knosses. The Minoan artists were renowned for their bold, beautiful use of color and their exquisite paintings depicting scenes from nature and the rituals of their people.

The people of Crete worshipped among many idols, the bull, for its strength and pow-erful stature. They performed several rituals, one such was called "Bull Leaping." Young athletes tried to grab a hold of a charging bull's horns, flip over his head, land on his back, and by flipping again leap off of the bull and land safely on the ground. Instead of reproducing a painting of this fresco, we produced our own version by cre-ating a painted paper collage. This technique involved several different steps and jobs which utilized each student's individual strengths and interests. The students were presented with many different organizational and sequencing problems to solve from planning the space on the board, making lists of colors and patterns needed, mixing paint, tearing paper, and applying the pieces with papier-mâché "goop."

At the same time, our "research staff" was looking up information on the Minoan Civ-ilization to include in the exhibit. The end result was a beautiful piece of artwork that the students are extremely proud of and historical content that they will carry with them forever.

3.   What abstract concept did you translate into concrete, practical activities?

The religion of ancient Mesopotamia is the oldest of which we have written records. The Mesopotamian view of the universe, which they called heaven-earth, consisted of the earth, which they believed to be a flat disk surrounded by a large hollow space enclosed in the overarching heaven. They believed that the universe was run by "unseeable," boundlessly powerful and immortal gods. Man, they were convinced, was fashioned of clay and created for one purpose only, to serve the gods by supplying them with food and shelter.

The Mesopotamians believed that in order to achieve a long and prosperous life, constant prayers to the gods were imperative. But such constant devotion was often impractical. To solve this problem, stone praying statues, or votive figures, were created as stand-ins and left in front of the altars. The important concept of symbolism, of these figures representing people and their devotion to their gods, was something that I felt needed a concrete activity to help make it more understandable for my students. Employing clay made the concept more real for my students. Using clay, each of my students created their own votive figures. Using rolled coils of clay, they formed the bodies on a cone shaped armature, then added the head, shoulders, and arms. I asked them to follow certain guidelines, such as large gazing eyes and folded hands expressing deep religious conviction. They were free to be creative with the clothing and hair. The votive figures are magnificent and help solidify an important concept.

4. What materials or situations that you set up produced some very exciting thinking?

According to Greek legend, King Minos was the ruler of the Minoan Civilization on the island of Crete. He received a gift of a beautiful bull for sacrifice to Poseidon, the great god of the sea, but his wife liked the bull so much that Minos decided to keep it. Poseidon was furious and as an act of revenge made Minos's wife give birth to a monstrous half-human, half-bull. This monster was called Minotaur, which means "Minos's Bull." The king kept the Minotaur in a huge indoor maze called a labyrinth, which he built under his palace. Every 9 years, the Minotaur received a sacrifice of seven boys and seven girls from Athens. This entire legend is known as Theseus and the Minotaur, after the young prince who finally slays the monster.

After reading this legend, we spent some time looking at pictures of various types of mazes and labyrinths that have been built throughout the world. The students had very interesting lively discussions about the various sizes, shapes, and materials used in mazes and advantages and disadvantages of each type.

As a group they decided that they would all like to try out their own ideas at building "the perfect maze." The students began by making several design sketches, using books and web sites for inspiration. This type of project is very diagnostic with regard to fine motor skills, spatial planning, organizational skills, visual memory, and problem solving. The students often used their own interests as the theme for their labyrinths. They ranged from a cross-country jumping course to the inside of an iMac computer, to the coral reefs at the bottom of the ocean. The unique ideas that the students developed were a testament to their creativity. I was also pleased to see them helping each other solve problems, offering advice, and trying out each other's mazes.

5. How have you translated the Academic Club Methodology to other teaching you have done?

I teach art to elementary and intermediate students during the school year as well as a Club. This year we have been focusing on specific holidays that are celebrated in other countries throughout the world. The Chinese New Year was a particularly successful project that we recently completed. The art projects that we completed with the students visually reinforced the content knowledge that was also being taught. As they were creating papier-mâché masks that depicted the animals from the Chinese zodiac, they were also learning about Chinese culture through stories told by an older student who had visited China many times with her father.

Characters from the Chinese alphabet were taught through the use of calligraphy painting. We built a huge Chinese dragon that needed many students underneath it to make its colorful body wriggle its way throughout the halls of the school. The students also used the masks that they made to act out their specific animal's movements and sounds as we had a huge parade outside the school. As in the Club that I teach, I try to use as many visual, kinesthetic, and auditory ways I can think of to reinforce a specific topic. The culminating activity for Chinese New Year was a banquet of many different Chinese dishes and a tea ceremony using ceramic teacups that the students built by hand and glazed with beautiful Chinese characters. The Academic Club Methodology immerses the student completely in a topic and was a perfect vehicle for bringing the Chinese culture alive for my students.

6. What do the students seem to enjoy most about their Academic Clubs?

The best part of being in a Club is walking into the room and becoming a completely different person. It's certainly not a typical classroom setting. In our case, it's the workroom of a museum, full of artifacts from ancient civilizations from all over the world. The students take ownership of their jobs and responsibilities and realize the fact that we are all important members of a team and must work together as a group to ensure that our exhibits will open on schedule and be successful.

As the students "act out" their jobs, it's great to see their "alternate personalities" emerge as they become the "exhibit designer" who creates the floor plans for the show or the "education coordinator" who plans brochures and lectures. The beauty of the Clubs is that the students become so involved in acting out the password to enter the room and the artifacts that they are creating that they don't even realize how much they are learning.

7. What is the most important advice you would give to a new Academic Club Leader?

My advice to a new Club Leader would be first of all to relax and have faith in yourself, even if you are feeling totally overwhelmed. Don't worry if you haven't learned everything there is to know about your subject matter. Teaching a Club is a learning experience that can be compared to the growth of a young tree; every year you will grow stronger and more knowledgeable, and every year you will add new branches full of ideas and projects. Keep copious notes about what activities worked well and what you would change for the next year. After we finish each civilization, I make lists of ideas for additional activities that might also have worked well.

Ask the kids; they have great ideas and will be your harshest critics. Incorporate your own specific talents and interests into your Club. If you are doing something that you enjoy, you and the students will have much more fun. Finally, the other teachers in the school are an amazing source of knowledge; use them. It has been a tremendous help to me to sit with the other Club teachers and just bounce ideas off of each other.

BETSY BABBINGTON

B.S. English; M.Ed. Special Education: Learning Disabilities; 12 years as a Club Leader

Academic Clubs taught: Industrialists Club, Covered Wagon Club, Inventor's Club, Treasure Island Club, Seven Wonders of the World Club, Rainforest Club, Development Club

1. What makes you enjoy being an Academic Club Leader?

Being an Academic Club Leader was the most successful and enjoyable way of educating that I have ever come across in my 35 years of teaching! I decorated the Industrialist Club as a Parlor Car, as instructed by the Director, which increased my enthusiasm even before school started. When the students arrived, they were clearly excited and ready to learn. They put on bowler hats and stepped into the late 19th century. They sat around a boardroom table and became Rockefeller, DuPont, J.P. Morgan, Vanderbilt, Carnegie, Ford, and Jay Gould. Each received a Million Dollar Trust Fund, which we monitored daily with rewards and fines. The Methodology tapped both the students' and my creativity, and we all learned new things. They learned geography as we illustrated their train ride around the country overseeing their investments and building the Transcontinental Railroad. It was very rewarding to see the students understand abstract ideas when taught through the Academic Club Methodology.

2. Describe the Academic Club activity that you are most proud of.

During the study of Henry Ford, we recreated an assembly line to demonstrate how Ford mass produced cars. Then, we raced the little roadsters we assembled on a ramp, emphasizing how Ford publicized his cars by racing.

3. What abstract concept did you translate into concrete practical activities?

When we studied Jay Gould, we attempted to give some understanding of the stock market to the 12-year-olds who participated in the Industrialists Club. We made clay bulls (representing rising stock prices) and bears (representing falling prices) to go above and below the line of the stock prices for the day. As the inflated bull market became a bear market, when Gould artificially created the crash resulting in Black Friday, all of the bulls ended up with their feet in the air and defeated while the bears stood triumphant and reigned supreme. This activity gave a visual reinforcement to the abstract concept of Bull and Bear Market.

4. What materials or situation that you set up produced some very exciting thinking?

While studying Vanderbilt, we made little sailboats out of wood and cloth and floated the boats in gutters filled with water placed on top of sawhorses. We used an electric fan to blow the boats down the gutter. After the students enjoyed this activity, we took away the fan. They realized right away that sailing was unpredictable because of the caprices of wind. The students said things like "What if we had to get the grain to market and there was no wind?" They appreciated the wisdom of the chance that Vanderbilt took when he sold all of his sailboats and placed his assets into steamboats. The project of sailing boats without wind demonstrated to them very clearly the need for a machine (steam engine), which ushered in the new machine age. The quality and liveliness of the discussion could not have been imagined without the experience of building and sailing the little boats.

5. How have you translated the Academic Club Methodology to other teaching you have done?

When I taught study skills/time management to seniors in high school, I used my experience in teaching Academic Clubs to lower school students. We used the project approach to study skills. We produced an Arts Pamphlet of local artists practicing in the Washington, D.C., area. Instead of just lecturing to the seniors, I immediately plunged into the project. We made a giant calendar of the school year on the wall. We made segments, visually on the calendar as to what we wanted to accomplish in each of the time slots. For example, from September to November we needed to identify the artists we would interview. From November to January, we needed to go on the interviews with the artists and photograph them. From January to March, we needed to type up and organize our interviews. From March to May, we needed to format and produce the book and sell ads. Thinking through the schedules and the deadlines began immediately to teach the seniors organization and time management.

6. What do the students seem to enjoy most about their Academic Clubs?

The students come to class every day looking forward to putting on their costumes and entering a new era. Play acting allows the students to actively learn instead of passively letting the teachers just tell them the information. Going back in time and becoming a historical figure stimulates their minds. They receive rewards for good behavior and learning. They get to become someone very important and in this new persona they are able to risk and learn.

7. What's the most important advice you would give to a new Academic Club Leader?

I would counsel a new Club Leader not to be too ambitious initially about the amount of information that they want to get across to the students. They need an outline of what information must be learned by the end of the year. At the beginning of the year, the teacher should pick a very important highlight and devise an appropriate project to go with it. The project should be large and enticing to capture the students' attention and hold their interests. For example, to begin our studies of the geography and history of the United States during the Industrialist Era, I made a huge map of the states and had a model train operating on it. With this project, I could teach the movement from an agrarian society to an industrialist society during the late 1800s, the significance of the Trans-Continental Railroad to the development of the United States, the Gold Rush, and geography of the states. Once the students understand the concepts from the train going around the map, I could show them the dramatic changes that occurred in people's lives due to machines, such as the steam engine, the cotton gin, and the telegraph.

One summer, at the end of the Treasure Island Club, I administered an activity that summed up some of the learning that had taken place during 6 weeks. The room was decorated as the island in Treasure Island. We could see a ship anchored off shore in the landscape depicted on the wall. The room was a jungle with the hut in the middle. I asked the children to first draw the room with everything in it. I then asked them to make a grid to superimpose over the room décor. I then instructed them to turn over the page and write the directions for discovering the buried treasure. In other words, go three squares to the north from the hut, then two squares to the east, and so forth until the actual treasure was located. Most of the children were able to draw a very successful treasure map. One child could not get beyond drawing a picture of the room, which was very diagnostic. The child's picture was very beautiful but showed no academic processing of the information. This is an example of a test that the Academic Club Methodology encourages on a continual basis. There are various ways to test children on what they have learned in a Club: through discussion, through art projects, through games, through reenactments, and through peer teaching.

11

Academic Clubs
Can Transform Schools

Dare We Do It?

We know that Academic Clubs are working because the students tell us. Graduates often visit The Lab School and tell us, "I lived for my Club. I couldn't wait to come to school each day." We hear frequently comments like, "I brought my Academic Clubs to college with me, even to graduate school. I could still visualize my Club rooms and the activities. I loved being Andrew Carnegie." Siblings of our students tell us that it is unfair that only children with learning disabilities get to be in Academic Clubs. They want Academic Clubs in their schools, too. Lab School students refuse to miss class. Eight-year-old Anais wanted to come to school with a 102° fever because he was Hercules in the Gods Club, and this was the day his Club was learning Hercules's Labors. Nathaniel, who was 9½ years old, declined to join his siblings to meet Grandma at the airport because he was determined not to miss the Battle of Hastings in the Knights and Ladies Club. He was playing the role of Harold, who was defending England against William the Conqueror's Normans. Jessica told her parents she could not leave early from school for a family holiday because she was Della Robbia. Club Members were all going to make ceramic tiles, as Della Robbia did, and decorate the door of the Renaissance Club with them. The opening of the Eastern Religions Exhibit at the Museum Club spurred Marielena to make cookies for the viewers. Jay Gould, alias Glenn from the Industrialists Club, was going to play his evil role as "The Mephistopheles of Wall Street," so he rushed to arrive very early at school that day. His parents had never seen him get ready for school so fast.

WHAT LAB SCHOOL SENIORS SAY

Lab School seniors got a chance to share their opinion of Academic Clubs with more than 500 professionals at a scientific conference on executive functioning, which took place on October 25, 2002, at The Lab School. At the conference, outstanding specialists on executive functioning discussed in detail the organization, attentional, and memorization problems of children with learning disabilities and teaching strategies that work for these students. The three last speakers were high school seniors at The Lab School. In a question-and-answer format with The Lab School's Director, the students made some of the following comments:

I loved having all the Clubs when I was little because they brought it in to where you were having such fun, but in the process you did not know how much you were learning. It was much easier to learn that way, or like even now when I am sitting as a senior in class reading Beowulf, *I remember Knights and Ladies Club where we heard* Beowulf *(and made Grendel's Arm) . . . As long as I have a picture or an idea in my head about something we did or made, I can grasp something new more easily.—Rasha*

Last summer, I went to Italy. I remembered the Renaissance Club when I was at Ghiberti's Gates of Paradise in Florence . . . I remembered that I was Rafael in the Renaissance Club . . . I remember like certain paintings everyone did and the art work everyone did. We sculpted miniatures of the David. We painted the ceiling like the Sistine Chapel. I went to all those places. I kept remembering all the experiences I had and all the things that I had learned through the Clubs, which is one of the strong points in the school. I was just astounded about how much I could remember from when I was so young because, to me right now, it feels like forever ago.—Jacob

Physically being a part of the Knights and Ladies Club, being a King, or physically being an artist doing what that artist did, walking in that artist's footsteps made learning a lot easier . . . It has a very strong impact on the kids because when you see the kids, it will look like they are playing but, in reality, while they're playing, they will say the most amazing things like, 'Oh, Alexander the Great did this and this' because they had played the character of Alexander the Great.—Laura

When I was in the Renaissance Club, we did a fresco on the wall outside of the window . . . sometimes I sit in my room and say, 'I want to paint this wall so bad!' I wish I could do a fresco . . . and I remember all the different time periods because of what we did. Like when I was in Cave Club, we made a woolly mammoth . . . When I am sitting down in front of the TV and I see a special [film] about finding woolly mammoths, or about the extinction of this and that,

I am like 'Goodness gracious, I know all of this stuff' . . . I feel like I am not as behind on things as I thought I was.—Rasha

I know I have a much higher regard for myself than I did when I was a kid. When I was a kid, I thought I was dumb, but I know I am not dumb. Because of the Clubs, I know that I am actually smart and there are some areas where I am stronger than many other people.—Jacob

As you can see from the kids' comments, 1) total immersion works, 2) identifying with a character helps children learn, 3) Academic Clubs demand total involvement and counteract passivity in learning, 4) having fun does not interfere with learning, 5) guided play can be scholastic, and 6) learning through the arts is rigorous. Academic Clubs take intellectual materials and teach the substance concretely, giving children many experiences that lead to understanding abstract ideas. They produce large storehouses of information, provide connections, and foster relationships between one idea and another.

Academic Clubs use visual, concrete materials to expand vocabulary and language skills. They provoke curiosity, reflection, and the asking of questions. They develop and employ strategies to trigger memory: color coding, kinesthetic clues, association, and repetition. Academic Clubs prize diversity; promote uniqueness; and foster team work, cooperation, and helping one another. The secrecy of Academic Club passwords and rituals promote a sense of belonging and membership. Subsequently, the Methodology builds confidence, competence, self-awareness, and self-esteem.

The Methodology promotes problem solving and critical thinking. Students with language learning disabilities, attention-deficit/hyperactivity disorder (ADHD), and related disorders become *educated*, not just remediated. Students are launched on successful pathways toward *learning* for a lifetime of inquiry.

CHANGING TEACHER EDUCATION

Academic Clubs and the Academic Club Methodology demand a different mindset from the usual teacher preparation of listening to instructions, reading textbooks, taking tests, and writing lesson plans. Employing all of the art forms and different intelligences to teach history, geography, civics, literature, and science requires a hands-on experiential approach. While teachers make sure that clear, precise, educational objectives are achieved, a student's body, mind, and all of his or her senses—the child's total being—are empowered to come alive.

Concrete visual programming takes over instead of the lecture method so that project learning, activity learning, object-centered learning, and reenactments of new information occur regularly. Children become partners in learning, following their curiosity, stimulating their sense of awe and surprise, and evoking their ability to solve problems creatively. Total involvement is the key, and total involvement of the teacher is required to produce total involvement of the child.

Teachers need to be taught in the same way that they are expected to teach children. The use of jump ropes, yo-yos, jacks, cards, and board games during teacher training should become as common as using textbooks, overhead projectors, slides, and study sheets. Club Leaders need to be immersed in a topic, such as immigration. They must decide which are the most important points for children of that age to learn, figure out an effective dramatic cover, and brainstorm with a group of 8–10 teachers about concrete, practical activities. The session should be fairly short because time pressure seems to produce a rush of unedited ideas that are often the most original.

One teacher in training might want to locate her Immigrants Club on a boat journeying to a specific country; another may locate his Club at a refugee camp on the border of a neighboring country, whereas another will center her Club on Ellis Island. They must figure out the authoritative role of the teacher, the roles for students to play, and the various rituals. They must know their content, present it through different intelligences, and seek ways within the Academic Club format to assess what the students learned. Enticing children to learn—especially enticing children who have experienced much failure—needs to be an important part of teacher education. It accompanies training on how to develop curricula and instructional tools. When discussing how the Academic Club lends itself to motivating reluctant learners, Club Leader Noel Bicknell said, "By creating a classroom that teaches social studies through pretending you are somebody else in the past, someone famous, the children become experts. That allows me a hook that allows them to learn. They feel 'Oh! I'm an expert. This information is important, and I am responsible for this.' From there, they are able to build their skills!"

TEACHING ABOUT CHILDREN WITH SPECIAL NEEDS

Training teachers to be Club Leaders for children with special needs requires sessions on relevant skills, such as management of ADHD. Club themes can be evoked from looking at the nature of the difficulties. Learning about auditory perception difficulties and language disorders from speech-language pathologists may encourage staff to seek ways to incorporate specific strategies into their Secret Agents Club, their Storekeepers and Pirates Clubs, their Seven Seas Club, or even their Disc Jockey Club. Applying strategies to help children remember a sequence of things (auditory sequential memory) has a role in every Academic Club. Teachers need to brainstorm together to come up with

concrete practical activities to teach auditory sequential memory in, for example, the Disc Jockey Club. They might have each Disc Jockey choose three
CDs and announce them, three at a time. In the Pirates Club, the Pirates may
have to remember four clues in order to discover some treasure on the island.

Because many schools are moving toward inclusive classrooms today and
are reducing the special education services that they offer, all teachers need
more training on typical learning difficulties and specific learning disorders as
well as on managing student behavior problems. Special educators need to be
brought in to impart some of this information. Teachers then need to turn the
information into useful classroom strategies or Academic Club activities.

SHOULD WE BE SAVING MONEY OR SAVING CHILDREN?

Although there is no doubt that states are saving money by reducing special
education services to children, enlarging classes, and cutting down drastically
on placements in special schools and special classes, children are not necessarily prospering. Our experience is that youngsters with severe learning disabilities, who are bright enough to see how poorly they are doing in inclusive
classrooms, tend to become depressed and may even develop psychiatric disorders. In the last few years, The Lab School has seen numbers of students
who were so overwhelmed by their failures in inclusive classrooms that they
needed intensive psychiatric help, sometimes hospitalization; several were
home schooled until they could receive the appropriate class or school placement. Sometimes saving money by not paying for special schooling costs more
because of the need to pay for psychiatric services, and the child and family
are the ones who suffer.

Our experience shows children from the inner city respond even faster
and more enthusiastically than most children to arts-based curricula and the
Academic Club Methodology. Their parents, however, seem considerably
afraid of this way of learning and worry that it is not real instruction. Intensive parent education on the efficacy of the methods is needed if arts-based
programs are to be employed with these students.

PRINCIPALS MUST BELIEVE

A school cannot incorporate the Academic Club Methodology if the principal
is not fully behind it. I had this experience in 1972, when a public school in
Washington, D.C., used the Academic Club Methodology every Friday afternoon. Every child was in an Academic Club, and parents were trained to be
assistants in the Clubs. The children adored their Clubs, and the parents were
totally enthusiastic. Unfortunately, the principal took ill and died that summer. In the fall, under a temporary principal, there were no Academic Clubs.

The parents petitioned the new principal to reinstate the Academic Clubs. The children, too, begged for them to resume, but the faculty decided that putting on Academic Clubs was too much work for no extra pay. Thus ended the Clubs. Had the principal lived, I believe that she would have found a way to support her faculty, encourage them, work with them, and help them see how much they and their students were benefiting.

The principal must help those faculty members who are not teaching Academic Clubs to become involved in the Club themes. The librarians and media experts provide excellent resource help. Often, physical education teachers have ideas for movement or exercises that fit the theme. The art and music teachers serve as important resources. The classroom teachers often choose books or activities to present to their students that tie in with Academic Club themes. All faculty need to be drawn in, asked for ideas, and encouraged to bring in materials (e.g., empty egg cartons, empty paper towel holders, sponges, all manner of throw-away items) that can be used as art materials in Clubs.

Speech-language pathologists at The Lab School keep track of passwords (when they can break the secrecy chain) so that they can review them with some of their students. Occupational therapists help students with eye–hand coordination problems, for example, by teaching them how to use implements on an archeological dig. Psychologists and social workers are often fascinated to see how different some of the children's behavior is when they are in the dramatic framework of the Academic Club playing an important role compared with their performance in the classroom learning to read or spell.

DRAWING IN MEMBERS OF THE COMMUNITY

With Academic Clubs, it is important for the students "to meet with a fellow lawyer" in the Advocates Club or "to share decisions with fellow jurists" in the Judges Club. The Museum Club turns to parents who are associated with museums to come in and talk about displaying artifacts or titling exhibitions. The Assistant Director of one of Washington, D.C.'s biggest museums is a Lab School Awardee with learning disabilities herself. She invited the Museum Club members for a behind-the-scenes tour of the museum where she worked. An Academic Club reaches deep into the community for its visitors and its field trips.

Journeying into the community sometimes brings accolades to the students, too. When they tour the National Cathedral, their guides are impressed by the extent of their knowledge, as are the docents in the National Gallery of Art when the students tour a Renaissance exhibit. Academic Clubs take students on a ride to high adventure. Norman Cousins, a famous American writer and editor, once said, "The growth of the human mind is still high adventure, in many ways, the highest adventure on earth."

DARE WE DO IT?

Most people are afraid of change, of replacing established routines with new patterns of learning. Many school boards and principals only feel comfortable if learning is a daily recipe of teaching that can be checked off in a book. In the month of November, 10 concepts will be taught in a prescribed order, with 85% of it learned by the end of the month.

When using the Academic Club Methodology, teachers do not follow one highly itemized syllabus or an exact set of academic regulations. Club Leaders and their Supervisor develop a set of objectives—a list of the information and concepts that the children are expected to learn by the end of the year. Then, they turn the academic material into a series of practical, concrete activities with evaluation instruments built into the curricula to ascertain that the children are learning what the Club Leader is teaching. How can this not make them better teachers?

Each Club Leader is encouraged to seek different approaches every year so that the teacher keeps on learning and growing. New reading material on the adult level is acquired along with reports of current research. Previously undiscovered children's books and new publications on the topic under study are sought after by the Supervisor and the Club Leaders. Club Leaders are urged to follow their interests in enriching certain teaching materials and dropping previous exercises. Once given the freedom to make up their own classes, Club Leaders frequently become empowered to come up with new ideas for activities or completely different approaches.

The Lab School experience is that Club Leaders like to work closely with each other, helping each other, sharing books and materials, decorating their rooms, developing a particular curricular unit, and finding a way to transfer a particularly clever exercise or art project into each Club. Club Leaders do feel their mastery, and that feeling can turn into a strong voice, which I believe is healthy for a school. I know that there are principals who do not want to hear from faculty, but my eye is on the children, and if Club Leaders become more competent and creative, my view is that it can only benefit the students.

Do not think for a moment that Club Leaders can ignore state regulations and requirements. Certainly, they cannot, but they do have the freedom to organize their teaching materials in original ways; present them in an orderly sequence that makes sense to them; and assess student knowledge through activities, projects, and teaching games. Student progress is difficult to quantify, but it can be tape recorded, filmed, and put in portfolios. Unfortunately, there are still professionals and school boards who do not believe students have gained knowledge if they cannot measure students' learning through paper and pencil tests.

I also know there are teachers who will hesitate to adopt the Academic Club Methodology because it contradicts their teaching styles and their need for traditional control over their class. There are parents everywhere who are afraid that pretend-play situations are not academic and that their children will suffer academically from this method. Parents who have never seen an Academic Club in action will likely fight the introduction of Academic Clubs into their children's school by labeling the Academic Club Methodology "the liberal approach," "watered-down education," "comic-strip learning," or "way-out alternative instruction." Once parents, teachers, and policy makers have seen the Methodology in action, however, their opinions change. Since 1967, The Lab School has not heard a complaint from anyone about the amount and type of information learned through Academic Clubs.

The more assessment data The Lab School can produce in the coming years, the more parents and teachers will believe that this approach builds structures of knowledge that allow highly sophisticated material to be learned early in life and in a thorough manner. Yet, 40 years of Academic Club successes that students, parents, teachers, administrators, and education reviewers have seen and heard themselves cannot be discounted. The Middle States Accreditation Team (that accredits independent schools) said in their March 2001 report that,

> The Validation Team observed an arts program with a finely tuned, deeply considered philosophy of how the arts can become the "way to teach and learn." . . . Strengths of the social studies program include small class sizes, stimulating and motivating activities, enthusiastic and well-prepared teachers, and the flexibility to adapt and modify curriculum to meet the needs of students. Teachers are given and enjoy considerable latitude to use their personal interests and talents to offer a highly creative and stimulating program . . . In many schools, the social studies program is a "weak stepsister" to other content areas. Not so at The Lab School! The social studies/humanities program is designed to enhance the students' understanding of historical and cultural content by providing experiential and multi-sensory instruction. It is a unique and exciting program . . . The content addressed in each Club includes history, geography, science, literature, and the arts. No textbooks are used. In the Academic Clubs, students experience total immersion in the time period being studied, thus, helping them to retain information and develop a larger fund of knowledge. Students assume the roles of historical characters to experience specific time periods for themselves. Carefully selected projects enable them to build skills of attention, following directions, cooperation, memory, organizing, and sequencing. Assessment is based on the observation of student progress over time. Anecdotal notes regarding individual student participation and progress are maintained so that comprehensive narrative reports to the parents may be written. The Middle

States Validation Team held interviews with high school seniors who indicated that these Academic Clubs were highly successful in making the historical periods meaningful. No greater testimony to the power of the Club concept can be found than the student the Team interviewed who plans to become a history major because his interest was sparked through his experiences in the Academic Club curriculum.

The District of Columbia has placed about 130 students per year at The Lab School, followed by Maryland and Virginia jurisdictions to a much smaller extent. The Baltimore Lab has students paid for by Baltimore City, Baltimore County, Anne Arundel County, Carroll County, and others. These jurisdictions are well aware of The Lab School's unique manner of teaching. Families have moved from India, Jordan, Kuwait, Norway, Sweden, Denmark, Germany, Israel, England, France, Switzerland, and Mauritius, as well as from California, Illinois, and New Hampshire, to enroll their youngsters at The Lab School.

The U.S. Department of Education from 1994 to 1996 and from 1996 to 1997 gave Blue Ribbon Awards to The Lab School and one other special education institution as Models of Excellence. The Academic Club Methodology is described in Janet Lerner's extraordinarily popular textbook titled *Learning Disabilities: Theories, Diagnosis, and Teaching Strategies* (2003) and used in many education departments in universities for training teachers to deal with students with learning disabilities. Dr. Lerner wrote:

> *An example of a school curriculum that makes good use of information about the child's psychological processing difficulties is The Lab School of Washington, D.C., a school for students with learning disabilities. Sally Smith, the founder and director of this school, recognized that many of the children attending it displayed much difficulty with auditory and linguistic learning, yet they excelled in the visual arts. Therefore, she used the arts and experiential hands-on learning to teach these children. Instead of learning through typically structured text-based lessons in social studies and history, these children are taught through Academic Clubs for grades one through six . . . The Clubs teach content, vocabulary, history and geography through the visual arts. For example, in the Renaissance Club, the children build scaffolding and actually paint a replica of the ceiling of the Sistine Chapel.*

ACADEMIC CLUBS BRING BOOK LEARNING

Eighty-five percent of children with learning disabilities cannot read or read poorly, according to The National Institute of Child Health and Human Development (NICHD). These children are deprived of the fascinating information that books provide. If they were better readers, then they could choose to be whisked away by books to embark on journeys into different cultures; solve mysteries; and look at a series of relationships between people of different ages, sexes, and genders. Through books, good readers learn how people have survived despite the worst hardships of nature. Through literature, students can be inspired by Helen Keller and Annie Sullivan, Gandhi, Mother Teresa, Florence Nightingale, and other dedicated humanists who helped mankind. Books take readers on journeys to places known and unknown where they can explore treasures and mysteries.

The Academic Club Methodology provides children with a rich curiosity, a passionate interest in the past and present, and the information they would glean from books if they could read. They learn and retain a behemoth amount of information and are empowered as learners. Their vocabulary and language fluency is stimulated. Their critical thinking is sparked. My belief is that the Academic Club Methodology paves the way for 90% of Lab School seniors to go to college. These students take with them the massive amount of information they have joyfully learned in their Academic Clubs. The Academic Club Methodology transports them into new worlds, where they play important roles in daily life and in productive careers, thinking, inventing, and producing ideas and objects.

MAGIC CARPETS OF THE MIND

Technology and Learning Magazine has named futurist, author, consultant, and Director of the Thornburg Center, David Thornburg, as one of the top 10 most influential people in the field of educational technology in the past 20 years. As a leading technology futurist he said, when talking about education, "I believe the role of education in this new age is to help students make magic carpets—magic carpets of the mind with which they can explore the infinite world of ideas at the speed of thought" (1996).

The Academic Club Methodology transports each Aladdin with his lamp and his magic carpet to a new world where he weaves ideas into the loom of history, geography, civics, science, and literature in order to produce the most brilliantly colored, substantial, and useful set of highly textured fabric content that will accompany him on his educational journey.

THE CHILD HAS LIVED IT.
THE CHILD HAS LEARNED IT.

References

Adams, L., Rassai, R., Shottenbauer, M., & Iseman, J. (2004). *The efficacy of The Lab School Approach in improving basic and applied academic skills in children with learning disabilities.* Unpublished manuscript.

Catts, H.W., & Kamhi, A.G. (1999). *Language and learning disabilities.* Boston: Allyn & Bacon.

Dewey, J. (1938). *Education and experience.* New York: Collier Books.

Fahey, K.R., & Reid, D.K. (2000). *Language development, differences, and disorders.* Austin, TX: PRO-ED.

Gardner, H. (1999). *Frames of mind: The theory of multiple intelligences* (10th anniversary ed.). New York: Basic Books. (Originally published in 1983)

Hirsch, E.D. (2003, Spring). Knowledge of words and the world scientific insight into the fourth grade slump and the nation's stagnant comprehension scores. *American Educator.*

Lawton, E. (1994). Integrating curriculum: A slow but positive process. *Schools in the Middle,* 4(2), 27–30

Lerner, J. (2003). *Learning disabilities: Theories, diagnosis, and teaching strategies.* Boston: Houghton Mifflin.

Manzo, K.K. (2003, May 7). Forum invokes heroes to help students learn history. *Education Week, 22*(34), 26, 28.

Middle States Association of Colleges and Schools, Committee of Institution-wide Accreditation. (2001, March). *Report of the Pathways to School Improvement.* Unpublished document.

Popham, W.J. (2001). *The truth about testing: An educator's call to action.* Alexandria, VA: Association for Supervision and Curriculum Development.

Schubert, M., & Melnick, S. (1997). *Thematic instruction: The arts in curriculum integration.* Paper presented at the annual meeting of the Eastern Education Research Association, Hilton Head, SC.

Schwebel, M., & Raph, J. (1973). *Piaget in the classroom.* New York: Basic Books.

Snider, J.H. (2003, May 25). Getting real on raising test scores. *The Washington Post,* p. B7.

Thornburg, D.D. (1996). *Technologies of liberation.* San Carlos, CA: The Thornburg Center. Found on-line at http://www.tcpd.org

Vellutino, F.R. (1979). *Dyslexia: Theory and research.* Cambridge, MA: MIT Press.

Yorks, P.M., & Follo, E.J. (1993). Engagement rates during thematic and traditional instruction. *Eric Digests* (ED 363 412).

Appendix A

Teaching Approaches Designed for Different Behavior Characteristics

The Academic Club Methodology was designed for children with learning disabilities and attention-deficit/hyperactivity disorder (ADHD) who need their intellects challenged and their imaginations tapped. Principles of programming and teaching approaches for Academic Clubs have been organized around the characteristics of neurological dysfunction (of learning disabilities and ADHD) as this chart demonstrates.

Characteristics	Principles of programming	Approaches
Short attention span	Use short-term activities. Give one direction at a time. Approach one idea from many directions.	Present 3–4 different activities within a class period. Use concrete materials. Use all of the senses.
Distractibility	Lure focus through drama. Entice focus through colorful materials.	Use pretend play. Preassemble materials. Set up routines.
Poor impulse control	Establish clear rules and clear expectations. Use short-term activities with tangible results.	Give a lot of attention to what is done well and how rules are followed. Use dramatic roles.
Hyperactivity, restlessness, and random movement	Provide active learning. Use short-term activities. Create special spaces for work. Limit the amount of stimulation.	Change pace frequently with varying activities. Provide visible results in short-term periods.
Disorganization	Design a ritual for orderly entry in the room. Assign seating. Use clear, nonwordy explanations to establish procedures. Have a well-organized room. Show how to approach a task.	Use color-coded shelves and containers for storage. Give each child his or her own system to hold materials (portfolio or shelf).
Poor understanding of sequences	Instruct what's to be done first, next, and last. Draw the sequence. Demonstrate the sequence.	Use order words (e.g., first, second). Ask students to discuss what they did first, next, and last. Ask students to teach others the steps of a task.

Characteristics	Principles of programming	Approaches
Poor transitioning and difficulty starting and stopping	Help children switch gears for transitions. Give early warnings.	Use colored papers or objects and signals to alert students to change. Use a particular percussion instrument to represent getting ready to change.
Poor auditory skills, poor listening, difficulty remembering information, and difficulty remembering sequences	Use visual, tactile, rhythm, and movement cues to help convey information.	Use project learning. Have students construct objects with all kinds of materials, then ask them to point to what they did first, next, and last.
Poor language skills, poor word finding, limited vocabulary, and poor fluency or language	Refer to experiences in the classroom. Have students draw pictures, then talk about them. Talk clearly and succinctly.	Make products or projects that children can point to and state how they were made. Increase vocabulary through passwords.
Poor visual skills, poor discrimination, poor remembering of visual information, and poor remembering of sequences	Explain what children are looking at. Outline objects so that they stand out.	Frame visuals by putting a border around groups that students should look at.
Poor visual–motor skills and poor hand–eye coordination	On some projects, pair students with others who have good coordination. Plan projects individually for quick success.	Have big projects, sturdy cardboard, wood, or metal to work against. Present simple tasks that increase in difficulty.
Poor motor skills, poor motor planning, and poor use of space	Help students position themselves in relation to the task.	Use assigned seating. Have designated areas for out-of-seat work.
Poor symbol formation, trouble assigning meaning to symbols, and trouble with abstract ideas	Break abstract ideas into concrete activities. Find objects to represent a concept.	Use concrete materials. Teach with different concrete materials and pictures to illustrate the same concept. Role-play.

(continued)

Characteristics	Principles of programming	Approaches
Immature social skills	Individualize projects. Have some students work alone, others work in pairs, and the rest work in small groups.	Use drama so that students work together against outside adversity.
Poor inhibiting functions, trouble putting on the inner breaks, and perseverating	Limit procedures, directions, and the amount of work. Discuss the amount of work.	Provide enough space so that students aren't touching. Change activities frequently. Assign dramatic roles to help children control their impulses.
Extreme immaturity	Program the most elementary skills into the most sophisticated guise.	Use play. Use concrete activities. Change activities frequently.
Inconsistent, erratic, unpredictable, and scattered performance	Avoid overloading students with work. Be aware of students' fatigue cycle.	Always have back-up materials and objects ready. Go over materials relentlessly to the point of over-learning.
Poor sense of time	Relate time to events. Relate tasks to be done in order.	Use pictorial representations of periods of history.

Appendix B

Some Principles of Effective Group Management with Students with Learning Disabilities

1. All students need to feel that their teacher is in charge, but students with learning disabilities have more disorder and are more fragile. Therefore, they need more order and structure. The teacher must be an authority but not an authoritarian.

2. Students with learning disabilities lack parameters and borders, so they need their teacher to provide clear limits (e.g., what can and can't be done, how things need to be done in this classroom).

3. Regular routines and consistent ways of behaving help students feel safe and in control.

4. Students with learning disabilities usually have poor focus, distractibility, short attention spans, and poor listening skills, so their teacher must speak with authority, brevity, and clarity and use a lower pitch.

5. Pacing is extremely important for students with learning disabilities. To ensure their success, have shorter work periods and give more breaks.

6. Know the students well—their strengths, their weaknesses, and their interests—so that you can individualize the program for their success.

7. Because they are concrete, objects, pictures, games, and movement activities work better than lectures to keep a group involved and effectively managed.

8. Because of their problems with space, students with learning disabilities benefit from assigned seating.

9. Students' egocentricity and self-absorption often prevent them from working well in groups. Start with groups of two or three students, if possible, and tell each student what is expected of him or her.

10. Comment positively and frequently about all behaviors you see the children doing in an effort to conform to your expectations. A lot of specific praise is an effective form of behavior management.

11. Students need a consistent, logical sequence of consequences that they are aware of and can see on the chalkboard or bulletin board. You can point to the consequences rather than discuss them because too much discussion about behavior takes away from learning.

12. Keep the most difficult students near you, at an arm's touch. Develop some unique signals (e.g., a "look") of warning just for these students to respond.

13. Remain respectful of each child's feelings. Do not humiliate, ridicule, or put down any student. Reprimands must be done one-on-one before or after class.

14. Have clear goals for each activity but be flexible enough to step back and take the room's emotional temperature. Be able to change, if necessary.

15. Plan ahead and anticipate problems; have back-up materials, games, and activities ready.

16. Prepare students for greater demands and changes in structure when you can. You can't always, though.

17. One child can disrupt a whole class and, at times, must be sent out of the room. It is not good for this child to feel as if he or she has the power to keep the class from functioning. The other children need to feel in control and to have the safety to learn. Sometimes the child that disrupts just needs to be sent out of the room to deliver a message or to do an errand, and the group becomes more cohesive and focused. Sometimes a student is losing or has lost total control and must be sent immediately to an administrator so that the student will not injure him- or herself or others and will not keep the whole class from learning.

18. Develop a class plan to attain something, such as a special trip or pizza. The class must help each other to stay in control to earn the reward. You want to establish a caring environment where students watch out for and help each other.

Appendix C

The Lab School of
Washington and the Baltimore Lab

For many years, The Lab School of Washington has been a national resource for all those concerned with the needs of the nation's 8–10 million children and adults with learning disabilities. This role was underscored in 1995, when The Lab School was identified by the U.S. Department of Education as a National Diffusion Network Model Education Program, and public school systems were encouraged to use The Lab School as a resource and to replicate its programs. The Lab School was the only independent special education school for learning disabilities in the country to receive this distinction. In 1994–1995 and in 1996–1997, The Lab School was one of only two private special education schools in the country to receive the National Blue Ribbon Award of Excellence for both the elementary and secondary school programs.

In September 2000, The Lab School opened an elementary school campus in Baltimore, Maryland. By September 2003, the enrollment had quadrupled (for students in first though eighth grade), and the school began to add a high school. The first graduation will be June 2008. The arts-based Baltimore Lab, a division of the Lab School of Washington, continues The Lab School's tradition of high-quality, information-centered, experiential, project-learning education.

The Lab School serves as a national and international resource on learning disabilities. In addition to its day school, The Lab School offers intensive tutoring services for children and adults, diagnostic assessment and psychotherapy for children and adults, college and career counseling, an after-school program, and speech-language pathology and occupational therapy, It also has a 1-year training program for tutors. The Lab School's Night School serves adults with learning disabilities. The Outreach Department offers professional development workshops for educators and mental health professionals; lectures for parents; and products including videotapes, audiotapes, books, and articles. The Lab School is currently providing faculty development for six inner-city schools in the District of Columbia.

Since 1985, The Lab School has honored individuals who have excelled in their chosen fields despite their learning disabilities. More that 1,300 people gather each November to honor these awardees' achievements. Their struggles, courage, and ingenuity to overcome great obstacles serve as an inspiration to the students and to us all.

The Lab School is planning to open other schools as well as an Academic Club Service that will help schools put into action this innovative program of study that has proven itself effective at The Lab School and Baltimore Lab. Please call 202-965-6600 for more information.

ACADEMIC CLUB
ADVISORY SERVICE

The Lab School of Washington and Baltimore Lab have developed a service for public, private, and charter schools; enrichments programs; at-risk programs; summer programs; children who are home schooled; and individuals who want to put the Academic Club Methodology to work in their environment.

Although the Methodology was developed for children with special needs—particularly those with severe learning disabilities and attention-deficit/hyperactivity disorder—we have found that siblings of Lab School students crave the Methodology as well. The Academic Club Methodology works effectively with all children and can be adapted for children with a range of abilities, from nonreaders to gifted and talented youth without any reading and writing difficulties. It can be adapted for children who are deaf and those with physical impairments. It can also be tailored to serve children from other countries and cultures.

We offer the following programs:

Visits to our demonstration center to see Academic Clubs in action and to participate in a 2- or 3-day intensive workshop, combined with on-site initial help from experienced Lab School Club Trainers to help start Clubs in your environment.

Visits by a Club Leader or a team of Club Leaders to your environment to support your Academic Club Leaders on a regular basis.

Newsletter to share activities, information on new Clubs, and different resources.

Subscription web page with on-line resources.

Because we practice individualization and pride ourselves on our creativity, we can custom-design Academic Clubs for specific purposes. We can help bring success to your institution.

Call 202-944-2220 or visit http://www.labschool.org

Index

Page numbers followed by *f* indicate figures.